SCITHAIN

Vampyric Witchcraft

of the Drakon Covenant

A. A. Morain

Copyright © 2017 Martinet Press

All rights reserved. No part of this work may be copied or reproduced in any way without the express written permission of the author and the publisher.

ISBN-10: 0-9978363-8-5
ISBN-13: 978-0-9978363-8-7

128yf

CONTENTS

Foreword	v
Haemodae	1
The Scithain Tradition and Vampyric Witchcraft	7
Ancestor Cults	28
Modern Witchcraft Vs. The Sevenfold Way	40
Sinister Witchcraft of the Drakon Covenant	47
Hermetic Initiation	56
The Path to Scithain	62
Mastering Vampyric Flight	75
The Astral Realms	87
Preparation For Hermetic Rituals	92
Sitheil	97
The Scrying Mirror	100
The Tree of Wyrd	105
The Vampyric Novitiate	119
The Chain of Devouring	135
The Vampyric Adept	151
Eremis	158
Myths and Legends of the Hebrides	170
Morgatha, Mother of Vindex	210

The Black Pilgrimage	223
Preliminaries of Lichcraft	227
Star Gates and Hebdomadric Astrology	242
The Moor II	250
Cuairt Coimhgí	288

Appendices

I - Tinctures and Correspondences	293
II - The Secret Tasks	299
III - Lanuwythe - Lycanthropic Praxis	303
IV - Coenobitic Vampyrism	317
V - Draumrúna	324

Contributors

A. A. Morain

Robert Brooke

Myrwyrdd

Artwork by

Princeps Guyhel

H. Nythra

A. A. Morain

SCITHAIN

"When doomed to death I shall have expired, I will attend you as a nocturnal fury; and a ghost, I will attack your faces with my hooked talons (for such is the power of those divinities, the Manes), and, brooding upon your restless breasts, I will deprive you of repose by terror."

-Horace, 5th Century BCE

SCITHAIN

Foreword

The information revealed in this book, particularly that relating to the culture of *Scithain* (conveniently called in lieu of an actual name for the spiritual beliefs and culture of the pre-celtic peoples who populated the British Isles, and in particular focusing upon the ancient inhabitants of the outer Hebridean isles of Britain) has been passed down for some time within the inner circle of the Drakon Covenant on a purely aural basis.

It pertains to the essence and nature of certain lich-like entities with whom the witches of the Covenant have communed over a span of time, and which entities made their presence known to the original practitioners of the coven's vampiric rituals and techniques.

In recent times, research was undertaken as to the etymology of the words and visions brought forth via Communion with these discarnate entities.

What was discovered through these communal rites was a very real locale - *Beinn Sciathan,* located on the outer Hebridean isle of Eriskay. What was of interest was the translation of this place name - the 'hill' or 'peak' 'of the bat' or 'peak of the winged', a symbol regarded as an inherent totem within traditions of vampiric magick of all stripes, and especially so within that of the Drakon Covenant.

The information gleaned via Communion hinted toward a connection with this site and a now extinct, chthonically orientated culture. Further research by the Covenant unearthed a little known pre-celtic society, with locales of interest around the outer Hebridean Isles within which Beinn Sciathan is found.

This region and society are known to archaeology as being unique in that these people mummified their dead and practised certain macabre rituals and traditions. This points toward a belief in the afterlife and communication with one's ancestors. Thus, there was perhaps a knowledge of post mortem existence and the veneration of a priestly caste (who were believed to reside at a site known as *Cladh Hallan* in the Outer Hebrides).

This priestly caste's abode contained various dead bodies interred ritually within the settlements; again, practises for which archaeology has no current definite explanation.

It is proposed in this book that they utilised such practises for necromantic communion, and the rituals and traditions uncovered so far fit within the already defined witchcraft of the Drakon Covenant.

Whilst some of the practises and ideas detailed in this book may seem fanciful or difficult at first to grasp or even perhaps believe at all, they are the solid result of insights attained via an attempt to further commune with the entities who first brought the region and ancient culture of the Hebridean Isles to the Covenant, as well as the accumulated efforts of initiates of the coven resulting from a strict adherence to the Sevenfold Way and the Sinister Tradition. No information has been added that has not come via some form of extranormal inspiration or diligent research (particularly in regards to the ancient activities of the Scithain peoples). The mythos can be accepted or discarded as one desires, and only wilful and genuine application of the rites and teachings in this book will bring the seeker to know the origin and authenticity of the writings herein, as well as the power such writings hold.

What is offered here therefore is the praxis of Sinister witchcraft of not only the Drakon Covenant but also threads of the long extinct culture of Scithain, whose priests have deemed it worthy to grant us an insight into their world, as well as various threads of Celtic beliefs which share similarity with the chthonic Scithain rites.

Alongside such insights is the advancement and exploration of other parts of the Sinister Tradition (most notably several developments of the Arthurian Grail mythos deriving from the legends of the peoples of ancient Albion).

The Drakon Covenant has since adapted several aspects of that which has been revealed via vampiric communion of the now extinct Hebridean culture and their religious beliefs - which were believed to be somewhat similar to the Sinister tradition and, it can be argued, gave rise to the beliefs which birthed the Sinister tradition itself.

To those unfamiliar, the Drakon Covenant defines itself as a *nexion* of the Order of Nine Angles, a Left-Hand Path occult society which proposes and utilises what it calls the *Sinister Tradition* - this tradition being the foundational basis upon which all magickal workings and ontological treatises within Drakon Covenant philosophy are based and derived from. More accurately, the Covenant follows the same Sinister tradition which the ONA draws its ideas and practises from as a whole. They can be regarded as facets of one world-view with their own distinctions and unique applications.

Combined with this is a unique interpretation of this ontology as a primarily *vampiric* one - rather than Covenant application and practises being a blend of the two occult currents, it is proposed vampirism (spelt *vampyrism* within our writings simply for clarity's sake) is simply a convenient name given to the various aspects and effects seen amongst magickal systems and workings, as well as evolution itself in a greater, teleological sense.

The rich tradition of which the Drakon Covenant inherits thus argues a deeper legitimacy in contrast to the common claims so frequent among other occult temples and covens of being privy to a long chain of traditional pagan practises. What is detailed herein are the dark and often-times obscure rites and rituals of a long vanished people, a people who represented the chthonic aspect of the Hyperborean culture of Albion, as detailed in the Order of Nine Angles' writings elsewhere.

It is expected that the reader be familiar with the mythos of the Dark Gods and other pertinent aspects of the Sinister Tradition. Some of these details will not be repeated here for sake of brevity and originality of content, and therefore it is assumed that the reader has a working knowledge of these matters, as outlined in *Naos, Hostia,* and the *Deofel Quintet* (see *Sources and Further Reading* at the end of this book).

This book is written with the solitary practitioner in mind, as well as the fully-fledged coven, with many rites being communal focused, deriving as they do from the inner workings of the central founding coven of the Drakon Covenant (currently based in West Yorkshire, England at the time of writing). It is hoped that as long as one person remains who puts these teachings into practise, the Drakon Covenant - our vision - shall live on.

It goes without saying that of all those who read these words, few - very few - will put into practise the complete set of teachings outlined herein, let alone undertake the arduous tasks of sacrifice, internal exploration, physical journeys to the sacred isles and all that which is asked of a witch of the Covenant's tradition.

This book is not written for those who simply wish to possess another dangerous and demonic grimoire, thrilling with delight at the infamy that perhaps surrounds its author/s or its contents; it is written for the few (perhaps only a small handful per century) who can recognise its merit above the plebeian outpour presently polluting the so called 'Left Hand Path community'; who can see it is not simply another tired and pleonastic vanity project replete with hollow invocations and fabricated sigils, recycling the same archaic dead ends of occult titillations.

Rather, like the Sinister tradition from which soil these teachings grew, it is a living current, a continuation of a genuine pagan philosophy and way of life. You may read these words and convince yourself you simply do not need to undertake the particularly difficult tasks, or that you can pick and choose which aspects to put into practise. But in the end, you are only deceiving yourself - you are forbidding yourself the chance to truly know what power and wisdom is, and thus relegate yourself to another somewhat curious but ultimately unremarkable member of that species so amusingly mislabelled *Homo Sapiens Sapiens*.

If, however you are like us, of our kind - if you possess that Promethean drive, that unique, stark grimness and focus of character; if you are truly willing to spend many nights away from the comfort of your home, months in isolation, years on a quest for wisdom, and to accept you have a long way to go till mastery (or even adeptship), then pursue the arcane echoes of Scithain, and come to learn that profound essence of what we have deigned to share with you. For he who sees furthest stands atop a pyramid of skulls.

To you, dear reader, I offer here the fruits of my quest, my *πάθει μάθος*, my personal $αναδος$; and hope you join us one day, upon the fateful moors - in person or in spirit - to presence the acausal darkness. *And ever darker, recall...*

Alexander Aristarchus Morain

West Yorkshire, 127 yf

Haemodae

The Ancient Hebridean Centre of Scithain

The Hebrides are a collection of islands off the western coast of Scotland in the British Isles. Despite their remote location, the islands are believed to have been settled as early as 8500BCE, according to conventional archaeology.

The isles incidentally contain remarkable evidence for a pre-Celtic culture that once flourished in the British Isles as early as the Mesolithic Era. Little is known of the people who lived in this region, though it is speculated that they shared at least some consistency with the later arriving Celtic tribes - particularly regarding beliefs such as burial rites, nature spirits and the alignment of heavenly bodies.

Later incursions by the spread of the so-called 'Beaker people' around 2500BCE brought the use of bronze and new religious beliefs, eventually supplanting that of the aboriginal peoples (these aboriginal people's beliefs being the primary - but not sole - basis of the historical and chthonic research contained in this book). These later settlers can be distinguished by their singular burial methods, in contrast to the previous inhabitant's communal burial habits.

Some theories posit one or both cultures moved west and

eventually became what are known now as the Pictish peoples, after having mingled with various later Celtic settlers.

The Hebrides are mentioned by several ancient scholars, including Pliny the Elder and Ptolemy. The Greek historian Diodorus Siculus called the isles *Hyperborea*, meaning 'far beyond the North'. Pomponius Mela, a Roman-Spanish writer of the first century, refers to a group of seven islands he named the *Haemodae*, which are believed to have referred to the Hebrides.

According to Greek myth, Hyperborea was a wondrous land which lay (as its name implied) to the far north, and was a land bathed in eternal Spring. Its inhabitants were said to live a life free from warfare, disease and any form of misery. It is said this is where the wisest of men travelled to learn the secrets of magick and astronomy. Through its land flowed the blessed river Eriadnos, the name also given to the god of that river and who was worshipped there in Hyperborea. Flocks of white swans were said to congregate upon this river.

Hyperborea was said to have two harvest seasons, leading to an abundance in food and grains. The south was guarded by mountains and fierce, icy winds and its surrounding valleys were home to tribes of one eyed, monstrous men.

Sinister Tradition holds that the Hyperborean Aeon which gave rise to the civilisation of Albion (preceded as it was by the Primal Aeon) spread historically southward from the British Isles, inspiring and seeding the European cultures such as the mainland Celts and ancient Greeks.

From such a model, it can be deduced that the Celtic and Scithain cultures share similarities due to the latter being the progenitor of the former.

Whilst unique aspects of this culture have been observed elsewhere in Britain (such as ritual practises and even mummification), it is believed the outer Hebridean Isles were home to one of the spiritual centres of the ancient culture - serving as a *Chthonic* counterpart, and perhaps even a precursor to the *Solar* tradition (which was allegedly centred around Stonehenge, and later the *Cosmic* tradition, based around the Welsh Marches).

At the Outer Hebrides, a community found its priestly centre based around certain sites. Two of these sites are *Beinn Sciathan*, on the isle of Eriskay; and *Cladh Hallan*, on the isle of South Uist. The former was believed to be a centre of great magickal power, whilst the latter was where the priesthood of this culture took residence for reasons currently unknown. There perhaps may exist more sites (such as the temple complex at Orkney), but the places mentioned have stood out as particular regions of noteworthy interest, as has the region of the Outer Hebrides in general.

Beinn Sciathan as mentioned is a barren mountain situated in the Outer Hebridean isle of Eriskay, off the coast of South Uist. The aural mythos of the Drakon Covenant relates that this is a sacred spot to the now extinct priesthood of the isles, and is a pilgrimage site for all those who follow the Covenant tradition. It is believed the word 'Sciathan' is a Gaelic corruption or development of the word Scithain. The meaning of this word is currently unknown, but is believed to derive from the language of the peoples who dwelt in the Hebrides during pre-Celtic times, and may refer to a power or potency associated with the Dark Gods.

Cladh Hallan is a settlement located at South Uist, and is believed to be over 4000 years old. It has been the site of a discovery of mummies, the only recorded instance in the British Isles (though archaeologists believe there may be more instances across Britain which were previously overlooked). The mummies were often composite - that is, they are made of different parts from separate corpses.

The ancient peoples of the Hebrides and the priests of Cladh Hallan revered their dead - in particular the dead priesthood, who strove to enter into a state of Lichhood upon death via the rites and rituals passed down to them through the mists of time. The composite mummification process may have been a way of binding the essences of several generations of the priestly caste. These mummies were kept in temple dwellings, where they were displayed and their essence communed with so as to understand the secrets the priests wrought from beyond. Often, at certain points during the year, they were carried out in processions which were believed to have involved the entire community. Other rites saw chants and offerings of incense left to the desiccated remains of the ancestors, who were left in the open air upon stone altars. The practise of mummification and veneration of these mummies clearly points to a belief not only in the afterlife, but in the ability of the dead to return and house within physical shells.

Cladh Hallan itself was made of seven houses, arranged in a terrace formation. Archaeological discoveries there have unearthed a strange mix between ordinary settlement and highly ritualistic activity. Many of the houses have sacrifices (some of them human) placed under their foundations - with one house having an infant buried underneath the main door facing north, as well as the ashes of cremated children's bones. The entire settlement is in effect built atop a cemetery or cremation ground. This is unheard of in ancient Celtic or Neolithic societies. There have also been suggestions that rituals which involved the deliberate smashing of pottery took place here, though the purpose of this ritual act is unknown. Some of these pots have been found to contain remnants of hallucinogenic herbs, which were assumedly ingested during certain religious rites.

Some of the houses were also dismantled and rebuilt a few metres elsewhere. The settlement contains many instances of animal sacrifices, including sheep and dogs.

The final standing house of Cladh Hallan was eventually abandoned in 400 BCE, making it the longest used house in British prehistory to date. This remote culture of mummy venerating shamanic tribes eventually faded into history.

Despite the settlement being occupied well into the Bronze Age, the activity there exhibits typically Chthonic rituals, suggesting that a somewhat unique culture and spirituality persisted here among the peoples of the Outer Hebrides for some time.

Discoveries across these isles continue to baffle and fascinate experts. There is also a high frequency of stone circles and cairns scattered throughout the islands pointing to an active community who placed spirituality at the core of their worldview. It is an established fact that inhabitants have dwelt on the Hebrides since the early Stone Age.

Current theories dealing with the 'Scithain culture' suggest their ritual and religious beliefs were largely comprised of the aboriginal British worldview.

As it stands, little else can be written regarding archaeological and historical peculiarities surrounding the Hebrides given how little is currently understood, by both academics and practitioners of the Chthonic Scithain tradition.

The Scithain Tradition and Vampyric Witchcraft

The unique teachings and practises of Drakon Covenant witchcraft are founded upon the Sinister Sevenfold Way (known also as the *Septenary Tradition* or *Hebdomadry*), which in turn derives from the aural tradition of the Camlad Rouning (known also as the way of the Rounwytha). According to its adherents, this way was passed down by reclusive adepts on a master-pupil relationship for many generations.

The Sevenfold Way was an attempt at codifying the aural teachings of the way of the Rounwytha, the practise by naturally gifted witches to guide the community and maintain the balance between Man and Nature. Often, what the adepts possessed was a rather garbled interpretation of the teachings (these teachings being believed to have been practised by the ancient civilisation of Albion, of which the druids were a later imitation).

During the latter half of the 20th century, a collective of the inheritors of the genuine tradition of Albion decided to unite their efforts and begin to make the teachings more public. Thus, the Order of Nine Angles was born, and the Sinister Tradition was ushered into public knowledge, as well as consequently making the way of the Camlad Rouning known.

Whilst many magickal traditions claim such an illustrious lineage and antiquity, the Sinister Tradition stands on greater merit, given that these other supposed traditions are always, without fail, inherently derivative Qabalistic systems - a system popularised by Rosicrucianism and the Hermetic Order of the Golden Dawn (of which Aleister Crowley was a member). From here, Gerald Gardiner, Alex Sanders and every other pseudo-witch derived and plagiarised ideas to create the varied forms of Wicca, Druidry, and 'traditional witchcraft' we see today - to mention nothing of the so-called New Age movement. In contrast, the system of Hebdomadry shows no reliance on these themes, and brings to light genuine and unique practises, portraying a naturally mature system composed of depth and insight.

Since the public emergence of the Order of Nine Angles as a distinct entity and system of occult philosophy and practise, several aspects have been forwarded as examples of its distinction between what it regards as its historically rooted teachings in contrast to other variants of Satanism and/or Paganism.

The first being that the Septenary system, manifest in the Sevenfold Way, is the genuine Western occult tradition pre-dating the Qabalah and the Order has simply made available this secretive tradition in modern times.

The second is that the Sinister tradition exists to be lived, being the way of practical and exeatic, experience and the subsequent learning from such experience forming the basis of pathei-mathos. This living also encapsulates several dangerous, real-world ordeals - such as the infamous Insight Roles and rite of Internal Adept.

The third is that the pantheon of Dark Gods are part of a previous and garbled aural tradition (a mythos) and like entities such as *Satan*, may or may not exist in the standard manner which we understand things to exist. As written elsewhere - 'it is for each individual to discover for themselves, via practical experience of sorcery, the truth of the matter.'

The fourth distinction between the Septenary Tradition and other magickal systems is that this unique Way and the insights attained through the gifts of the Dark Gods and adherence to the practical, exeatic experiences are geared toward the creation of actual Adept-like individuals, a new human classified as *Homo Galactica*, among other names. This widespread creation of such a type of human will of course take some time to accomplish (within the span of centuries or more).

Another distinction (and many more exist, though only several here are highlighted out of context and brevity) is that the system is not sacrosanct or dogma; it exists to evolve as an entity in its own right. This does not mean however that individuals can extract the safer aspects and create an empty aesthetic and rhetoric out of them, but rather that the stages of the Way and the insights accrued from such stages can and should lead to further developments within the tradition. This is an important aspect to understand - it is an evolution, not a simple morphosis or mutation of the essence of the Sinister-Numinous.

Many more unique facets and such exist which serve to demonstrate how the Sinister tradition is in itself a self-contained whole, exemplifying an inherently Western ethos and philosophical Weltanschauung. These facets will become clear to the initiate who diligently pursues the Sevenfold Way in an honest and earnest manner. From here, the touch of the Dark Gods simply cannot fail to go unnoticed.

The Dark Gods and Literary Intimations

Modern notions and reactions to the mythos of the Dark Gods invariably turn to similarities among writers such as H.P. Lovecraft, et al.

Lovecraft created a very loose mythos to add to his short stories, based upon the various fragments and recollections of intense and at times lucid dreams he had experienced for many years. Modern attempts to structure such a loose mythos into a genuine occult system are extremely forced and more telling of the nature of such individuals who attempt to do so, the systems crafted are always - without fail - based upon the Magian, Qabalah derived ontology and theology of pseudo-western occultism.

The Dark Gods are chaotic and timeless entities, who by Their very nature can intrude upon the unconscious of the individual should They so desire. That various intimations and hints of Their existence and nature have surfaced amongst those few sensitive enough to intuit Them, as well as being articulate enough to attempt to render Their essence into written form, is of course feasible and not surprising.

The ontological and theological treatises of the ONA

regarding the Dark Gods do possess a coherency, one which can be understood and thence experienced by the initiate providing they follow the stages and ordeals of the Sevenfold Way in a correct and whole manner. Several authors and thinkers are now starting to consider the possibility that humankind came into contact with certain non-terrestrial forces sometime during our early stages of rational awareness.

In the ONA mythos, the Dark Gods - along with other acausal entities - are said to have travelled to Earth at several points in the distant past, giving rise to various myths and legends. Primitive magick arose, so some say, out of early Man's attempts to emulate the technology of these acausal beings. The interaction between the two species is believed to have advanced our evolution in a considerable manner. Some of these acausal species known to Adepts of the tradition are said to have copulated with humans, which led to the creation and bearing of half-human offspring. We see such notions abound in ancient literature, from the stories of famed demigods and heroes such as Heracles and Perseus in Greek myth, to the terrible monsters such as Grendel in Norse saga.

A study of such writings within ONA texts, as well as more mundane speculations on ancient visitors may help the reader grasp the truth behind such legends.

The Sinister tradition is therefore rather simple, and draws into itself influences from several traditions itself, such as Arabic, Hellenic and Celtic mysticism, as well as European Alchemy and the black magickal shades of traditional witchcraft and what is nowadays termed the

'Left Hand Path'. The Order itself defines the term Left Hand Path as:

The amoral and individualistic Way of Sinister Sorcery. In the LHP there are no rules: there is nothing that is not permitted; nothing that is forbidden or restricted. That is, the LHP means the individual takes sole responsibility for their actions and their quest, and does not abide by the ethics of mundanes. In addition, the LHP is where the individual learns from the practical deeds and practical challenges that are an integral to it.

The vampyric elements of such black magickal traditions have always existed; however, an overt focus on this particular aspect was always the preserve of a few, given its demanding and essentially hidden nature. A cursory study of hexes, spirits and typical powers of the traditional witch according to folk tales and historical accounts often show a markedly vampiric bent - the draining of life from victims and cattle, the life sapping effects of blights upon crops, the use of blood in many pacts and rites, and other various examples which can be discovered via a study of the history of witchcraft.

Vampyrism is the natural extension of the witch's power. It is the direct acquisition of that which animates life - the very acausal Blood Essence. The most feared spirits and deities of many ancient cultures were always perceived to possess vampiric powers. It is proposed that principal focus upon this mechanism and the worldview it entails is a charged path to obtaining results far above and beyond non-vampiric orthodox applications of spellcraft. Experience has shown this assumption to be true.

The Heresy of the Witches

Within the tradition espoused by the Drakon Covenant there are several markedly different and essentially heretical viewpoints (as far as the mundane apprehensions are concerned) added to the ontology and theology of the ONA's 'Traditional Satanism' as well as their Sevenfold Way.

Traditions exist to guide the individual toward a certain desired point, with the individual's consequent learning (their essential *pathei-mathos*) adding to and enriching that tradition over time. Thus, to belong to a tradition is to continue the work of those who have gone before and to recognise one's self as a chain extending from the past to the future.

Within most traditions several distinct ideas, symbols or forms are used to denote the essence of that which the guide or tradition itself is attempting to impart. The point of the traditional way is to lead the initiate through varied and/or distinct grades or degrees until they arrive at a point of apprehension where the symbols no longer need to be relied upon and the essence of that which is being imparted is recognised, understood, integrated and utilised. It is for this reason that a tradition (and a workable path to Mastery) can only truly be created by a collection of individuals living out across a span of causal time a distinct set of rites and modes of living.

However, this is not to say that all symbols are useless - they are in fact often more powerful than the individual could ever hope to be, being immortal numinous entities in their own right. What the tradition can or should do is guide the initiate to the point at which they understand and can rationally grasp the essence behind the form - perhaps in time, using such a grasp to weave new forms to express such an essence. This point cannot be arrived at via shortcuts; it requires years of learning and living, and those who attempt to change or shortcut the Sinister tradition from the beginning of their journey have often usually only done so out of a desire for banal self-expression, with such attempts at crafting new forms quickly dissipating, given that they lack the necessary numinous energies which bring them (the symbols) to life.

The traditional aspects of the Drakon Covenant therefore are distinct not in their attempts to advance the Sinister tradition *per se* (though time will tell if they do so), but rather come about as a result of initiates apprehending the essence and forces of the cosmos through a particular lens (being that of vampyrism/wamphyrism) and hoping to not only shed more light upon such forces via such a way of living, but by also allowing the initiate to advance along a particular vector, and arguing - whether some agree or disagree - that such aspects are inherently a part of the ONA's nature - as evidenced in the depiction of Baphomet as a vampiric goddess, among other such pertinent examples.

The primary and noticeable distinction of the Covenant tradition is the belief in several additional 'Dark Gods' or such similar acausal entities - be they aspects of Wyrdful forces within the cosmos (such as Morannis and Lanus) or acausal beings believed to be on a par with the Dark Gods themselves. Such Dark Gods are similar to those already known by us - they are indeed perhaps aspects of the Dark Gods themselves. They serve the same basic function - the integration and understanding of cosmic forces to lead the initiate toward the stage of Adept. If such forms and symbols are continued with beyond this stage, that is up to the personal judgment of the Adept. Some of the Dark Gods are approached in a particular manner within this vampyric tradition, thus seemingly going against one of the Covenant's maxims of forbidding the post-initiate to describe or attempt to express the essence and nature of the Dark Gods in an explicit manner (a notable example is the veneration within the Drakon Covenant of Nythra as the *Void Mother*, the primal vampiric arch-deity). However, direct communion with and understanding of such ordinances and teachings, as well as direct communion with the entities themselves quickly reveals to the sagacious just why such manners of approach are undertaken.

It should be stressed however that these unique entities and traditions are by no means exclusive to the Covenant teachings - indeed, it is encouraged and hoped that such traditions in time spread to become accepted by all adherents of the Sinister way.

The most prominent of these acausal entities which are unique to the Covenant tradition are of course *Morgatha* (regarded by the Drakon Covenant as *Mater Vindex*, as well as an earthbound distillation of the Sinisterly-Numinous archetype in its entirety and bearer of the Grail).

A Historical Tapestry of Medieval Witchcraft

As proposed, traditional witchcraft has always been essentially and often overtly vampiric in its essence. When applying a vampiric lens to the classic accounts of witch activity throughout history, many things begin to make sense. Most interpretations from both sides of the fence woefully mistranslated the nature of these rites and rituals. To understand this, we must first study the nature of several phenomena - sleep paralysis, astral predation and Communion with the Undead.

So-called 'night terrors' are explained scientifically as the mind remaining awake whilst the body has fallen asleep, this paralysis being an inbuilt mental process to stop the sleeper from acting out their dreams and thus unintentionally harming themselves. This theory is flawed for three main reasons. It fails, firstly, to explain why people do sleepwalk and thrash about in bed. It also fails to explain the pseudo-scientific notion of the 'body falling asleep' when the mind is still awake (a woefully inept description), as well as why this would induce hallucinatory effects. It also fails to explain why the paralysis occurs nowhere near the REM cycle (when we actually dream). Finally, it fails to explain why people from diverse cultures across the world all experience the same entities and sensations (shadow figures, cats, old hags and so on).

According to the occult explanation for such phenomena, sleep paralysis arises from the individual's consciousness focus switching from the physical to the subtle *astral body* and thus the primary mode of perception is thence based in the astral body. Often the astral is still locally to, or still firmly within the confines or region of the physical body. Most people experiencing this phenomenon will have little to no knowledge about these astral mechanics or how to switch back to the physical. This engenders fear and thus panic. As in any natural environment, a struggling prey would attract the notice of predators and thus many people experience being attacked at this point.

The 'predators' in this case are the entities which led to, and inspired the myth of vampires. Some are simple entities. Others are far more powerful and it is those the witch is encouraged to attempt to gain Communion with.

In medieval times and earlier, this out of body astral experience and subsequent Communion was achieved with the use of drugs (such as the infamous 'witch's salve', this concoction often including potentially fatal ingredients if mismanaged, such as Monkshood, Deadly Nightshade and psychoactive mushrooms possessing varying hallucinogenic properties). The witch's Sabbath was one example of this communion, as was the witch's flight, which was representative of the effects of the hallucinogens themselves, often said to give the sensation of flying (as depicted in many sensationalist and religiously motivated woodcarvings of the time).

The gathering of witches was often presided over by various shadowy beings, often equated with Satan or other chthonic indigenous deities/entities, who were later maligned and reinterpreted by the Nazarene church. These deities/entities were no doubt analogous to the vampiric spirits dealt with in this book, and given the nature and method of the techniques employed to contact and beseech them, the modern witch will be continuing a dark and potent tradition in this regard.

The relation of such vampiric powers to the dark and chaotic spirits of the wilderness is thus evident in this natural predatory hierarchy, which humans long ago sought to honour via offerings and treaties made with such entities. These rites later became the basis for the persecution of witches in medieval Europe.

To this day, modern wiccans and practitioners of neo-paganism are quick to fall into the role of eternal victim, claiming such rites are wholly myth, and believing they are persecuted in today's society as some form of hangover from these Christian prejudices. Whilst those practising the black arts were maligned and indeed tried and executed for their crimes, many witches in Europe were simply often imprisoned or forced to pay fines for their arts. The so-called 'Burning Times' is simply a histrionic modern invention

What such modern practitioners also tend to overlook is the historical accounts of witches being burnt and executed throughout ancient pagan, non-Christian societies such as Greece and Rome. In the Roman Empire for instance, the *Lex Cornelia de sicariis et veneficiis* was written up, and which banned the trade, procurement and possession of not only occult literature and paraphernalia but also of poisons - as most witches functioned as poisoners and assassins alongside the provision of skills such as hexing and soothsaying. In 31BCE, the Emperor Augustus ordered the confiscation and burning of every magick book in Rome (the number of books gathered supposedly being around 2000).

Interestingly, the *Sibylline books*, a set of oracles written by the Hellespontine Sibyl (the head priestess of the Oracle of Delphi) were not subject to such burning, perhaps due to them being consulted during times of crisis within the Roman Empire.

As can be seen, the power of witches and magick has been feared and respected since antiquity. The persecution does not stem from solely Christian ignorance, but simply that of human ignorance. It is for this reason that genuine practitioners of witchcraft have isolated themselves throughout history and kept their practises hidden from the masses.

The Witch's Salve

Traditionally, the 'flying ointment' used by witches to meet various shadowy beings (be they demons, nature spirits or the Dark Gods themselves) was a salve or paste applied to the skin and containing many ingredients which were potentially fatally toxic if ingested in large amounts.

The ingredients in traditional recipes often utilised members of the *Solanaceae* family, and usually included plants such as hemlock (*Conium Maculatum*), deadly nightshade (*Atropa Belladonna*), wolfsbane (*Aconitum Napellus*), and henbane (*Hyoscyamus Niger*). How these were treated was supposedly via extraction, with the ingredients being applied via an animal fat base.

For the intrepid witch, the recipe for making such a salve is given here, as well as later in Appendix I.

Firstly, the plants themselves need to be acquired. This will involve a certain degree of research and/or travel in order to harvest them, after which they should be stored somewhere dry and allowed to air, so as to dry them sufficiently. Those more invested may opt to grow the plants in their garden.

Next, the herbs would be ground up with a little boiling water in a mortar and pestle. Then, the witch would proceed to blend these and mix them with the animal fat into a paste and left for a week. The resultant salve was then topically applied to the skin.

Another method involves the creation of a tincture. Witches in the middle ages would have traditionally used vinegar to procure extracts (modern extracting methods often use vodka). The herbs are placed in a jar which can be sealed airtight. Vinegar is poured over the dried herbs until submerged. The jar is then sealed and left in a cool, dark place, being shaken slightly every two days for two weeks.

Certain traditions claim that witches would smear the ointment along the length of their brooms, grinding their genitalia along the handle, thus providing a sexual gnosis as a preliminary to the drug's effect, and signalling to discarnate entities the witch's desire to copulate with the attendant shadows. From these practises, the church drew clams that witches bred with demons during their infernal Sabbath rites.

The use of herbs and drugs for ritual purposes has a long and documented history throughout Europe and elsewhere. Often the very plant's energies were perceived as intelligent forces which taught the ancestors their properties, which were handed down and preserved.

Sacramentum Sinistrum

Several psychoactive herbs and plants native to Europe and the British Isles can be employed to bring about trance states and visions during rites and meditations within the Covenant tradition of witchcraft. Often the plants are either smoked, drunk in a tea or (as in ritual form) burnt on a brazier, with a shawl or cowl covering the head hung over the burning herbs so as to inhale the smoke as efficiently as possible.

Plants are natural teachers which possess their own unique spirits, a muted wisdom which the Rounwytha can tap into with persistence and imbibement. The plants should be respected and recognised as ancient guides through the earthen darkness. Some plants such as Datura possess a very palpable aura bordering on sinister consciousness, and should never be treated with candour or flippancy. Cultivating these plants in a greenhouse or garden is one way to develop a close bond which will in time be repaid through the insightful journeys undertaken upon ingestion of these sacred herbs.

Cannabis is one of mankind's oldest cultivated plants. The plant generally comes in two distinct strains, *Cannabis Sativa* and *Cannabis Indica*. Sativa is generally regarded as more psychoactive than Indica, with Indica having more physiological effects which lead to mellow feelings and a general state of relaxation. Cross pollination between the two has created a variety of unique hybrids. Cannabis Sativa is the form generally employed for ritual purpose.

Every part of the cannabis plant can be utilised. The flowering bud of the female variety of the plant is dried and smoked. The leaves can be used to make an earthy drink or for bulking up the collected bud. The resin glands are used to make hashish. The stalks can be kept and ground up for making a mildly intoxicating tea. The oil is also widely regarded as a panacea. Cannabis Sativa is a powerful aid to visionary experiences and exploration of the self in relation to others and the world (it has been used extensively alongside chant and dream magick by initiates of the Drakon Covenant during the discovery of several rites and historical threads which are detailed in this book).

Mugwort (*Artemisia Vulgaris*) has historically been used by witches for inducing lucid dreams/astral projection with potent results, and thus can be used for vampyric flight and various draumrûna rituals. It can be drunk in a tea or smoked (often mixed with cannabis and/or tobacco).

Mandrake (Mandragora Officinarum) usually refers to the root of the Mandragora plant. It grows mainly in Southern Europe, and has been used in the British Isles since the 1500s. Witches would often mix Mandrake and cannabis together. Given that this plant contains scopolamine (as found in belladonna and Datura) it is unsurprising that it was utilised during the witch's flight.

Many myths and legends abound regarding Mandrake. The plant was believed to possess a sentience and could vanish at will should a wandering botanist come looking to dig it up. If one were to chance upon it, digging it up would result in the plant giving an ear-shattering scream which would kill anyone unfortunate to hear it. Eventually medieval seekers of Mandrake developed a method of harvesting it safely - they would tie the plant to a dog and run away, with the dog immediately giving chase. The plant's dying scream would thus kill the animal, and the owner (now at a safe distance) could return when it was safe to fetch the root.

The root was often kept as a talisman for all kinds of purposes, and worn to rid the body of ill health or demonic possession. According to folklore, the root must be bathed in milk or wine, and wrapped in fine silks or other such fabrics.

Mandrake became a characteristic symbol of the superstition which abounded during medieval times, and following the Enlightenment consequently fell out of favour altogether.

Ergot is a fungus belonging to the *Claviceps* family and is noted for its ability to induce hallucinations. It grows on crops such as rye and has historically been accidentally ingested due to this. It has since become a useful fungus in various medicinal treatments, and can easily be cultivated by those wishing to experiment and use it in a ritual setting.

***Psylocibin Mushroom*s** grow in a variety of forms, the most prevalent within the British Isles being *Psilocybe semilanceata*, known commonly as 'liberty caps'. Mushrooms are perhaps one of the most useful and powerful psychoactive entheogens at the witch's disposal and should be experienced by any with a serious interest in developing a closer connection to the land and the forces of Nature. They can often be found scattered in fields and other grassy areas and start to appear in Autumn. They have a characteristic yellow-brown hue, with a long stalk that can be either straight or (more often) slightly crooked.

Many witches find the psylocibin mushroom becomes a firm favourite for traversing between the worlds, given the potency and ease with which they can be harvested and tolerated by those who know what they are doing.

Datura is a perennial plant native to several regions throughout the world. Its most commonly used species are *Datura Metel* (growing in warmer climes such as India), and *Datura Stramonium* (which is found throughout Europe and North America). *Datura Inoxia* is also popular.

It is identified by its beautiful white or purple flowers. Its leaves and flowers can be dried and smoked, or made into tea via simply brewing them in hot water, and its seeds can be also eaten. The species which is recommended for use here is *Datura Stramonium* (it is advised that research is done to ensure this is the strain in one's possession prior to ingesting it).

Datura is often reserved for use during the Eremitic rite, when communion with the chthonic forces is sought after. This is a risky endeavour for the practitioner due to its potentially intense hallucinogenic effects and resultant photophobia, which can last for up to three days. The drug's actual effects can last up to 48 hours, though - like the potential photophobia blindness - this is a rare occurrence. Therefore, the nocturnal nature of the rite is suited to taking this powerful sacrament. The plant is traditionally brewed into a tea or the smoke inhaled via the use of a brazier or 'smudge bowl' during the Eremitic rite, prior to which a fast and meditation on the plant's essence itself should have been observed. Such prior communication is key to the success of the rite and the resultant insights. Demonstrating a healthy level of respect and will to communicate with the plant will ensure the spirit of the Datura will guide the witch through the experience.

However, in order to ascertain the correct dosage, the witch must experiment in preparation for ritually taking the drug (which will usually involve taking the highest tolerable dose). Some will drink Datura tea and receive no effects, only to find smoking the plant or eating the seeds yields success.

The seeds are ingested for their ability to assist in astral projection and lucid dreaming states. Beginning with a small handful of seeds (usually 5-6), a natural dosage limit can be worked out by the individual. More than 10 are known to bring about more intense effects, though some individuals have been known to take up to 100 in a sitting - with terrifying and revelatory consequences.

Making a tea from Datura is as simple as placing several leaves and flowers in boiling water, preferably leaving it to steep for around an hour (the recommended dosage for beginners is 1 flower or leaf. This is usually too mild for any effect to take place but serves as a useful baseline from which to build and ascertain the safety and efficacy of stronger doses).

A salve can be made from the leaves, flowers and seeds which is then applied to sensitive areas such as the temples, genitalia and armpits (as outlined above). This is believed to be the safest method for ingestion alongside eating the seeds.

Datura contains chemicals which are fatally toxic if allowed to build up in the system. Ingesting or inhaling the plant should be done no more than once every two weeks.

Within the Drakon Covenant tradition, Datura is held to be especially favoured by Nythra, and it is regarded as one of Her cherished symbols.

These plants as stated are intelligent entities in their own right, imbued with a form of life extending into the Acausal spaces in ways the average human simply cannot begin to understand from a normative and waking state consciousness. These intelligences, manifesting as wise teachers and guides through the various recesses of the Abyss can teach the initiate/Adept much about the sheer depths of the Natural world and Cosmos as a whole.

These plant intelligences often manifest as feminine entities (especially Datura and Ayahuasca) and demand respect, lest the 'trips' involved via ingestion turn into hellish odysseys. Primitive man soon learnt to hold these plants in high esteem, understanding the various magickal properties they possessed (and which understanding has degraded in latter days to a bland categorisation and use of various 'magickal herbs and oils'). Within Covenant tradition, the life-force of these plants and their attendant intelligence and properties is generally honoured under the auspices of the dark goddess Azanigin.

Alongside this recognition of the untamed elements and vegetative intelligences that lurked on the periphery of society was an intense awareness of Man's spiritual aspects and existence beyond death in other non-physical worlds. Thus, a general cult of ancestor veneration was observed, with similar offerings and sacrifices made to beseech the long dead relatives, so that they may continue to guard over and guide the community from their ghostly vantage point.

This focus upon the realm of death and the communication with the deceased became the Chthonic tradition of Scithain, as a priestly caste arose, ever refining the ways with which they could contact the ancestral dead.

Ancestor Cults

It is a staple aspect of most ancient cultures to appease the native spirits so as to receive assistance if and when their help is required. The spirits were generally regarded as those of the ancestors for the most part, and the lineage of one's bloodline was seen all around the individual, existing in the natural world in a perpetual cycle of rebirth and harmony.

In Celtic myth, the general term for such spirits is *sídhe* (pronounced *see-thuh or shee-tha*). They are often equated with the dead, and are said to dwell in the barrow mounds which were built for the deceased.

These spirits were more often than not hostile in nature, and various charms and prayers existed to thwart them or at least keep them at bay. Among the grimmer variants of the sídhe were the *Dearg Dûl* and the *Sluagh Sídhe*. Within Drakon Covenant literature, these are but two terms used to denote certain acausal vampiric entities (the other descriptive term being *Draugr*, with these Draugr making up the type of Undead entity commonly referred to - whence named to a degree and known to the practitioner - as the *Ascended Masters)*.

Returning to the vampiric worldview of supernatural phenomena, we can see the prevalence of such predatory entities and forces particularly with the *Dearg Dûl* ('blood drinker'), vampiric spirits of the wilderness who were described as terrifying and apparent female creatures which thirst eternally for blood. These entities are said to be responsible for the death of livestock and lonely travellers. Little is written or known of the Dearg Dûl, but vampirism in ancient times - particularly in Celtic Europe - was a real concern. It was common for the Celts to pile stones upon the graves of the dead so as to prevent them from rising again. This folk superstition arose out of the reports of the deceased returning to feed upon the living. Such precautions were often observed especially when a witch or sorcerer of some sort was buried, as it was believed such individuals were more likely to return from the dead (which it could be argued is rather true, according at least to the model proposed herein regarding magickal ability). The pronunciation of *Dearg* (duh-ruh-guh) shows quite a similarity to the Norse *Draugr*.

Lonely places, such as caves, cliffs, lakes or forests as well as cemeteries are traditional regions to leave offerings to the Dearg Dûl and the Sluagh. Both are believed to be appeased by blood.

Simple offerings of incense or other gifts, such as fruit or coins are also acceptable tokens to the Sluagh. Offerings were normally given in a small bowl, often left atop a rock, cairn or similar stony makeshift altar, which was decorated and adorned. This practise is still observed today, particularly in Ireland, and is referred to as *Creideamh Sí*.

Origins of the Creideamh Sí

The practise of leaving offerings to the spirits of the dead stems from the ancient ancestor cults which flourished during the prehistory of Albion.

As humans began to move from a lifestyle of hunting and gathering to one of agriculture, land became a highly valued commodity. Land was one's livelihood, upon which livestock could be grazed and crops grown.

The land was integral to the survival of the clan, and was passed down through the generations. Ancestors were often buried in their land, with a belief that their essence would continue to watch over the clan, and bring forth fertility and a good harvest.

The land literally became a part of the clan identity, and thus a natural integration with Nature was born along with an appreciation of the cycle of the seasons, leading to a solar based religion which founded its centre at Stonehenge. This religion, which grew from the fertile soil of the chthonic ancestor cults of Scithain eventually evolved into draíochta (druidism), which soon spread throughout the lands along with the Celtic peoples.

The veneration of the natural cycle later became ossified into a distinct ritual practise, one tied in to the bond between man, nature and folk, represented by a necessary sacrifice, whereby a young initiate would be raised to the level of priest or king and sacrificed at the end of the year. The reason for initiation was to ensure the sacrifice (the willing opfer) was not only aware of his place in the scheme of the ritual, but also ensure that he was possessed of a sufficient acausal saturation. His ritual slaying would thus bring about change for the entire land and those who lived there.

The sacrifice was traditionally either thrown into a bog in earlier times, to bring him close to the chthonic earth forces, or in later times, a particular rite arose (which formed the roots of the Ceremony of Recalling), which culminated in the head of the opfer being removed and displayed as a token and symbol of fertility and assurance of good crops and a restoration of natural balance. Often, the head was decorated and the mouth stuffed with oak leaves and other such effigies of nature. Thus, the symbol of the Green Man came about (this being the root of the florid face seen adorning medieval churches and new age shops, and is not - as some sanitised urbanites have claimed - a personification of natural forces or virility).

The Celts in particular were famous for their veneration of such symbols and historians have written much on the supposed 'cult of the head'. Celtic warriors would collect skulls and display them at thresholds and the perimeters of their homes. To passing travellers, a celtic settlement would have been an unnerving sight to behold. Strabo, a Greek philosopher and historian wrote of this activity among the Celts:

"There is also that custom, barbarous and exotic, which attends most of the northern tribes, when they depart from the battle they hang the heads of their enemies from the necks or their horses, and when they have brought them home, nail the spectacle to the entrance of their houses. At any rate Posidonius says that he himself saw this spectacle in many places, and that, although he first loathed it, afterwards through his familiarity with it, he could bear it calmly."

Julius Caesar records his witness of a Druid grove near Marseilles in Gaul:

"Interlacing boughs enclosed a space of darkness and cold shade, and banished the sunlight from above. ... Gods were worshipped there with savage rites, the altars were heaped with hideous offerings, and every tree was sprinkled with human gore. On these boughs ... birds feared to perch; in those coverts wild beasts would not lie down. ... Legend also told that often the subterranean hollows quaked and bellowed, that yew-trees fell down and rose up again, that the glare of conflagration came from trees that were not on fire, and that serpents twined and glided around the stems. The people never resorted thither to worship at close quarters, but left the place to the gods. When the sun is in mid-heaven or dark night fills the sky, the priest himself dreads their approach and fears to surprise the lord of the grove."

Ancient Irish peoples especially were known to subject their kingly sacrifices to visceral ritual torture prior to killing them. The opfer was garrotted, often cut up before having their throat slit and thrown into a bog during sacrificial ceremonies. Other instances, as discovered in archaeological finds in Ireland show victims such as 'Croghan Man' had holes carved through his arms, with a rope then pulled through these to restrain him. He was then stabbed several times before being literally cut in half.

The Irish god Crom Cruach (whose name was believed to mean 'crooked bloody one' or 'bloodied head') demanded human and even infant sacrifices in order to spare the withering of crops.

Altars to the gods were often anointed with the blood of sacrificial victims, with the Roman historian Tacitus describing the druid altars of Anglesey being drenched with the blood of prisoners. Strabo also recorded the sacrificial activities of the Cimbri tribe, describing a highly ritualised method of offering:

"Their wives, who would accompany them on their expeditions, were attended by priestesses who were seers; these were grey-haired, clad in white, with flaxen cloaks fastened on with clasps, girt with girdles of bronze, and bare-footed; now sword in hand these priestesses would meet with the prisoners of war throughout the camp, and having first crowned them with wreaths would lead them to a brazen vessel of about twenty amphorae; and they had a raised platform which the priestess would mount, and then, bending over the kettle, would cut the throat of each prisoner after he had been lifted up; and from the blood that poured forth into the vessel some of the priestesses would draw a prophecy, while still others would split open the body and from an inspection of the entrails would utter a prophecy of victory for their own people."

Strabo also noted grisly methods of divination, observing how 'for example, they would strike a man who had been consecrated for sacrifice in the back with a sword, and make prophecies based upon his death-spasms.'

Caesar also famously noted such practises amongst the Gauls designed to appease the gods and keep the cycle of the seasons in check, describing great 'wicker men' in which men and beasts would be burnt alive as offerings.

These accounts detail human sacrifice among the Gauls as if it were a regular practise, flippantly employed to elicit answers for every question or ailment. Whilst the writings of Strabo and Caesar may very well be embellished or exaggerated to a certain degree, there is of course 'no smoke without fire', and on all other matters, such historians are generally regarded as sound sources.

Human sacrifices were regarded as a worthy choice, though were often reserved for times of calamity or necessary seasonal observations. One notable example of such a sacrifice (and which example also showcases the Druid's role as antagoniser and freedom fighter against occupying Roman forces) can be seen in Suetonius Paulinus's attack on the isle of Anglesey (just off the northern coast of Wales) in 60CE, an attack designed to nullify the power the Druids had over the rebellious Britons.

Upon reaching the island, the Roman troops were greeted with a grim spectacle - the Druids were stood, their arms uplifted and chanting ancient magical incantations. Accompanying them were women, chanting and savagely beating their bare breasts, and armed only with flaming torches. The entire scene paralysed the Roman soldiers with fear, who did not advance until Paulinus shouted his orders and snapped them out of their daze.

The Romans, their senses restored, swiftly cut down the maniacal women, before massacring the sibilant Druids. It was then that they realised their doom, for the beach where the Druids were stood was in actuality a pre-prepared pyre. One of the women who had survived the bloodshed threw her torch upon it, and the bodies of the dead, along with the Roman soldiers, were lit up in a fiery sacrifice.

It was said around this time that the river Thames ran red as blood, and the Roman inhabitants truly believed they had been cursed by the act of the Druids at Anglesey. Shortly afterward, the entire city was decimated by the fury of Boudicca and her army.

Interestingly, according to the Roman historian Dio Cassius, prior to the invasion of London Boudicca invoked a goddess known as *Andraste* to augur the fate of such a battle. She produced a hare and, cutting its entrails and scattering them, deduced from this divination a good omen.

Many modern authors on witchcraft and Wicca include this goddess in their pantheon of deities supposedly worshipped by the Celts. However, careful study of Celtic belief and history indicates clearly that this translation is quite inaccurate - the goddess invoked was 'An Dras De', which is Brythonic celtic for 'the tribal god'. We can see a similar example in 'An Dag De', which refers to the Dagda.

The connections to war and prophecy suggest the goddess Boudicca invoked was perhaps an aspect of the goddess Aosoth.

Witchcraft in the World of Ancestor Veneration

Covens of witches were known to exist during those times when the types of prophesying and conduct of rituals normally reserved for the magickally initiated were observed by all members of a community, even if it were often through the intermediary of an appointed priesthood.

However, these covens of (mostly) female practitioners were regarded as distinct even from the celtic religious castes such as the druids and other wise folk. Belonging perhaps to the pre-celtic chthonic tradition from which the Camlad aural Rouning derives (and thus the Sevenfold Way), evidence exists of particular covens functioning upon the fringes of Celtic religion. Pomponius Mela in his *De situ orbis libri III* (circa 43CE) for example writes of a college of nine priestesses from the Gaulish Osismii tribe capable of summoning storms and transforming themselves into animals.

Another example, known as the Larzac tablet (dating from around 100CE) records a curse made against one group of sorceresses by another group. The tablet is made of lead and is inscribed in Gaulish language using Roman cursive lettering. Found in Aveyron, southern France in 1983, it is now kept in the museum of Millau.

The tablet was buried after construction, a chthonic practise common during ancient times, in the hope that the curse's magick would reach the underworld, perhaps to increase its power or have the curse reach the ears of the gods.

The text inscribed upon the tablet directs a curse against

Severa Tertionicna (the head witch) and a group of other women, presumably her covenmates.

The text roughly reads, 'Behold - The magic of women, their special underworld names, the prophecy of the seer who weaves this magic.'

The rest of the tablet is tentatively translated to call to an underworld goddess named *Adsagsona* to enact a binding spell against two women who left the group.

These covens or groups of witches have been described by historical authors and geographers such as Strabo as distinct parties, living communally and somewhat separate from the rest of society. Amidst their practises we can see threads of magickal rituals which hearken back to those preserved from the Chthonic tradition which arose during the Neolithic times, a tradition arising out of a synthesis between Aboriginal British and Neanderthal beliefs and practise. This continuation was later preserved in garbled form throughout the middle ages and then carried through the subsequent centuries to the modern era via the aural recollections of the roots of the Sinister tradition. We can therefore see much more clearly just how this semi-unbroken lineage developed and sustained itself throughout the centuries.

These solitary and communal bands of witches were buried in a very different manner to the druids, male or female. Often they were decapitated after death and their heads placed beneath their feet. Some also had their lower jaws removed, to perhaps prevent them from speaking evil magick post mortem. Such superstitious practises are observed among communities who wished to prevent the buried dead from returning from their graves as vampiric revenants. They were perhaps seen as powerful but untrustworthy women, capable of rising from their graves to continue their maleficent works, so long as they could sustain themselves upon the blood essence of the living.

With the arrival of Christianity, the wild witch and the female druid were cast as one and the same - evil satanic entities whose power had to be broken.

Whilst Roman and later Christian scribes sought to demonise the druid class (given that the druids held so much power over British resistance to both invaders), this is not to say that the darker aspects of their rituals were wholly fabricated.

Modern practitioners of the wiccan derivation of 'Druidry' have gone to extreme lengths over the years to dispel these historical accounts of ritual killing, claiming that the inherent bias of Roman and Greek writers was the reason for such depictions of violent sacrifice among the druids. This is of course a natural reaction of an urbanised and Christianised milieu who seek to portray their icons of roleplaying as ethereal and grandfatherly soothsayers. They arrogantly delude themselves into believing that the belief system they are most attracted to conveniently adopted a modernistic form of pacifism and universal love, whilst all around them the peoples of the time engaged in violent warfare as a natural course of life. It is a telling remark that amongst these unsettled and pallid practitioners, the feminine role in the druid caste is often overlooked or even entirely ignored. Regardless of modern sensibilities, the visceral elements of worship were certainly not shunned by our ancestors.

According to one tradition, the slayer of the opfer priest was often selected as the next sacrifice, this title appearing in several classical texts as 'Rex Nemorensis'. J. G. Frazer in *The Golden Bough* claims this is representative of a worldwide ancient fertility myth, though some anthropologists are sceptical; it is however likely that variations of the theme of regular sacrifice to ensure natural balance pervaded most ancient peoples, sprouting from an intuitive understand of the Wyrdful blood and soil to which a people were bound.

Those trees in whose dim shadow
The ghastly priest doth reign;
The priest who slew the slayer,
And shall himself be slain.

Modern Witchcraft vs. The Sevenfold Way

The stark differences between what passes as witchcraft in modern times and the genuine western tradition of the Sevenfold Way are clear to anyone who has studied both currents of thought.

Whilst the modern, urban interpretation of witchcraft claims to have derived from centuries old practises and ways of life, most if not all books on the subject of Wicca and the like are little more than modified forms of the Qabalistic rituals which Gerald Gardner and the originators of modern witchcraft borrowed from the writings of the Golden Dawn, an influential occult group of the late 19th century.

An interesting development has arisen in which individuals claim to follow traditional witchcraft, as opposed to Wicca; yet an inspection of their works reveals they possess nothing which differentiates themselves from the innumerable 'traditions' gathering dust in every new age bookstore across the world.

All these writers offer are slightly modified circle castings, correspondences detailing lists of rocks, angels, spirit animals, and other items plagiarised from a dozen cultures. At their core, they all prescribe the same *essentially Magian* paradigm of magick and the occult forces. What is revealed is a basic understanding of the forces of the cosmos - and an inability to think beyond the illusion of form.

Colourful variants, such as 'Druidry', 'Green witchcraft' and 'Eclectic Wicca' show little more than superficial differences on this Qabalistic theme. Curiously devoid from these forms is the vital element of human sacrifice, which was seen throughout many pagan traditions (most notably that of Druidry). These pseudo-traditions often espouse ideas such as karma, which our pagan ancestors never gave thought to. Indeed, the modern notion of karma stands far apart from the original Vedic belief; the current interpretation is nothing more than exotic clothing on an old Christian concept. The progenitors of Wicca had their 'Rule of Three', an essentially patronising idea that any negative magick would return on the caster three-fold. What proof they had for this was never offered, but as most followers of Wicca come from a Christian background and society, the idea of Divine Punishment was adequately clothed for them to at least pretend to be different from everybody else.

The Druid Myth

On the 21st June, 1972, a group of bards staged an invented ceremony at Primrose Hill in London. Amidst a hastily constructed stone circle made of pebbles, they claimed to be enacting a ritual which resurrected an ancient Celtic, druidic cult which had its roots in ancestral Britain.

In stark contrast to these claims, it is argued by some scholars that the word Celt was first used by Herodotus in 450 BCE, to describe the natives of the Danube valley. The British people were referred to by the Romans as Britanni. The use of the term 'Celt' in English dates only from the 17th century, when a Welsh linguist noted the similarities between Welsh, Irish and Scottish and Cornish languages (though it is now recognised that the pre-Saxon Britons were of Celtic stock). The Greek historian Strabo described the people of the British Isles as being somewhat distinctive to the Celts of Europe. It is believed they may also have also been distinct from the Gaelic speaking Celts of Ireland and Scotland.

The image of defined Celtic patterns, benign white robed druids and horse-loving tribes was itself an entire fabrication of Gaelic Romanticists created during the 18th Century.

As such, any claims by groups who espouse this modern interpretation to having some ancient knowledge or connection to Celtic past are most often deluding themselves. There is no record of the druids (mentioned in Roman texts often simply as 'priests' of the British) venerating a god called Anywn, of holding the triplicity sacred or of having specific ranks and titles.

What we do know of the druids and thus of the religious beliefs of the ancient British are that they honoured Nature and the cosmos, and practised human sacrifice in order to aright the natural balance of these factors. The image of the white druidic robe and headdress is also a fabrication, and not a single historical text describes the accoutrement of the druidic caste.

Thus, whilst the beliefs and practises of the ancient British resembled that of the Celts, it can easily be argued that history is far less certain than modern druids claim it is. The Celtic origins of several aspects of the Drakon Covenant's rituals are taken as part of an ancestral pathei-mathos, as well as a continuation of those beliefs which appear to have been influenced by the Neolithic cultures present in Britain prior to the arrival of Celtic or Celt-like tribes to the isles.

The New Age Marketing Scam

One movement which has influenced and distorted the modern trend of witchcraft has been the so-called 'New Age movement'. This was born out of the convergence of the drug fuelled rebellion of 1960s youth and the exploration of exotic cultures in typical urbane fashion, and the capitalist understanding that you can sell anything to anyone.

As a result, we see a consumerist attitude to Nature proliferating, where we find convenient lists of stones and crystals which possess any power and solution one can think of - if only one would purchase them all; endless 'new age bookstores' selling the same mish-mash of Native Indian, Wiccan and Buddhist paraphernalia; and a thousand variations on the Tarot deck, none of them remarkably revelatory, and nearly all of them modelled on the Golden Dawn deck of E.A. Waite.

Another example would be in the so-called path of Shamanism, a patronising cultural appropriation by largely urbane individuals who write endless books offering pathworkings to meet one's spirit guide or 'power animal', failing to understand the necessary prerequisite to a shamanic experience being social isolation and physical ingestion of substances often illegal in their country of residence. A complete misunderstanding arises in the assignment of spirit animals and these animals' supposed qualities and thus the supposed character traits of the pseudo-shaman. Again, it merely suffices to make boring, urban individuals feel special and unique.

The glaring issues with all these attempts to formulate a genuine magickal tradition are threefold:

α - The desire to make money eclipses the genuine desire to pursue the magickal path (notable examples of this would be nearly every American occult and 'wiccan/satanic' author).

β - The authors and practitioners still function within the social and moral paradigm of the society they find themselves within, despite what they may argue otherwise.

γ - And most importantly, these 'nature-based religions' are often the invention of wholly urban dwelling individuals, whose approach to Nature is typically consumerist. Nature, to them is viewed as a novelty, an arena in which one can enter in safety and play at being witches. Nature, in its primal, untamed form, is virtually unknown to them. They would last little longer than a few days when placed in the wilderness with only their supposed connection to nature to keep them alive. Because ultimately, the Magian brand of witchcraft we see today does nothing to develop the individual; there is no test of character, no insight gained, no true evolution of the self. We see the same arrogant, pretentious embarrassments who ordain themselves as 'High priest' or 'Grand Druid' or other such empty titles. These individuals, for all their magickal power, still live in mundane dwellings and work mundane jobs. Beyond their gothic attire and a dozen pentagram necklaces, they are simply average, unremarkable, uninspiring humans who have found a delusional outlet for their weakened grip on reality - the exact opposite to what an adept should be.

The Sevenfold Way and the Path to Wisdom

In contrast to this, the Sevenfold Way of the Sinister tradition places the understanding of Nature and the Cosmos upon the individual and his/her experiences. The social norms, taboos and beliefs of the society they have grown within are irrelevant and seen as unhealthy symptoms of the Magian worldview. Furthermore, real magickal tasks and development are encouraged (such as living in the wilderness for extended periods of time, engaging in the art of culling, and discovering the nature of the Dark Gods through the Spheres and Pathways of the Tree of Wyrd). Within the Sinister tradition, there is no distinction made between 'black' and 'white' magick, for no distinctions exist; this abstract dichotomy exists only within the dualistic worldview of the Magian.

The Sevenfold Way is an integration - a becoming with the forces of the cosmos, bereft of causal symbology - an evolution of the integral part of who you are and what you strive to be. The beliefs, hopes and dreams of the shifting mass of mundane society becomes little more than a predictable sea of misdirection and slow, uncertain progress. And it is when this understanding, this Aeonic insight comes about, that one attains a true sense of magickal power. Adeptship has been attained.

Sinister Witchcraft of the Drakon Covenant

As aforementioned, the practical system of the Drakon Covenant is founded upon the Sevenfold Way of the Order of Nine Angles and the Camlad Rouning. Coupled with this is a lens of a decidedly vampyric context, which sheds light on many aspects of the Sinister tradition which the witches of the coven have advanced over recent years.

In addition to this (and as a by-product of the vampyric practises), there are also the chthonic rites and traditions as revealed by what are referred to as the *Ascended Masters of Scithain*. There is thus a natural connection to the ancient practises of these Isles (Albion and the northern isles of the Haemodae), as well as an intimation with the spirit of the land.

From this intimation arises that unique Rounwytha nature; and it should be recognised by the initiate that these diverse strands of explication - be they the Rouner, the Vampyric witch or the Traditional Satanist - are all strands woven into an unbreakable whole which we refer to as the Sinisterly-numinous essence, and all come to the same destination, the same fruits. They arrive at that same goal, which is wisdom, the Grail: *Lapis Philosophicu*s.

The most convenient and relevant way toward this stage is of course, the Sevenfold Way.

The Sevenfold Way proposes a system of seven fundamental energies, forces, archetypes and powers - present both within the cosmos and the individual's psyche (the psyche being the latent aspects of the conscious mind, which magical initiation seeks to bring forth - making the unconscious conscious in Jungian terms).

These seven fundamental forces and their interaction with the world and each other are described in the Tree of Wyrd, a map of the cosmos' fundamental energies according to the Tradition.

The Tree of Wyrd

The Tree of Wyrd is a convenient description of the cosmos, the psyche and the pathways which link these to the acausal realms. The Tree contains seven spheres and twenty-one pathways. Each sphere relates to a planet or fundamental cosmic energy, and each pathway relates to a Dark God (three 'hidden' pathways are not mapped on the 2D image of the tree, but their properties are often given alongside depictions of the tree).

The Tree of Wyrd serves as a map of the unilluminated aspects of the mind and the Self; initiation being the awakening of these latent aspects within the mind. This awakening allows a greater apprehension of the psyche and the acausal, thus presencing within the initiate a higher degree of acausal energy. In essence, the mind moves furthermore into the acausal realms.

The Acausal Realm

Alongside this is the unique apprehension of magickal energy known as the Acausal. The Acausal is a realm parallel to the ordinary world of our five senses and general laws of physics and chemistry (the causal). It is from this Acausal realm that all life and consciousness originates, and Acausal energy presencing within the causal gives rise to what we refer to as a living organism. Magickal adeptship is the increase of this Acausal energy within the causal confines of a living being - the 'Acausal charge' being thus increased over a period of causal time. The Adept thus has a larger degree or complexity of acausal energy to draw upon and is able to comprehend a greater knowledge of the cosmos as a whole. However, it is advised such quantitative apprehensions of energy are foregone when trying to understand how acausal energy works upon the individual. To put it more elegantly, magickal adeptship is the consciousness of the adept moving more into the Acausal. Acausal time itself is the natural growth of Life according to its own unique nature, which causal abstractions cannot govern nor presently understand.

There is therefore no banishing, cleansing or shielding rites; the correspondences are aligned not according to our relative and skewed view of the universe from our singular point on earth; rather, the correspondences and combinations of magickal energies are derived and understood according to a cosmic view. There is no placing upon certain collocations of stars the behaviours of animals or forms which we deem them to look like. They are intuited as they are, the energies made manifest and understood via direct experience of the initiate.

The whole system and ontology of magick and magickal ritual is thus simplified into a progressive and elegant model, one in which the cosmos is bifurcated into a causal and acausal universe, with these each possessing energy and matter of their own nature. The Acausal is manifest in our realm via living entities, with this energy capable of manipulation by living entities - either causally or acausally bound. Evolution and magickal ability is signified by a greater intrusion of Acausal energy into a specific point in the causal - these points being described as *nexions* and such nexions being of varying types. Nexions can thus be opened, and in the case of a non-organic occurring form, lead to the creation of sacred spaces or regions where the forces of the Acausal can seep into the causal, causing subtle and widespread change upon living beings. In the case of organic forms, the opening of a nexion leads to a greater degree of magickal ability and understanding, and from there - evolution. Nature itself is regarded as a type of nexion, and the topic of nexions in general is detailed in other ONA texts.

Within the Septenary system therefore is a genuine

understanding of Nature beyond urban appreciation of the novelty of the wild. The wilderness is understood as a challenger, a mentor, something to become one with. Nature does not comply with transient moral ethics which humankind imposes upon it according to societal trends. She is the eternal mistress of change and evolution. Satan, as the archetypal master of the wilderness and conflict sits reposed, deep within the dark forests and moors, awaiting His children who are worthy to discern the hidden mysteries of Nature.

Ritual Method

Most rituals and rites of the Vampyric tradition, as exemplified by the Drakon Covenant, follow three forms:

I. Magickal rituals, designed to yield effects or knowledge which would not normally occur without magickal interference (scrying, hexing, weather spells, divination and so forth)

II. Offerings at certain places and times as part of a bond the witch has with a specific entity or Dark God

III. Seasonal rites, designed to strengthen tradition and pay homage to the ancestors and the cosmos

Not included are the trials and grade rituals which mark the progression of the witch through the degrees of the Septenary tradition.

Ritual is divided into two modes: Hermetic (solitary), and Ceremonial (those performed with a congregation of 2-3 or more). Most rites within the Septenary tradition involve the witch entering a trance state and manipulating the energies of the Acausal directly, via his/her use and knowledge of the energies of the Tree of Wyrd.

The entering into a state of trance is a necessary requisite for attaining success in your magickal rites (as well as unique practises, such as vampyric flight). Trance states are those states which differ from ordinary waking consciousness. They represent a shift in brainwave function (usually from Delta to Alpha wave activity) and as such, allow the consciousness to tune into differing modes of existence.

Trance states were historically obtained via various methods, such as the use of drugs, working the self up into a frenzy, dance and song, self-mortification, or sleep deprivation and fasting. That most modern magickal traditions ignore this necessary aspect and prerequisite (and that it is still a staple ingredient of primitive societies shamanic workings shows how far the civilised urban pretender has come from the reality of Nature's greatest mysteries).

A simple example of a ritual within the Sinister tradition would involve the practitioner having fasted and reduced sleep to some degree prior. Then, either the imbibing of a mild drug (such as cannabis or other naturally occurring substances, outlined later in this book) or performing a circular repetitive dance accompanied by a chant (usually of the Dark God who presides over the theme of the ritual - such as destruction or hidden knowledge). The trance state is entered and a fixation upon the energies of the aspect of the Acausal or Dark God is made via the use of a sigil and chant - combined with the ubiquitous use of a clear quartz crystal, which acts as a gate to the Acausal energies, allowing the energies to come through to the causal realm. The traditional, and most effective shape for this crystal is that of a tetrahedron. The fundamental formula is this: crystal, image, chant.

Vampyric applications to ritual method (as evidenced in the ancient Greek mystery rites of which the Sinister Tradition draws connection to) include the whipping and cutting of the flesh to shock the mind and body into the necessary trance state. This method is often chosen over the other methods by the followers of the Vampyric tradition as it also draws near and pleases the vampiric spirits of the Sidhe, who may choose to impart extra beneficial knowledge to the practitioner (if the Rite was not solely aimed at drawing their attention in the first place). Often, a combination of trance inducing dance, drugs and bloodletting is used.

Communion Ritual Method

Most communion based ceremonial rituals within the vampyric tradition of the Drakon Covenant (and this particular method can be employed in a ceremonial setting when seeking whispers from the Draugr or the Dark Gods Themselves) generally consist of a specially trained witch, known as a *Lamia Naturalis*, who was selected for his/her (though mostly female) natural skill and affinity toward medium abilities (this was usually a girl of around 13 -18 years, this demographic often noted as being particularly conducive toward Undead and spiritual contact). The Lamia Naturalis would enter a light trance using drugs, chant or music, oftentimes sealing herself from sensory input via a head dress or black cowl over her head.

The other participants to the ritual would then beseech particular Undead entities via the above outlined methods. The entities, upon approaching, often make their voices known to the most sensitive member present - in this instance the Lamia Naturalis. She would write down what was relayed to her and provide correspondence with the spirits in this manner. The function and role of a Lamia Naturalis is an inherently dangerous one. It is essentially an extreme form of mediumship which can bring about a certain degree of psychosis if the witch is not adequately prepared.

However, all adherents and practitioners of the vampyric tradition of Drakon Covenant witchcraft will come to possess traits similar to that of the Lamia Naturalis (a prime example can be seen in the communion with the Dark Gods during Dark Pathway rites). This structure use of a Lamia witch often occurs within a generally formed coven or temple, the Lamia witch being able to devote her path to the unique grasp and attunement of the subtle arts of trance communion, under tutelage of the coven's Morain.

A Note on The Use of The Quartz Tetrahedron

As stated, the most efficient key to opening the acausal gates is a tetrahedron made of clear quartz. However, other suitable methods include a quartz chunk of natural shape (not polished or rounded). As well as this, several other materials within the spinel and quartz groups can be just as effective.

Among these are spinel, pleonast and morion. Spinel can take a variety of shades, but generally takes a transparent crimson colour. It can be seen in a tetrahedral shape in the hand of the Mousa of Swords on Christos Beest's Sinister Tarot paintings. It is particularly treasured by vampiric practitioners and often used in place of quartz, for its association with Baphomet via the depiction mentioned, as well as resembling bloodied quartz stone. Pleonast (also known as ceylonite), is a black, glassy mineral in the spinel group, and morion is known also by its common name smoky quartz.

For more detail on the conduct of rituals, see *Naos: A Practical Guide to Modern Magick* (Order of Nine Angles, 1974 EV).

Hermetic Initiation

Initiation into the Drakon Covenant's vampyric tradition can take two forms; either the standard rite of initiation as given in *Naos* followed by a subsequent adoption of vampyric practises alongside those of the Sevenfold Way; or the explicitly vampyric rite as given in *Codex Aristarchus*. For those choosing the vampyric rite of initiation, a secondary step taking the form of a pathworking meditation follows.

The rite evokes the essence of the Drakon Covenant path as one bearing a continuation of the mysteries of the Blood Grail, numinously upheld by the entity we honour as Morgatha, the Mother of Vindex. A direct spiritual lineage stretches from the Sinister Adepts of Albion to the modern-day novitiate, actualised in the form presented here, but one which is merely a current within the stream of life extending from past to present to future.

Initiation is essentially a bestial event. The willed and forceful evolution of an organism into something else is an abhorrent creation in itself. It creates something wholly singular and new, thus making the vampiric entity a direct intimation or seedling of divinity by this very act of self-apotheosis.

The shifting of essence during (genuine) initiation is an almost therianthropic process. Within the Covenant's tradition, several entities are therefore honoured during this transformative event - Satan and the Void Mother.

Satan is the great initiator, the awaiter-in-the-woods. It is He to whom all practitioners of the Black Arts come before to be anointed and sworn to the Tradition at the beginning of the initiatory quest, signified and symbolised by the ritual in itself. The Covenant tradition rite advances this further, forcing the initiate to summon the energies of Satan directly but within the predefined form as witnessed in the Tarot Atu *Azoth*.

The Void Mother is the end consequence of all vampiric power, a seething vortex of incomprehensible hunger and is brought into being here in a form to be rationally understood, despite such forms generally being utterly beyond abstraction. She anoints the Initiate, binding them to the Chain of Devouring utterly and completely, and which anointing will bestow a new apprehension throughout the quest to Mastery, namely that of the Vampyric current.

The Initiatory Rite

For several days, the witch must reduce their food and sleep to minimal levels. Each night, the *Sanctus Satanas* must be chanted before sleep, followed by meditation on the word *Azoth* quietly uttered slowly for several minutes.

On the night of the ritual, prepare yourself with a ritual bath. Having then meditated quietly for some minutes, sit down with your crystal in hand, marking it with blood and marking your forehead in a similar manner.

Burn a mixture of Oak and Henbane, ensuring to fill the area you are meditating in with a heady amount of smoke within comfort.

Next, begin to intone the word *Drakon* seven times.

Now, imagine yourself at the foot of a large oaken door. It is old, with large iron bolts and a heavy door handle. It bears upon it the sigil of the Covenant. Open the door and step into what resembles a medieval church nave.

You walk down the shadowy aisle, feeling the cold and ancient stones beneath your feet. The stained-glass windows let in only minimal light, windows which depict grim and half human, bat-winged knights in the frenzy of battle, drinking the blood of their enemies and holding up a chalice which flows with the blood thus spilt.

At the end of the chapel is an altar. On either side of the altar are ancient and tattered banners bearing the Covenant's sigil, and upon the altar itself is a large goblet of intricately wrought iron.

Behind the altar on the wall is a large painting, depicting a wraith-like entity, a feminine skeletal figure clad and veiled in tattered robes. About her feet are many bones and upon her head is a wreath of flowers. Her hands drip with blood. She is the primal vampiress, the Void Mother. Bow before her and take the goblet.

You look into the goblet, and see it full of blood, almost black in its fullness. Scry now and visualise your destiny.

Take the goblet in your hands and drink of the blood until nothing is left, and place it back upon the altar.

The Void Mother's image from above the altar moves toward you, filling the chapel with a cloying presence as she places a skeletal finger on your heart. You see crimson, fading to black.

With that, the rite is finished. Return to normal consciousness and say, '*Agios O Drakon.*'

This rite initiates the novitiate into the esoteric aspects of the vampyric tradition, one which unites this particular path with the historical roots of the Western Tradition of Albion.

You may return to this chapel during meditation whenever, to reaffirm one's ties to the mission of Covenant. The Void Mother may also be invoked during this time, for she answers the vampire call of all those who are Her children.

Secondary Initiation

The following night, prepare a ritual area with candles and incense or oils somewhere outside (preferably a wooded area). Intoxication using alcohol or other substances is often recommended for this ritual.

Take the soil from the earth and mark your arms and face with it, saying, *'Ecce Terra.'* Then vibrate the word *Satanas* seven times.

Next begin a circular dance, during which you will continue to chant until exhaustion compels you to finish and sit upon the ground.

Having regained composure, take a sharp blade, and making an incision upon your arm allow the blood to hit the earth, saying as you do so, 'It is from this blood that the soil shall be renewed. Let the Dark Gods come forth and anoint me for this quest.'

Sit in silence, allowing any thoughts to enter your mind. Note down anything intuited or gleaned during this time.

The Void Mother is of particular importance within the Drakon Covenant ontology, as will be seen throughout its writings. She is the paradoxical source and devourer of all phainomenon within the Cosmos. Signified by the causal name of *Nythra*, She is the inevitable pull toward baselessness and entropy within all matter. All things which bring subtle death are sacred to Her, especially poisons and deadly plants.

She anoints and enthrals the vampyr, making him/her a filament of her deadly Abyssal impulse. As stated, the Form used in this rite is simply to familiarise and allow the initiate to comprehend the essence of things (as is the nature of all Forms, at least in the beginning of the occult quest). Any attempts at symbolism as an end goal are utterly irreverent and incomplete.

Not to be confused with theological and wholly banal concepts of a primordial void, the Void Mother is the absolute source of vampiric potency, the *essential* vampiric wraith whom all vampiric entities are mere reflections of. It is no coincidence that vampires were long associated as bringers of plague and death, just as Nythra delights in the spread of sly, cloying deathly odours and diseases.

Of course, She has no form as we can understand - any causal depictions are simply gestures designed to elicit an understanding of Her essence. She is utterly beyond depiction in Her essence.

The correct (and only) way to come before Nythra is one of utter surrender and devotion; certainly not a difficult task given Her natural magnetic pull of all things into Her sublime dark essence. As such, all genuine novitiates of a vampyric bent pay homage to Her at the beginning of their quest toward Mastery.

The Path to Scithain

Every witch and infamous Adept of the Sinister tradition began at the foot of the dark mountain of struggle and progress. The grasp and mastery of the various distinct practises put forth within this tradition are but garnishes to the subtle and wordless power that arises and germinates within the Initiate as the Ego dissolves away, leading through a painful and tumultuous series of crises which the Initiate must resolve and rise above if they are to succeed and ascend above the morass of mundanity, giving birth to the Adept as a genuine entity.

It is outlined in Drakon Covenant texts such as the *Codex Aristarchus* just how one begins to enact a vampyric praxis in the real world and start upon that hallowed path toward Mastery. The principles are simple - the application of a distinctive predatory mindset and the subsequent methods which develop this (insight roles, objective analysis of one's thought processes, and baleful living, to name but a few); there is also the cultivation of certain abilities and heightening of subtle senses, such as the Wamphyric Tendril and the mastery of the conscious stream of thought.

These methods shall be outlined again here to serve the practitioner with a ready set of practises to begin their pursuit of Vampyric Metamorphosis.

Previous selections of teachings and practises such as those enshrined in the *Codex Aristarchus* so mentioned were initially distributed and published to expose the would-be novitiate to the energies of the Undead entities, not to mention the granite-hard bedrock of discipline necessary for staying the course. However, such publications were simply fragmentary, hiding much of the essence and totality of the Covenant tradition which was consistently and steadfastly practised by the members of the inner coven.

With such a foundation, the knowledge offered in future publications such as this will allow a depth to be appreciated far above and beyond the simple (though fruitful) masochistic worship of arcane bloodthirsty entities.

Meditation in Dead Stillness

The meditation in dead stillness is a deceptively simple practise. It involves sitting and remaining unmoved for a set period of time. Humans spend much of their time fidgeting, tapping and engaging in other unnecessary movements which use energy which can be better cultivated elsewhere. Vampyrism is concerned with the increase and cultivation of energy, and therefore this meditation can serve as a preliminary example of stillness and conservation on the lower physical level.

Simply sit comfortably, and do not try to control the breath or the thoughts which may arise (this comes later). Simply enjoy the feeling of absolute stillness. Think of the vampyr sat amidst the shadows - unmoving, silent and ancient. This is what you strive to become. If itches or discomfort arise, attend to them and return to your stillness. Do this for as long as you wish. It will in time become the foundation for future exercises and meditations.

Power comes from a reduction of the superfluous - unnecessary talk and unnecessary movements when eliminated create an aura of power for which the vampyric witch is idolised. You will find in time your energy levels increase when superfluity is removed from the mind and body. Let this serve as a mundane reflection of the power you will cultivate in more sinister ways yet to come.

The Unwavering Eye

The Unwavering Eye is the next application to be added into the process of Metamorphic practise. It involves picking a spot in front of you (this could be anything, such as a sigil described on a piece of paper, a point on a wall or a candle flame). Simply stare ahead, not straining the eyes or will. Combining this with Dead Stillness, you should feel calm and balanced. There should be no physical or mental exertion (though a little mental effort may be required to remain).

This practise of cultivating an ability to remain still for periods of time shall not only allow one to understand how energy is expended unnecessarily, but also be used as a cornerstone for further practises which shall be detailed herein.

Lich Breath

The focus and direction of the breath is a vital component of several aspects of the vampyric tradition. The harmony between the physical and astral bodies is regulated primarily by the breathing process. The still, centred cultivation of the Lich breath (also known as *blood breathing*) leads to a myriad of powers being bestowed upon the practitioner. It is no coincidence that the powers of the Undead were historically often rumoured to be linked to their breath, which could bring death and paralysis to their victims.

Begin your meditation as usual, clearing the mind and focusing upon the breath. The mind and body should be stilled by the inward and outward tides of your breathing. Feel yourself become the centre of the vortex, the still blackness that is the vampiric archetype. Be at one with your breath.

See about you a swirling mass of crimson energy. This is Blood Essence and it adorns your aura as a vampyric predator. Your will draws it from the Acausal realms, marking you as one of Them.

Begin to draw this in with every intake of breath, feeling it dispersed through the body - from the core outward, into every limb, invigorating your very essence with the outward breath.

This meditation can be modified, as mentioned above, to infuse the Blood Centres. Indeed, this preliminary practise is utilised as a base method when seeking to attain astral flight, with the Blood Essence being absorbed through the feet and upward toward the Blood Centres.

In time reduce visualising it and simply feel it, focusing on the inward breath and the outward breath. Focus upon the breath entering the nostrils and exiting, if it is too complicated to feel the full process. The Blood Essence fills your entire being, invigorating you and subtly changing you, speeding up your evolutionary and involutionary path towards the Lich state. This ability to master the mind, body and its energies will serve as a precursor toward drawing energy from opfers as you begin to feed upon the human mass.

Tendril Feeding

The Wamphyric Tendril is a sacred and hallowed aspect of our Vampyric tradition. The practise of Feeding via the Tendril creates within the psyche and within the astral body proper a subtle alchemy, changing the individual and aligning them with the Ascended Undead spirits; simplistically speaking, it transforms them into an astral beacon. Whether this is the goal of the practitioner of this method is irrelevant, as it will occur either way. Most magickal techniques are essentially attempts to call forth and speak with certain powers, entities or spirits, hoping to elicit effects or knowledge from them which cannot ordinarily be attained. The art of Vampyrism (and its attendant praxis) ensures an inevitable confrontation and communion with such entities and thus it can be seen as an extremely pure and powerful magickal discipline when compared with other traditions and practises, stemming from the simple application of the tendril itself.

Among the more pallid iterations of the vampiric current, the use of tendril feeding is either neglected or outright forbidden; we of course hold no such qualms, and it is indicative not only of the mindset of such groups and individuals but also of the efficacy and glamour surrounding the Tendril that it is regarded with such disconcertment and fear.

Several scholarly minded adherents of the Covenant tradition and its predecessors have taken time to pen various theories regarding the tendril and its nature. Its origin of use is currently unknown, but it has been a staple teaching within the inner core of most vampiric lodges within living memory. Some have suggested that the mind moulds the subtle astral flesh, creating within it a new and distinct organ which develops a penetrative nature and a magnetic ability to feed upon targeted living hosts.

Others have suggested it is perhaps a latent astral organ which most complex living creatures possess in rudimentary form, and cite several examples of the sick and dying exhibiting vampiric tendril-like powers in order to sustain their life as evidence of this theory. Others still have posited a theory that the tendril is implanted via direct interference by vampiric entities, or that it is a simple organism itself which latches onto the living vampyr, with the vampiric practitioner and the tendril forming a long lasting symbiotic relationship - this theory however holds least weight, and most agree that the tendril is an elegant formation of the vampiric mind, which over time forms into a distinct pathway of feeding.

Esoteric Chant

The specific use of chant within the Sinister tradition is one of the many features which defines the system as distinct from others.

Chant can be divided into three versions or methods, all of which have the same general goal - to produce or increase magickal energies.

The first method is simply the correct vibration of words. For example, 'Aosoth' would be vibrated *Aaaa -ohhhh -sooothhh,* with the voice being deep and extended, and the word drawn out, as opposed to being shouted. The word should almost 'vibrate' the body and be visualised to do the same to the immediate surroundings. Each syllable is vibrated individually, an exhalation of the breath devoted to each. With sufficient practise and training, this simple vibratory method can be honed into a powerful utterance of magickal potential by the witch.

The second method is the chanting of specific chants, such as the Diabolus. This is performed in roughly the same manner, with the words being vibrated (though no vibrato should be employed, as utilised in contemporary singing and sustainment of notes). The chants should be sung monotone, akin to monastic chants.

The third method of Esoteric chant involves the chanting of specific chants within the correct modes, and is the more difficult of the three. The attribution of the modes to the corresponding chants (as seen with chants attributed to the seven Spheres of the Tree of Wyrd) is outlined in *Naos - A Practical Guide to Modern Magick*, and is often taught to the Novitiate/s by the master/mistress of a coven, who ideally has experience and practise in this unique form of magickal intonation.

Within the system of Esoteric Chant employed by nexions and adherents of the Sinister Tradition, the method of plainchant is employed. This method is designed to record vocal melodies and is a precursor to modern notation systems. The notational method of chant is a simple one and involves a staff, a clef (which denotes the relative pitch of the chant sung) and the notes themselves.

The next step in the novitiate's quest is the mastery of the night side of the mind - the dreaming world and the unconscious.

Draumrûna - Lucid Dreaming

Lucid dreaming is regarded within the ontology of the Covenant tradition as an imperfect form of astral travel, one projected into the inner realms and subconscious landscapes of the dream world created by the unconscious, hence the name for this art, *draumr* meaning 'dream' and *rûna* meaning 'mystery' or 'working'. Another similar word used is in the tradition is *Draugrûna* or 'death-workings' - rites and rituals which bridge the gap between black magick and Lichcraft.

The projection into dream worlds is a highly useful skill to master, one in which entire worlds can be crafted by the witch during their sleeping hours. The primary difference between this and astral projection could be said to be that draumrûna is an inward projection into the psyche - as such, it is a powerful tool to cultivate upon completion of the Dark Pathways and Sphere meditations. As any serious student of the tradition will know, the unconscious is itself a gateway to the Abyss. Draumrûna therefore is a potentially powerful and dangerous magickal ability. Whilst vampyric feeding will need to take place in the physical world (and thus require projection into the causal realms), inner projection holds a store of vast knowledge for the daring explorer.

Given the fluid and acausal nature of a world such as the dreaming unconscious, little can be offered in the way of structured advice on the individual level. The methods to attain lucid dreaming however can be outlined and are proven to work repeatedly, given the practitioner provides adequate effort.

Simple gestures, such as regularly questioning the reality of one's immediate surroundings and whether one is in a dream state or not are useful tricks to employ several times a day - conditioning the mind to be critical of its surroundings. In time, you will find this reality check arising during dream states, and lucidity will be attained. This method must be practised for at least a month before effects begin to take place (or even longer for some).

Experimentation with herbs such as Mugwort and small doses of Datura are also incredibly useful aids in attaining the lucid dream state. Upon achievement of draumrûna proficiency, the only limits are those placed upon the self.

Alongside lucid dreaming (and often coincidental in its development of such), the next skill to master is that of astral projection, the infamous vampyr's flight across the nocturnal world.

Treading the Wildling Path

These preliminary practises will provide the practitioner with the basic skills necessary to begin transformation into a witch of the Scithain tradition.

This transformation will begin to separate one from the restless everyday reality so familiar to waking consciousness. In its place will be a lifetime of experiences which will drastically awaken the psyche into genuine Initiation of the vampyric condition and bring one into direct communication with ancient forces.

What then can be truly written, in the sane and rational manner afforded by literary text, of those silent and deadly beings which haunt the peripheries of the vampyric practitioner's world? What can truly be said, in a definite and logical manner, of the nature and intentions of those beings whom we are inevitably and indelibly drawn into contact with upon the gradual and insistent practise of the dark arts of vampyric witchcraft?

For those who have mastered the gifts of the Wamphyri, to take flight during one's sleeping hours and see the nightside of reality, these entities will be well known - as either stalwart teachers or terrifying pursuers, depending on the gall of the astral sojourner. The mastering of the potent and wretched arts of astral vampirism will transform the witch into such a nocturnal terror, and it is such transformation that is the primary focus of all those dedicated to these black arts.

By these arts we do not speak of the half-hearted and rehearsed scripts of modern occultism with its safe ploys, its words of power and its concept of 'protective circles'; above and beyond autistic fantasies whereby one sits and talks to themselves, deluded in their sanitised and urban ideas that demons are 'fun' and can be made friends with. Rather, we look back to the primal traditions of wordless rites and bloody sacrifices, ceremonies which rose out of the thick smoke of Mankind's earliest intimations with the raw powers of nature.

Just as humanity learnt to live among the wild beasts and the untamed elements of his environment, so then did a cadre of blighted individuals amongst him begin to recognise and ally themselves with powers and entities which had been watching from the shadows as a curious ape-like creature stood upright and began to mutter its way to self-awareness.

The few wild places that remain still hold those primal echoes, roots which have not been touched for untold millennia, if ever at all. The witch must leave the comforts of civilisation and be immersed into the wilderness, the domain of the ancients. The soil of these lands can teach the sensitive individual far beyond any sophistry contained in the world of words.

The shreds of rationality must be discarded like a garment; civility must be abandoned during this time. The witching rites must become a time of teeth grinding and of claws dug into the soil if the proper mindset is to be invoked.

You thus come before the threshold of infinity with much baggage, traveller; far too much to allow passage into the earthy secrets nestled in the vines and roots of these old lands. The Dark Gates through which you must pass will cleanse you time after time like tides of blood essence, refining your core until what has mutated in place of the once drab and mundane novitiate is now a sovereign walker of undreamt dimensions. This however is not the final aim of the vampyr. We have always been those who inspire myths and tales, the legend of the weald-wicce who haunts the forests at night. There will come a time when you find yourself moving from the position of prostrate observer of terrifying natural forces, to one of stepping forth as the total symbol of nightly terror. You will become the witch of the wild, the vampyr lurking for blood across the night-shrouded moors and forests. Initiation will bring you to the nightside of consciousness, and over time you will pass through many Gates of Earth, emerging as a bloodied Rounwytha.

Whilst these words may seem superfluous or florid, the message cannot be driven home enough: you must create within yourself a state of savage adherence to the forces of Nature, a state which the ordinary man cannot and would not dare comprehend, a state beyond the dimensionless posturing of sociopaths and misfits, a state of Man aware of his place in a vast natural order which exists within and yet without him. You must remove the limitations fostered via a life-long reliability upon an external system. How many could survive, let alone thrive were the comforts of urban civilisation suddenly snatched from under them? How many who claim to be of Sinister ilk, for that matter? Very few undoubtedly. Very few indeed. Nature will give everything one needs if She is listened to and obeyed. A striving against Natural Law is a death warrant for any living organism. And whilst modern civilisation may seek to operate in such a way, living as they do on borrowed time, there will come a day when Nature comes to collect Her debt and returns us back to a primal state. This reign of Azanigin will see many fall by the wayside, but for those who remain, a Numinous balance will be found.

Remember then, the wilderness - the swamps, the woods and the moors; these are your nests and eyries. It is away from the chatter and lights of civilisation that you will find the challenges you need to transform into what you have been seeking for so long.

Mastering Vampyric Flight

Vampyric flight is a form of astral travel experienced much more intensely due to the clarity brought about by astral feeding whilst in this discarnate state. This is the ultimate act of vampyrism, the pinnacle of predatory ability. Undertaking this is the natural birth right and next logical progression of the living vampyr. Astral travel in itself is a truly liberating act; but in the context of vampyrism, in which the vampyric witch ascends with the primary aim of feeding, a much darker and malevolent spectre is born.

The methods for attaining astral travel, as outlined in *Codex Aristarchus,* follow a simple formula: the manipulation, familiarising and raising of Blood Essence within the body and directing it so as to strengthen the astral self and leave the physical shell at will, usually under a particular gnosis.

Thus, can this be broken down into four distinct sections:

I.   Familiarisation and raising of Blood Essence/energy

II. Gnosis

III. Astral Fight

IV. Feeding in the astral

The entire methodology of conscious astral projection outlined herein is one which seeks to firstly enliven the subtle astral form and develop a familiarity with the energies related to it, and secondly to move the consciousness into the sphere of experience of astral projection itself, moving awareness from that of a collection of half-remembered dreams and lucid experiences in the beginning to one of total mastery of the discarnate state. The initial development of energetic manipulation is necessary for the second stage to be realised in its full potential and should not be overlooked, especially in the preliminary stages of occult development.

The standard method toward attaining a gradual mastery of astral projection as taught by the Drakon Covenant is rather simple, but takes time and consistent practise to master:

"Begin by lying down and focusing attention to your breath. Follow it passively as it flows in and flows out. Do this for a few minutes until you feel content and your mind is clear. With the regular practise of the novitiate exercises, this should not be too difficult.

Now, begin to feel your descent into the Abyss with each external breath - like you are sinking in a black ocean of infinite depth, one tiny point in a vast darkness. This is a useful method to induce a deep state and shift to Alpha brainwave functioning.

Do this until your mind is clear and you feel relaxed.

Next, visualise the sigil of Drakon above you, raining down Blood Essence, crimson-violet in colour with filaments of plasma arcing through it. As you breathe in, this Blood Essence bathes you and fills your being, clearing tension from you on the outward breath.

Now visualise the Blood Essence around you being pulled through your feet to the first Blood Centre, opening it and infusing it with energy." (Codex Aristarchus, *Ascending as Wamphyri*)

From here the novitiate is instructed in this raising of energy, leading to an activation of the Blood Centres of the astral body, followed by a mental exercise in which the activation is associated with a conscious leaving of the physical. Success will manifest itself firstly in the sleeping-waking threshold, as well as in lucid dream states. In time, the ability to ascend at will may be achieved. This is one of the hallmarks of the vampyric adept, a state referred to within Covenant tradition as the 'Master Elite'.

Familiarisation and Raising of Blood Essence/Energy

Breath work should become a regular discipline - 5-10 minutes each day, preferably twice a day, should be spent simply sitting or lying comfortably and observing the breath flowing in and out. Still the mind and feel any thoughts leave the mind with every breath. Some novitiates envision a river during their meditations, which they visualise any distracting thoughts being swept away in. The goal is to achieve greater and greater periods of time when there is mental stillness. The mind is powerful tool and is a conscious aspect of the psyche (the psyche itself being a subconscious aspect of the

Acausal). Thus, any willed direction of the mind (such as during energy raising or magickal ritual) must be honed to a single point of awareness, or else energy is being dissipated amongst stray thoughts. Discipline is one half of our doctrine.

During astral projection experiences, the body will lay in a catatonic state. The mind is easily pulled back to the physical body and consequently into a state of dreaming sleep. Given the proximity to such a dream state during projection, the disordered mind which flies from one thought to another in a regular pattern will swiftly clutter the objective experiences of the projector, leading to a subjective and confused experience during astral travel and causing a lesser focus on the immediate and a slipping back into dreaming. This is another reason for training the mind in a single pointed manner. As meditation and energy raising (and vampyric feeding) increase in depth and frequency, so till with the success and clarity of astral flight experiences.

Another useful technique for the activation and manipulation of the astral body's energies is known as the *subtle touch* or *tactile imaging*. This is a practise which is often taught in its rudiments within various schools of witchcraft and occultism with the ostensibly vague aim of 'increasing psychic ability'.

It involves the witch visualising an object and striving to 'touch' it in their mind, imagining as best they can how the object feels. Eventually a very real textural ability within the imagination develops, and a synesthetic sensation can be conjured upon command.

This ability to 'feel' with the mind is then applied to brushing or touching the astral body, often in a directed manner - starting from the tips of the toes, a brushing motion is visualised along each toe, leading up to the feet, then the legs, and finally the entire body. This energetic stimulation is useful when performed prior to the opening of the Blood Centres during meditations designed to prepare the subtle body for astral flight. This method is unique in that it requires no actual visualisation - simply a textural apprehensive ability within the focused mind. It can thus be practised for far longer than standard visualisation techniques (as such techniques tend to tire the mind and can become difficult over extended periods of time - this is especially so among novitiates or the meditation novice).

Breath awareness meditation should be adhered to for at least two weeks, after which you should begin working with the Blood Centres during your meditations (incorporating the actual sequential opening of them after a preliminary breathwork session each time). Performing these set of practises before sleep will often result in vivid dreams, which will be a pointer toward success. Sometimes, sleep paralysis will set in, often during the mornings or between REM cycles. This is also a sign of success.

Also, to be employed are of course the meditation in Dead Stillness and the Unwavering Eye. The novitiate is encouraged to work out an order to implement these practises in according to their preference. All these will assist not only in preparation for astral travel, but for also for vampyric feeding.

Some practitioners experiment with fasting during astral projection attempts, which helps clear the mind but more importantly provides an impetus to force the astral consciousness to become preoccupied with the notion of feeding and consequentially associate hunger with such attempts at flight.

Gnosis

Deep sessions of meditation will often lead to states of gnosis, trance states which in time will become easier and quicker to immerse into. The ancient peoples of Britain beseeched their seer and druidic priest castes to prophesy, who would fall into a trance and give predictions and insights. Though the spiritual training methods of the druids and their chthonic predecessors are now lost to us, we can assume similar methods as outlined here were utilised.

Besides the stillness of breath based meditation, the more exeatic practise of self-discipline (flagellation) is also known to attain trance states. This method is often used to achieve gnosis in the context and setting of Communion, where the Draugr, Sluagh Sìdhe and other vampiric entities are explicitly called forth to commune with. This method is effective, but can become a very dangerous pursuit, with some entities refusing to answer the call without ever more drastic measures of self-mortification being enacted by the practitioner. Thus, the witch should pay heed, and learn to facilitate a working relationship (or as close as one can be forged with these alien intelligences), and communion in the astral is the most effective, if not the most terrifying solution to this problem.

The use of mind-altering drugs also played a crucial role in rites designed to attain gnosis. This unique and potent subject is dealt with later on in this book.

Astral Flight

The ubiquitous Wamphyric tendril plays another role in the retinue of vampyric praxis, this time in regards to leaving the physical body. The given method for achieving astral flight within the teachings of the Covenant involves visualising the sigil of Drakon above you, showering your form in Blood Essence, and filling your being with this energy. A tendril is then visualised emanating from the sigil, and having attained a deep state of stillness, the tendril is grasped with the mind and the projector pulls their astral body out of their physical form. This can be attempted several times, and in the early stages should be practised before sleep (with the regimen of breath work and Blood Centre opening coming prior to this). During the dream state, or in between, results may be achieved. It is purely down to experimentation at this point as the novitiate learns to recognise the pointers and furthers their pursuits. Later, when the astral body becomes used to loosening during consciousness, involuntary, partial or fully intentional projection may become frequent and even the norm.

(As outlined earlier, a more explicit method is given in *Codex Aristarchus*.)

It is also during this loosening of the astral body, when combined with consistent vampyric feeding, that the attention of the Ascended Masters may sometimes be drawn by particularly talented practitioners or those possessing the nature of a Lamia Naturalis. These encounters will convince the witch of the dark reality of the vampyric tradition, and hopefully provide a marker toward more success and a spur toward more diligent practise.

It is important to recall your senses during your astral experience. Diligence, discipline and persistence of effort *will* in time yield results. However, the overwhelming and wondrous experience of moving around in a non-physical context can often override one's mind and cause one to forget why they worked to attain this state at all. Thus, the witch must employ consistent vampyric practises, forging in the subconscious an unbreakable link between astral projection and its *raison d'etre* - feeding and genuine consequent vampyric evolution.

The practise itself will first begin to manifest during one's sleeping hours before any success is attained at projecting via willpower and meditation. This will lead to much confusion - a dream journal should be kept therefore to spot pointers toward success. Success itself will be acausal, in that it is not followed on directly from regular praxis. The experiences will become more pronounced, more regular and more intense, but they will also come about via their own admission. Do not worry too much if results are not obtained straight away, but instead stick firmly to the methods and teachings. From such a solid foundation, failure is simply not possible.

In time, and with a mastery of meditation, the more skilled vampyric adepts will be capable of projecting at will, thus affording them a certain degree of omnipresence. Until then, most projections will be achieved around the threshold of sleep and within the dream state itself.

Feeding in the Astral

This most hallowed of practises forever marks the witch among the ranks of those who have stepped upon the black path of immortality. The astral body is subtly changed, distorted and reborn via the act of draining Blood Essence and imbuing it within the self. This takes its ultimate realisation during discarnate states. The feeding itself should be performed above a living target the witch has sought out during their astral travels.

Extend your tendril, and tear deep into the core of your sleeping victim. Draw up the Blood Essence and enjoy the clarifying and life giving properties. This will lead to a deepening of the astral experience.

Some practitioners of the vampyric tradition of the Covenant have reported that feeding (most often first time feeding) propels them into a staggering and almost psychedelic experience, where the astral landscapes of the Undead are glimpsed for a brief time. Of these glimpses, little can be written, given the sheer absurdity of what is seen, though the witch reading these words will come to be familiar with such experiences in due time.

In certain instances shades may be encountered attempting to expel the astral vampyr from their grim task. These shades (often the deceased relatives of the target you are draining) can pose quite a challenge, and should either be avoided or - if the witch is skilled or brave enough - seized upon and slain, or at the very least driven from sight.

As well as this issue, some targets may prove difficult to feed upon - sometimes feeding can lead to awakening the target or awakening their astral senses. In this instant that your target is aware of your presence, you will possess an upper hand, given the sheer horrific nature and reason for your being in their place of rest. Fear not only weakens the prey, but makes the Blood Essence all the more relishable to partake of.

According to one theory, it is possible to inhabit the body of another, forcefully supplanting their will and thus come to replace the consciousness of the victim for a degree of time (the length itself perhaps coinciding with a variety of factors, such as the skill of the witch, as well as the willpower of the victim). This is the basis for cases of 'possession' and can be a difficult and potentially dangerous practise to the astral vampyr if unprepared or unfamiliar with the workings of astral mechanics. This practise takes place as part of the Rite of Transference in its neotic version - the placement of the Master's lich essence into the physical vessel of a new-born infant, thus doubling their lifespan:

"...the infant would then be raised within the care of the lodge, who would name the child by his/her former name, and in time hope to bring the child to recall its previous life. This continuation of consciousness within a specific physical parameter is but one way in which the tradition and teachings were preserved through harsher times, when adepts of all pursuits were under heavy persecution by the Nazarene church.

The traditional title of Morain, (meaning *'great'* or *'dreadful'* in the Celtic tongue) was passed down to each head of the vampyric lodges, the title rumoured to have originally been the actual name of the first vampyric master to successfully attain Transference. The epithet is used nowadays in the same vein as the Roman usage of the title Caesar, as both a name and title." (*Lamia Naturalis*, Codex Aristarchus)

As with all aural mythos, it is left to the reader to determine the truth of such statements, though certain hints can be found amongst certain occult literature throughout the ages. Such mythos also serves to demonstrate how these practises can and should be applied by the ascendant lich and his/her coven.

Sleep Paralysis

This is the dreaded gateway toward astral mastery, the paralysing cold fear which clutches at the body prior to expulsion into nocturnal flight. Whilst a normal side effect of astral projection, its connotations of fear arise due to its alarmingly powerful hold over the body, not to mention that certain vampiric entities are able to induce this effect upon their victims.

Despite the pseudo-scientific drivel attempting to explain

the nature of sleep paralysis, its cause is rather straightforward - it is the mind shifting into active awareness of the astral body and away from the physical. Thus, conscious effort has no direct bearing upon the flesh. This can be a worrying feeling if unused to the phenomenon, or if unaware of the astral mechanics behind it. The witch should learn to recognise this stage as awareness moving into the astral, and from there, use it to project. It is essentially a window of opportunity, guarded by fear.

There will also arise a secondary issue, namely the sensing of a presence, the 'lurker on the threshold', which often forces projectors to return to their bodies. This should also be ignored. It is simply the mind becoming aware of two distinct selves - the sleeping physical, and the astral emerging from the physical. It is not a malevolent entity waiting to seize or possess the sleeping projector. It is the hitherto unexperienced phenomenon of a dual consciousness.

Once these two feats and others are surpassed, it is time to assert one's dominance upon the astral food chain - no easy feat by any measure, but one well within the grasp of the ascendant vampyr.

The Astral Realms

The Astral realms are a complex subject, and an entire book could be devoted to detailing their properties and relative interior dimensions. Often, books dealing solely with astral travel and the astral realm can be found to be rather useful resources. The books which touch upon it within a magickal setting are often woefully simplistic and deal only with it in a brief fashion. Thus, to avoid such simplification, and whilst hoping to bring clarity to the novitiate, this chapter shall seek to outline in depth the nature of the astral, whilst avoiding unnecessary complexities and superstition.

The astral realm can be arbitrarily divided into several levels. Many distinct models exist, and the model provided here is a general one formed via experience and study on the part of the author.

The Astral Pylon

Acausal

Astral/dark astral

Liminal

Physical

The Liminal is an intermediary level where the astral realm blurs with the physical. This is the realm most familiar to lucid dreamers and astral projectors. It is in essence a focal region where mental energy transfers onto the physical. Thus, the projector may see objects which appear out of place (such as doors where they should not be, as well as items which may have existed in the past).

The Liminal intermediary zone is the prime hunting ground for the ascendant practitioner (an ascendant practitioner here being one who has achieved vampyric flight successfully on numerous occasions, and begins the process toward vampyric adepthood alongside the orthodox methodology of the Sinister Sevenfold Way).

This is also where the majority of earth-bound spirits such as ghosts, vampiric entities and even other practitioners may be found and encountered. These entities should be regarded as prey and nothing more (especially other projectors - who will appear ordinarily human, either wandering around or floating, believing themselves to be in a dream or at even sometimes possessing a modicum of awareness of their discarnate state).

Confrontation with other astral entities must be met with extreme hostility. In the predatory paradigm, offense is the best defence in all cases.

The astral body submits to the thoughts of the projector. Transform hands into talons, bat wings, tearing claws; eyes into raging pits of fire - make the astral body into a veritable Baledrecan killing machine, hell bent on striking fear into your targets. You are the peak of evolution, take the mantle and become a majestic embodiment of Satanic terror.

It should also be worth mentioning that awareness (or lucidity) can be vastly sapped if meditative disciplines are not developed sufficiently. There will be a general fading of consciousness back to dream state sleep within a few minutes of conscious projection, and the astral body will be drawn back into the physical, which is often felt as an intense pull or fall from a great height.

Confrontation all depends on who possesses the most energy and lucidity. The witch will find him/herself fading back into unconsciousness during an astral battle if he/she does not possess an adequate energetic charge. It is therefore important to practise energy raising meditations (such as the opening of the Blood Centres, tendril feeding and Lich breath) on a regular basis.

Astral Travel and the Dream Realms

As outlined above, the astral transforms according to the mind of the projector. Consciousness has the ability to directly mould the astral, which is in itself a denser product of acausal energy, just as the physical is a denser product of the astral. This is one of the keys of magick, and it is in this way that powerful Undead entities such as the Ascended Masters can create entire dominions from which they operate within what is known as the dark astral.

The Ascended Masters make Their hallowed eyries

among the fragments of mankind's dreams and the astral regions these dreams border upon and mould via the creative properties of acausal consciousness.

These dark corners of twisted non-spatial, non-temporal dimensions and illusory depth are the prime hunting grounds, a base from which They propel Themselves into the causal world of the dreaming masses.

The shadowed moors and iron forests of the Undead landscape are littered with the scattered conclaves and garrisons of the Ascended clans and houses. Their worlds and customs are alien to us, Their towering astral spires are prison to the countless opfers They have stolen away to serve as eternal food in these blighted lands.

And when They encroach upon this world, They bring with Them all the hosts of Their world, its darkness and mire spilling out and polluting this realm, opening further the jaws of the black gates which strain and groan without cessation.

To open a gate to these dimensions requires a tremendous effort on the part of the witch. For this reason, they historically bonded into covens whose collective efforts could, for a time, open a nexion into the limitless darkness and bring forth these ageless ones who would anoint them, and write their names in the books of black earth, so that their deeds would not be forgotten and they would be remembered when they called again.

A principal method to do this was via the aforementioned 'witch's flight'. This was a ritual involving the ingestion of a particular hallucinogen, which facilitated astral flight. Often, the witches would steal into the homes of sleeping humans, seizing upon them and feeding upon the terror thus wrought. This gave rise to the phenomena of the 'night hag', the 'succubus' and so forth. Whilst sceptics today have attempted to explain away the phenomena as a REM cycle related glitch of the body, this does not account for people all over the world experiencing the same symptoms - a fiendish feminine force attacking and paralysing without mercy the helpless sleeper.

The method of such astral travel can, however, be stimulated upon demand, without the use of intoxicants. It requires a certain degree of discipline and effort, but can be mastered in a relatively short amount of time.

The witch must be prepared for the terrors which he/she will face upon mastering this technique in this vampyric manner. You will be taking your place upon the Chain of Devouring and confrontation with very ancient, and wholly evil entities will occur.

Preparation for Hermetic Rituals

Hermetic rituals are those rites and practises which are performed by the practitioner individually - that is, not in a ceremonial setting with others present.

Most rites within the vampyric tradition as outlined above require a preliminary discipline set - usually this could involve mild fasting, reduction of sleep and social activities, fixation on certain chants, as well as bloodletting and self-mortification. The reduction of one's sleeping hours (or at least the sleep cycle being broken up so as to afford more time to prior meditation) is often the most effective, alongside mild fasting, with the mortification rites usually employed prior to or during the ritual being performed.

Ritual attire will usually consist of black clothing, with the addition of a black robe or cowl if the witch prefers. Within Covenant tradition, a piece of black silken gauze material (known as a nythran shroud) is draped over the hooded robe. Both the robe and the shroud are preferably buried in dry, earthen cemetery grounds - either when not in use, or upon obtainment for six days so as to suffuse them with chthonic death energies.

For those standard hermetic rites such as divination, spellcraft or cursing, the correct incense blends need to be procured or acquired. A locale also needs to be ascertained (unless the practitioner has a designated place where they can conduct their rites in privacy).

Locations usually include forests, hills, moorland, or other places in nature which are isolated (or at least undisturbed at night time hours). Certain rites serve best when they are performed in places conducive to their nature - such as caves for chthonic rituals and meditations. The ideal locale for vampyric magick is a cemetery; those newly built and neatly laid out are somewhat unsuitable, if only for the fact that they do not provide adequate cover for the witch and lack the energies which age naturally brings. Cemeteries of some age also tend to be surrounded by high walls or at least thick tree cover so as to facilitate some degree of privacy. (Again, *Naos* will outline in further depth the necessary requisites for Hermetic preparations.)

Whilst such funerary environs are perfect for communion with the Undead, certain natural locations are just as suitable, and sometimes more so (if seeking to attain a connection with a specific cultural deity, for instance). One example would be of course Cladh Hallan for its connection with the lich priests of Scithain.

The area you choose must be somewhere you will not be disturbed, particularly at night. The ritual *Sìtheil*, as detailed later on, is to be used to consecrate and dedicate the area you set aside for your rites.

Ritual Structure in the Scithain Tradition

Contrary to the modern fables and hasty reconstructions, the ancient peoples of Europe and the British Isles did not share a rigid and official set of customs and ceremonial rites. There is no evidence of these cultures sharing much in the way of ritual beyond funerary practise. The tradition was kept secret, and only the myths of their gods and heroes gives insight to the ritual practises.

The Scithain culture was a chthonic one - in contrast to the Solar tradition centred at Stonehenge and upheld by the druids, and the Cosmic tradition which began to flourish in the Welsh Marches after this, following a sharp decline classified elsewhere as the 'Magian Distortion'.

The chthonic aspects meant a focus upon ancestral links and the bond between generations, even past the point of death. This bond allowed secrets and teachings to be gleaned via shamanistic practises and meditations upon the remains of the ancestors - in essence, a proto-necromancy evolved out of the primitive shamanic cults which permeated the Hebridean Isles and the British mainland.

Thus, most rituals would have been crafted as a propitiation toward the spirits of the wilderness, the dead ancestors and the natural entities which guarded the regions uninhabited by humans. We see a remnant of these practises continued throughout the Gaelic peoples of Ireland, in which offerings are often left at isolated spots as gifts to the Sluagh Sidhe and other morally ambiguous or even hostile entities. This respect for the dark power of Nature was a necessity. Most have forgotten the link with Nature, and have sanitised and rationalised it into a safe novelty.

Within the Septenary Tradition, rituals are usually worked out in accordance with which Sphere they fall under. The spheres' correspondences, as outlined in the Tree of Wyrd are as follows:

Moon - Terror and sinister knowledge

Mercury - Indulgence and transformation

Venus - Ecstasy and Love

Sun - Vision and understanding

Mars - Destruction and sacrifice

Jupiter - Wisdom and wealth

Saturn - Chaos

Of course, the Dark Gods Themselves may also be invoked during a ritual to manifest the will into reality. Some examples include:

Noctulius - Enchantment and hidden knowledge

Nythra - Terror and sinister destruction

Shugara - Destruction

Aosoth - Works of passion and death

Azanigin - Very useful to invoke in works of personal destruction

A more extensive list is given in Naos, and the insights which arise during the Dark Pathways will lend more to utilising the Dark Gods during magickal workings.

Standard form involves the vibration of *Agios O Atazoth* for 'dark' workings, or *Agios O Baphomet* for 'light' workings three times. The incense to be burnt can be consulted in Appendix I - *Tinctures and Correspondences.*

During incensing of the area, the following path is to be walked. During this walk the following should be chanted:

Aperiatur et germinet Atazoth for destructive workings.

Ad Gaia qui laetificat juventum meam for constructive workings.

Following this, the key chant is chanted twice. These key chants are the chants associated with the corresponding planetary sphere.

Most rituals involve a frenzy on the part of the witch; dance or chant is employed, during which the appropriate chants are utilised (the Dark Pathway rites are excellent examples on which rites may be built upon and elaborated further).

The use of a crystal and the correct chant practised to a degree of proficiency are often the main keys employed, as well as a formulation of the ritual's intent.

Sitheil

The following rite is designed to acclimatise the practitioner to the general energies and touch of the Undead and the accompanying astral shades which arise from consistent practise of vampyric magick, as well as acting as a ceremony of devotion for your ritual space.

The rite involves spending at least one night (three nights is preferable) within a local cemetery. If a suitable cemetery is not available, a similarly secluded natural area will suffice. This place will become your area of magickal working, and the area for future novices whom you may take as part of your future coven. If a coven exists, this will become their communal ritual space, the combined energies leading to the creation of a veritable nexion.

A tent and other sleeping equipment may be brought - though the more fanatic may wish to choose a warmer season and bring only a blanket to cover themselves with.

The rite begins one hour after sundown, or alternatively one hour past midnight.

Sit cross legged and begin to chant the Communio. This chant is to be intoned for as long as one is able to stay awake. Take breaks to flagellate/incise and burn incense. The appropriate incense for this rite would be frankincense. Petrichor serves well, but is somewhat more difficult to acquire.

It is preferable to have reduced food and sleep, even if only slightly, the day before this rite. Similar measures apply during the extension of this rite. It is generally advised to practise the rite for one night, then attempt it again for two (or even three). If in an isolated spot, a campfire may be lit. During the day, remain isolated in your locale and do not return to normal activities. Stay and occupy yourself with reading or meditation, or any other pursuits which do not involve communication with the outside world.

The next step is to acquire a decent sized piece of clear quartz (the ideal shape would be a tetrahedron - but if this is impossible, a natural chunk, i.e. not polished, is just as effective).

Take the crystal, and following the usual preparatory rites, mark it with your blood, whilst chanting *CHAOS*. Visualise the crystal coming to life, and feeding upon the Essence your blood carries. Follow this with the Diabolus three times, and wrap it in a black cloth. This is also to be performed on the second night and third night.

Next, remove the crystal from the cloth and bury the quartz, making sure to conceal the act (by placing twigs or grass back over the earth). This crystal, properly consecrated, will serve as a beacon and a delayed 'time bomb' of sorts, suffusing the area with chaotic acausal energies. In time unusual, paranormal or even life threatening occurrences will take root within its vicinity, feeding the Undead which will congregate there following your rites, and which will lead to the creation of a place regarded by mundanes as 'haunted'. Your ritual space will be consecrated and serve you well.

Further along the path toward adeptship, the witch may choose to perform the Rite of Nine Angles at the very same spot, unearthing the crystal for use, before burying it again as is instructed in the rite itself (alternatively, the witch's coven may opt to exhume the crystal and perform the Eorthe Gate in its vampyric version, as detailed later in this book).

The Scrying Mirror

One of the witch's most useful tools is the scrying mirror. These are not ordinary reflective mirrors; rather, they are composed of a slab of glass (the larger the better). Paint one side with black gloss paint until it appears like a mirror which does not reflect but stares into blackness. Several coats of paint will need to be applied to the back of the mirror. Set the mirror in front of you so that you stare through the glass and into the blackness. The mirror should have its border marked with the blood of the witch, and incense may also be burnt in front of it. It is important to keep this mirror covered when it is not being used.

The mirror can be decorated with the sigils of the Covenant; however, minimal distraction is preferred. This is not to be an altar, but a living gateway to the myriad depths of the dark astral.

Use of the scrying mirror is essentially an extended meditation in which the witch comes to develop the natural ability to gaze into the ethers and intuit events normally unavailable to him/her. It can also be used to empathically connect with a person or entity. It is in essence an advanced divinatory aid.

Prior to its regular use, a simple rite should be undertaken where the mind and the mirror are inextricably fused together in order to foster an innate ability in the art of scrying. The rite is as follows:

Having preferably fasted, or awoken at night (sleep deprivation is especially useful for rites such as this which will involve staring into the mirror), sit before the mirror (or have it placed before you on a stand if it is small) and chant the Communio. If other disciplinary rites are employed, these should be undertaken prior to the chant being called.

Stare deep into the mirror, and passively observe as your vision begins to note subtle changes and movements within its darkness. Keep chanting the chant, staring deep. Do not pull away your gaze, even if movement is seen elsewhere beyond the mirror's border.

The mirror will in time come to yield images and sensations which the witch will use to further his/her understanding of the gates beyond and the Undead spirits which linger there. Incense burnt before the mirror will travel through the ethers, admitting a suitable gift to Those who wait Without.

Practise scrying with your mirror each night, awaiting any signs or knowledge which you may glean through this exercise. As you improve your skill in scrying, you should select someone and focus upon their image in your mind. Allow the mirror to act as a gate to their psyche, and implant thoughts and suggestions into their mind. The mirror can in time be used to observe individuals, should the witch be sufficiently skilled in this area.

The mirror should be thus charged as a focal gateway via this method, and when successfully ascending into astral flight, the witch should direct their movement toward the mirror and actually pass through it. The mirror, saturated with acausal energy, will function as a rent into the darker realms of the astral. The scryer will, if the rites have been performed correctly and consistently, find him/herself in time at the foot of the towering basalt steps which lead to the shadowed halls of the Ascended Masters, nestled deep upon the blasted moors of their dark astral landscape.

This will be achieved via the following rite.

Constructing a Gate to the Undead

The scrying mirror, having been consistently used over a period of time, will have become charged via the vampyric magick wrought through it. It will now be fit to establish it as a portal to pass through into the astral darkness.

For this ritual application to succeed, the witch should have mastered the art of astral travel and successfully fed at least several times. The mirror will be prepared as a doorway into the astral realms, where the witch will journey to find the hallowed ground of Their abodes.

Sanctifying the Mirror

The mirror should be laid on the ground in your ritual area, and a blend of frankincense and petrichor burnt (this being lit during the Offering).

The usual preparations should have been observed, along with a ritual of Offering to the Ascended Masters.

Take a dagger or ritual knife and wave it through the incense whilst chanting *Nythra Kthunae Atazoth*.

Next, a live bat must be sacrificed upon the mirror by removing its head. The blood must then be used to anoint the edges of the mirror.

Chant *Agios O Noctulius* as you mark the mirror with the blood.

Next, place your quartz crystal upon the mirror and chant *Aperiatur Terra et germinet Scithain* nine times. Do this whilst visualising a darkness growing within the crystal and spilling out to cover the mirror and infuse it with acausal energy.

Cease your chant and wrap the mirror, taking care that it stays out of the light from this point onward.

Leave the incense burning as an offering to the entities which will have drawn near during this Rite.

The mirror should be taken and set in the place where the witch will attain astral flight (usually their bedroom - most have success in astral flight during the period of falling asleep or waking up).

When the witch next attains vampyric flight and leaves their physical body, he/she should attempt to fly through the mirror, focusing on the darkness and making sure not to cloud the mind with preconceptions. The witch should record their journeys via this way and work through the astral darkness toward the shadowy eyries where They wait.

Other Scrying Methods

Several other options exist for practising scrying besides the use of a black mirror. One method is to take a large handful of nettles and boil them in water until the water turns black. This is then poured into a bowl. Alternatively, ink can be poured into clear water.

Another method involves digging a hole in the earth so that the bottom of the soil cannot be seen, thus making a dark depression which can be stared into.

The Tree of Wyrd

The Septenary Tradition utilises the Tree of Wyrd as a key to all magickal workings. Correspondences, chants and planetary relationships are chosen using the Tree before beginning a Rite (these correspondences are given later in the book).

"The spheres of the Septenary may be said to be the Nexus between causal and acausal (or 'Being' and 'nonbeing') and the paths linking the spheres may be regarded from a magickal point of view as zones of energy. This energy is according to tradition symbolized in an archetypal way since it is through such symbolism that control of the energy is possible." (*Naos, A Practical Guide to Modern Magick*)

Crystal, image, chant - these are the three necessary ingredients for magick according to the Septenary tradition.

To each sphere is attributed a particular area of governance and the corresponding attributes and qualities:

Moon - Terror and sinister knowledge

Mercury - Indulgence and transformation(s)

Venus - Ecstasy and Love

Sun - Vision and understanding

Mars - Destruction and sacrifice

Jupiter - Wisdom and wealth

Saturn - Chaos

To increase the efficacy of the rite, the *Table of Correspondences* should be consulted. Esoteric Chant will also be employed. Esoteric chant may be divided into two parts: vibration of names and magickal chant. The first type requires less skill and is the form most often used in ritual – for example, to create or 'draw down' a particular force or entity in a magickal working. The second type requires some musical ability or training since mode and tempo are important.

Thus, for example, a ritual designed to bring a vision of a future event (this desire falling under the dominion of the Sun sphere) would involve the usual preliminary measures, followed by the entering into a trance state and utilising Esoteric Chant. The incense used would be Oak, the initial chant would be *Agios O Olenos*, and so forth (see *Naos* for further details of the technical aspects and modes of Esoteric Chant).

Part I - The Dark Pathways

A necessary step along the path of initiation within the Sevenfold Way involves coming to know the energies and archetypes of the Tree of Wyrd (and the Cosmos as a whole) via a walking of the Dark Pathways and an exploration of the Spheres. This is a demanding set of rituals, which will take a considerable degree of time for the initiate (seven spheres and twenty-one pathways will result in twenty-eight weeks).

As aforementioned, a certain degree of fasting and/or reducing of sleep is beneficial. The witch may awake at night and spend an hour in devotional meditation to the Dark God they are preparing to call forth. Burning incense appropriate to the specific entity will facilitate a stronger link during this stage. The incense should be created according to the correspondences and planetary relationships via the Tree of Wyrd (See *Table of Correspondences*). You should also spend a few minutes each night before going to sleep meditating on the sigil of the Dark God. The goal is to imagine the several days prior to the rite as being an extension of the rite in itself - the fasting, nightly meditations and sleep deprivation all being aspects of the ritual proper.

You should begin by starting with the Sphere of the Moon and its related pathways (Noctulius, Nythra, Shugara). The recommended form is to walk the Pathways in their entirety, then approach the Spheres. The order of the Pathways can be found in Naos.

The Dark Pathways are essentially an archaic and organic method of communication with chthonic forces represented by the symbol-images and names given to the Dark Gods which have been imparted to genuine adherents of the tradition since the days of the first Rouning practises. They are essential tools in striving toward individuation and self-knowledge and function as 'gates'; each Pathway opened providing more direct insight into the nature of life and the Dark Gods Themselves, initiating the practitioner along the path which leads toward the Acausal itself, the 'Land beyond

Night'.

As Iamblichus writes in *De Mysterii* - 'An innate knowledge of the gods is coexistent within our very essence; and this knowledge is superior to all judgment and deliberate choice, and subsists prior to reason and demonstration. It is also co-united from the beginning with its proper cause, and is consubsistent with the essential tendency of the soul to the good.'

It is during these Dark Pathways that unique revelations and insights will be gleaned, and perhaps will lead to new additions and developments to the tradition; such additions and developments can only ever genuinely arise from practical adherence to the Sevenfold Way. No alternative exists to direct apprehension of the forces so outlined. These insights will not only lead to such evolutions of the tradition as a whole, but will affect the individual, either via knowledge gained through non-ordinary means, or by the literal opening of the Pathways that exist latently within the Initiate's mind. This is of course the core essence of what we call magick.

That the Dark Gods can only be known via an experiential exploration of these practises allows the initiate to advance *sans* abstraction, avoiding the muddied dogma, endless conjecture and pseudo-philosophy which plagues other forms of occultism. It is a useful indicator of an individual's progress to note the quality and quantity of words they use to describe the Dark Gods and their supposed essence. A mundane who has never experienced Their raw energies is easily recognised by the same tired clichés and usage of such backward terminology as 'evil' and 'infernal' when describing these timeless entities.

What the Dark Gods represent, what They *are*, it is up to each individual to come to uncover; and with that knowledge, learn to achieve true transformation along the difficult path toward genuine Adeptship.

Walking the Dark Pathways

If you have performed the Rite of Sìtheil and have devoted an area where you will use for your rites, it is important that the twenty-one Pathway workings are performed here, as well as the Sphere workings.

It is best to perform during the late hours of the night, as with all rituals within the Sinister tradition.

Incense should be a blend between the two planetary incenses which the dark pathway links. For example, pathway I (Noctulius) will be a blend of Petrichor and Sulphur (alternatively, the incense associated with the pathways' ruling sphere can be chosen - in this instance, solely petrichor).

For hidden paths, the incense blends are as follows: a blend between the two connected spheres along with petrichor in the following proportions (using the example of Lidagon) - three parts petrichor, two parts Sulphur, two parts Civet.

In absence of these, a generic incense may be employed (if the witch even chooses to use incense for these rites).

Having spent 3-4 days reducing food and sleep and

spending several minutes before sleep meditating on the appropriate sigil, the witch will be prepared to enter into communion with the Dark Gods via the Pathway rite.

Sit and meditate for a few minutes on the sigil of the Dark God, then chant the name nine times. Following a short pause, chant the name another four times. (For some Dark Gods there is usually a key which the chant should be sung in - such as G minor for Noctulius. This can be figured out quite easily and should preferably be adhered to for maximum effect).

The chant should reverberate throughout your entire body, and be felt to activate the energies surrounding you in your magickal area. If you have suitably reduced food and sleep, you will notice this taking place.

Next, begin a slow circular dance, which gradually increases in speed and which gradually spirals inwards. Make sure to continue the chant, using as much energy as is possible for this. Continue this for some time until exhaustion impels you to stop. You should then fall to the ground and chant the name a final time, forcing all your energy into this act.

After this say: 'Come ... (entity's name) to me! And bring me my desire!' Briefly visualize your desire, and verbalize it using a short phrase (such as 'bring me knowledge of...' 'kill...' etc.).

Begin your dance again in the opposite direction whilst saying: 'I am the power, I am the glory, I am a god!' Sit once you have done this and clear your mind, allowing any images and thoughts to enter you in this trance state.

If no desire is present during the working to call out, focus upon greater and deeper knowledge of the nature of the Dark Gods Themselves. This is always a suitable and necessary pursuit.

For the trance inducing part to the ritual, the dance can be potentiated with a combination of mild drugs (such as Cannabis, Salvia, liberty cap mushrooms or other such substances tested and experimented with beforehand by the witch - any aversion to this should be overcome, as there is little difference between this and the ancient practitioners testing the potencies of various unknown herbs and plants). There is also the rather grim and preferred method of ritual cutting/flagellation, which will yield extremely potent results.

The order of the Pathways to be undertaken is as follows:

I. Noctulius

II. Nythra

III. Shugara

IV. Satanas

V. Aosoth

VI. Azanigin

VII. Nekhela

VIII. Ga Wath Am

IX. Binan Ath

X. Lidagon

XI. Abatu

XII. Karu Samsu

XIII. Nemicu

XIV. Mactoron

XV. Velpecula

XVI. Kthunae

XVII. Atazoth

XVIII. Vindex

XIX. Davcina

XX. Sauroctonos

XXI. Naos

Part II - The Spheres

The Spheres of the Tree of Wyrd are the next stage following the pathways, and represent much more archetypal patterns than the more 'active' pathways.

As before, observe the usual disciplines of reducing food and sleep.

Place the three tarot cards appropriate to the Sphere in front of you, and burn the appropriate incense.

Now, visualise the tarot image in your mind, and try to imagine yourself in the image itself. This open-ended meditation, akin to a daydream, should last no more than 15-20 minutes and no less.

Then visualise the scene change into the next card, and perform the same; then the same with the final card. Write down any impressions afterward.

The order of the Spheres is as follows:

I.   Moon

II.   Mercury

III. Venus

IV.   Sol

V.   Mars

VI.   Jupiter

VII. Saturn

The Nythra Gate

The following rite is detailed to provide an example as to the creative license with which the Sphereworkings can be undertaken, as well as showing just how powerful these deceptively simple meditations can be.

The Rite is based on those attributes and correspondences gleaned via the workings of the inner Drakon Covenant, within which Nythra is a particularly venerated patron deity. The witch may even opt to utilise his/her own intimations of this Dark God's essence to function as a gateway to the nexion the Void Mother resides within (in astronomy, the star Arcturus where the Nythra gate resides is in the constellation of Boötes. In the vicinity of this constellation exists what astronomers call the 'Boötes void', a vast and unexplainable region devoid of stars and galaxies which extends to around a million cubic parsecs).

To undertake this rite therefore, an image must be painted depicting a scene crafted from the images and intuitions gleaned during one's Nythra pathway working.

For several days prior to this rite, gradually reduce food and sleep, and meditate for fifteen minutes on the Nythra sigil before going to sleep.

Incense burnt should be a mixture of Ash and Henbane. One black candle should be lit. No other light may be used.

Adopt a comfortable position, holding your crystal in the palms of your hands, having either cut the palms or other part of your body and applied a liberal smearing of blood to the crystal's surface.

Begin with some moments of measured, deep breathing. Now vibrate softly and rhythmically the word *Nythra*.

Next, imagine a misty landscape, devoid of any details beyond the dry and cracked soil under your feet and the sparse trees which line the path you are walking along. It is night, and the air is cold and heavy. Continue the Nythra vibration as you envisage the scene.

Walk through the mist, feeling the still cold earth

underneath your feet. There are sickly flowers growing up out of the earth, which is littered with various human and animal bones. Observe the scenery, taking in the image.

Now begin chanting the Diabolus. This must be chanted seven times, followed by a short pause, and then chanted again a further two times.

The path eventually leads slowly upward and into a clearing which opens on to a vast expanse of starry space, depicting the constellation of Boötes. The star Arcturus glints in the abyss with a silvery light.

You step into the blackness, compelled by the void's intense pull. You are drawn toward the star system and drift toward the great void-like nexion which has opened and which exists near it. As you approach start vibrating *Nythra* with as much resonance as possible. On the edge of the nexion cease vibrating, and enter the screaming silence of the Void Mother's embrace.

Other images from the Sinister tarot may be employed; what is important is that a 'gate' to the lands is located within the image. The key to the working lies in your maintaining a measured, controlled pace. Truly successful workings will induce an astral projection - and indeed, the rite should be performed during lucid dreaming states brought on by the ingestion of the Datura seeds.

Following from your Dark Pathway rite with Nythra, you may create your own meditative rite leading one through an archetypal gateway from the images and insights which Nythra may deign to bestow upon you. What is important is that a gateway is envisioned and a striving toward the star nexion is made the primary focus of the rite. The more capable may choose to fly to this point during astral sojourns.

It is said some witches may opt to travel to the Nythra gate upon death, shirking the other death rites and instead seeking to become one with the Void Mother directly through transit into the Acausal spaces via the Boötes nexion. This requires of course a sufficient skill in astral projection, as well as the witch choosing to pass over (via ritual suicide) during the time when Boötes is overhead in the night sky. This would be around August time for the Northern Hemisphere.

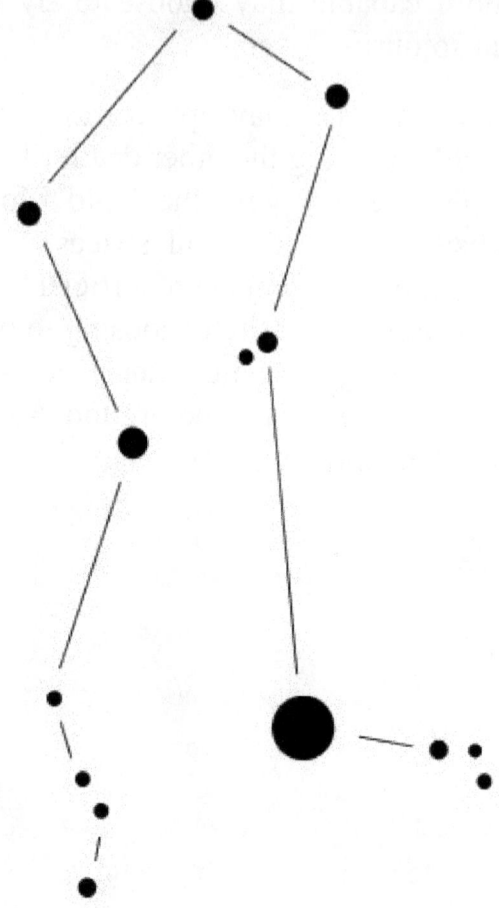

Boötes Constellation (Arcturus being the largest star to the bottom right)

Tarot

The creation of a Tarot deck is undertaken by the novitiate and these images are used to apprehend archetypal forces during the Sphere workings. For those possessing little or insufficient artistic skill, the cards may be commissioned to be painted by someone else.

The standard images as given in Naos are notably different from the standard 'Major Arcana' as exemplified by the common Qabalistic decks so prevalent today. For such a reason, these Arcana decks are unsuitable for genuine Sinister witchcraft.

As seen in certain examples (such as Christos Beest's *Emanations* tarot deck) some adherents choose to create tarot decks based on their insights and visions which arise during the Dark Pathway rites.

The Vampyric Novitiate

The Covenant structure of individual advancement within the vampyric application of the Sevenfold Way consists of *Novitiate, External Adept, Eremitic Adept, Internal Adept, Master/Morain* and *Ascendant/Lich*.

The stage of Novitiate within the Drakon Covenant tradition has several tasks within it the witch must accomplish before adeptship can be said to have been achieved.

These include:

- Performing the Vampyric rite of Initiation

- Mastering the basics of meditative practises designed to conserve and raise personal energy levels (breathwork, Lich Breath, the Unwavering Eye and Meditation in Dead Stillness, as well as opening the Blood Centres)

- Practising and achieving success in Feeding via touch and via the Wamphyric Tendril

- Achieving at least one successful astral projection and maintaining this experience long enough to feed whilst disembodied

- Dedicating a ritual area according to DC tradition and performing rites for personal desires (as outlined in the MS *Sitheil*)

- Performing pathworkings with all the dark pathways and spheres of the Tree of Wyrd and receiving insights from doing so

- Practising and successfully discerning messages and visions via scrying with the black mirror

- Selecting an individual you feel is fit for culling and performing a vampyric leeching curse upon them (or the traditional Death Rite)

- Studying and being able to answer certain questions related to the Sinister tradition (such as planetary incense blends, locales pertinent to the tradition and so on)

- Undertaking an insight role and seeing it through for at least six months

- Learning and practising at least three chants of the Dark Gods/Spheres

- Successfully training for and achieving a demanding physical goal

- Undertaking the secret tasks associated with the stage of initiate (as given by the ONA and the secret rite given by DC - this can be obtained upon request once the novitiate has proven their worth)

Once these are achieved, the initiate may then attempt to undertake the rite of External Adept as outlined within the Sevenfold Way.

As is clear, the way of the Drakon Covenant and the

Sevenfold Way is not an idle club for anyone to partake in. It is a powerful, alchemically charged path which will make you into something you have always dreamed of but never dared to achieve. Any posturing and/or attempt to make those around you think you have attained Adeptship without the achievement of these and similar tasks so required simply makes you not worth our time. No excuses, no clauses - you are not an Adept. Some individuals may lie and feign such achievements, but in the end, they are only lying to themselves, robbing themselves of the chance to truly attain what they long for deep down.

Accept your place in the Chain of Devouring or strive for higher.

Dark Pathways - Further Notes

The working of the Dark Pathways is the most prominent and extensive part of the Novitiate stage. It is during this time that real inner growth begins to occur, as the dark forces of the acausal become comprehensible in a definite way. This extended rite will take some time to complete (on a scale of months or even years, 1-2 if the novitiate is dedicated). They must not be rushed through so as to begin work on the rest of the stages - no more than one per week. The Pathways will take time as stated, and thus the other tasks should be pursued alongside them (such as physical preparations, developing a proficiency in astral flight, finding a suitable area for workings, and so on).

The pathway preparations will be physically taxing, and

thus a period of 1-3 weeks will perhaps be necessary in between each working - especially if one does not wish to experience significant weight loss (which will impact negatively upon one's physical progress).

A period of at least three days should be spent reducing your food intake and sleep. Meat should be avoided during this time. A useful technique is to reduce meals each day - having three meals one day, then two the next, then one the next, aiming for as little food as possible on the day of the working. The same goes for sleep - reducing one's sleeping by 2-3 hours each night, with the night before the rite having only 2-3 hours of sleep (with much of the night time being devoted to meditation on the Dark God's sigil).

An alternative method of fasting involves the same method above, but eating only small amounts of meat based foods. This ketogenic diet will help maintain the body's energy levels and is very suitable for those treading the vampiric current of the Sinister path.

You will feel drained, and thus no physical exercise should be taken during this time. Vitamins should be supplemented to negate any ill health. Green tea and small snacks of fruit will help push you through the final stretch of the preparation.

This will all be necessary; simply deciding to perform the dark pathworkings as a simple meditation rite will not suffice. Not only will the method outlined allow the witch to attune further to the subtle energies which will become present during the rite, but it will also teach self-discipline and self-honesty at this early stage in development. Both are highly desired skills for the would-be adept.

The Dark Gods are unknowable via the ordinary means of abstraction and analysis - no words should ever be wasted upon Them by those who have not come to know Their nature directly via walking the twenty-one Pathways. Insight is attained into the essence of the Dark Gods only through initially exploring these Dark Pathways. With this also comes a greater understanding of the Self and a slow dissolution of the Ego. In this way are the Dark Gods a means to self-understanding and self-fulfillment. Without Them and the gifts They bestow, Adeptship is simply impossible.

Once all twenty-one pathways have been explored, the witch's next stage is to explore the spheres of the Tree of Wyrd. These are seven in number, and one should be practised per week (thus taking seven weeks). This involves a simple meditation, prior to which particular disciplinary measures, as explicated during the pathworkings, should be observed according to one's desire and discipline

The other tasks are exercises in self-teaching and initiative. Preparing for and achieving the physical tasks demanded requires that the novitiate research various avenues of fitness and health, eventually coming to develop a certain degree of knowledge which they will carry with them for the rest of their lives.

If you cannot find an answer, attempt to answer it yourself.

Forming A Coven

One of the tasks for External Adept involves forming and running a magickal temple.

As detailed in *A Complete Guide to the Sevenfold Way:*

"The Temple must be run for a minimum of six months, as you yourself must seek out, recruit, instruct and train, the members of this Temple. There must be at least four other members, excluding yourself and your companion, during these six months, as you must strive to obtain an equal balance between men and women. It is at your discretion whether or not you are honest about your intentions, and inform recruits/potential recruits that this Temple is one of your tasks as an External Adept, and that you yourself are not yet very advanced along the Satanic path. If you choose not to so inform your members, you must play the appropriate role. If you are considering keeping and expanding the Temple beyond the minimum period and into the next stage, that of Internal Adept, it is more practical to be honest from the outset. The crux is to decide whether you wish your Temple to be solely for your own External Adept purpose, or whether you want it be truly Satanic, with your members guided by you to become sincere and practising Satanists."

Given that you will be following the vampyric branch of the Sinister tradition, this temple will of course be structured as a vampyr coven, with all that this entails. In place of the *Black Book of Satan* will be *Scithain,* and other texts of the Drakon Covenant which may be in the Adept's possession may be consulted.

The development of a coven is a deceptively simple task, but one made greatly difficult due to the ineptitude of the majority of individuals. Many may enjoy the thrill of being part of a secret temple, but unless effort and self-sacrifice are willingly engaged in, then there is little reason for them to participate. The running and maintaining of a successful coven is thus a lesson in self-insight, as well as in others, and will teach the witch more about people than any other tasks required of him/her up till this point. Patience and dedication will be needed for this task.

This of course requires several other members - at least two. Founding a coven before drawing in members is generally advised against as it is not an efficient nor natural approach. A genuine coven following the Sinister vampyric model should strive for integrity, self-honesty and absolute mastery.

If the witch is unable to find others willing to assist in his/her endeavours or students seeking to be initiated and develop, then it is best to continue in a solitary manner. Wyrd willing, others will appear when the time is right.

Further instruction and guides for running covens and temples are given in the ONA's *Codex Saerus - The Black Book of Satan*.

Conducting a Coven

A coven of witches should regularly meet and seek to form bonds with one another via social outings and general in group cohesion. Individual skills and traits among your members should be identified, and used most effectively to aid the coven's growth - be it one's artistic skill, or ability in manipulating the opposite sex; the unique skills of each member should be considered vital and utilised accordingly.

Monthly rituals should be conducted, such as the Crimson mass, as well as other smaller rites (such as Sidhe and Dearg offerings). More importantly, the Chain of Devouring should be implemented as soon as possible, with each witch being taught and becoming proficient in feeding via the Wamphyric Tendril. It is necessary that the coven thus establishes a living Blood Current, which will amplify your rites and generally confirm the coven's power.

Other bonding experiences involve the exploration of the aforementioned psychoactive plants with covenmates; this not only serves as a uniquely bonding and insightful social experience, but also allows each individual to explore the plants which will be used during their path within a safe setting, often under the guidance of more experienced members of the coven.

Each coven member should assume a distinct name which they will be addressed with by other covenmates. They are, in effect, a spiritual family whose bonds transcend mundane affiliations.

A list of possible names:

Male

Aulwynd, Caerdwyn, Mairon, Camoran, Ailidh, Aethol, Caedmon

Female

Aioslin, Caithmora, Myrwydd, Temora, Caethwyn, Morna, Morgatha

Leading a Coven

Leading a coven is a learning experience; the master/Morain must be aware of the solitary and aloof nature of this task. Your students must be able to look up to you and learn via your lead. Thus, you are to lead by example.

An image and code of conduct needs to be upheld. The difference between student and master should not be muddied by friendship. You may very well be a friend to other covenmates - but ultimately you are their teacher and handler. The role of Morain is therefore not as glamorous as first intuited. It requires patience, inner strength and resolve, as well as the ability to have utter faith in your own judgment.

It is for this reason one is advised, as above, to pursue the Sevenfold Way to some degree alone, rather than attempting to title oneself as a teacher, especially if one is simply at the level of their supposed students.

One task the coven should undertake is to identify and target 'white magick' covens or wiccan groups within their regional vicinity. This directed focus of attack will serve to unite the coven and give them a useful method of training in magickal ability, whilst also helping to eliminate rival powers and seeing that any malefic magick cast by the coven transforms the land with minimal thwarting of the powers unleashed.

This attack can take the form of active infiltration combined with magickal acts aimed at the group, their location of practise, or the individuals themselves. The only limit is the coven's imagination.

Another important aspect of the coven is in its ultimate binding to the will of its Morain or Moraina. This is done in several ways, though two distinct rites exist to increase such a bond on a subtler level.

The Oath of Fealty

It is generally expected that this rite is performed as an official declaration and codification of the coven's existence and purpose, with the swearing of fealty sealing the intent. From here on out, the bonds of the coven transcend all others - legal, familial, social and cultural. This ritual is only ever performed once (that is, this rite is representative of the official founding of the coven).

This rite involves all covenmates taking their place before the Morain/a. One after the other, the witches kneel before them, and he/she asks the following:

You, child of Noctulius, son/daughter of Chaos. You reap among men like a wolf among sheep, and no law can constrain you, save the one I place above you now. Do you swear allegiance to me and my coven, above all else?

The witch replies with *I do*.

The Morain/a then cuts their forearm and offers it out to the witch who drinks of the blood.

This is conducted by all members until it is complete. There then follows the Rite of Feeding (see next chapter *The Chain of Devouring*).

For those who break the bond sworn into upon entering a coven or betray those members so involved, and when all intermediary methods have failed, the only suitable punishment should be a cursing by all other covenmates.

Traditionally, an unofficial tribunal should be held, where the member of the coven in absentia is judged by those present. One covenmate is allotted the task of advocate, whereby they attempt to defend the covenmate who has wronged the coven. This is to give them a fair hearing.

After the hearing is finished and the charges have all been adequately gone over and decided upon, the covenmates vote upon banishment or death. The Morain/a gets the final say in this matter, given his/her experience and leadership within the coven.

If deciding upon death as charge, The Death Rite should then be employed to drain the target of their magickal power and Blood Essence, eventually resulting in the death of the covenmate.

Sometimes the coven member may be kept close and manipulated subtly by the other covenmates for reasons known only to them. But most often, a statement must be made and an opfer claimed in this way. If employed correctly and with enough dedication, the offending target will be sapped of life and will die some time thereafter.

The Death Rite

The rite is to be performed on the waning moon. The congregation gathered chant the *Diabolus* seven times, during which the witch priest/ess and Morain/a make the preparations.

An altar should be placed in the centre of the ritual area. Incense burnt should be henbane and ash. On either side of the altar should be placed black candles which are lit during the chant.

An idol, either of wax or other material should be fashioned the night before by one of the witches.

The Priestess lies upon the altar, and the Morain/a takes the wax figurine, placing it upon her womb. He/she then moves the figurine downward, symbolically birthing it, laying it to rest between her thighs.

He/she anoints the idol with a musk oil and says: *I who have made you and delivered you in birth now name you (victim's name).* The priestess and Morain/a visualise the idol as the victim.

Upon the altar should now be placed be a small wooden box covered with a black cloth which will serve as a mock coffin for the opfer idol. Around and upon it is scattered grave soil by the Morain/a. As he/she does so, he/she says: *Tua est terra.*

The Morain/a turns to the congregation and says: *Veni, omnipotens aeterne diabolus!*

Congregation: *Veni, omnipotens aeterne diabolus!*

Morain/a: *Nythra Kthunae Atazoth!*

Congregation: *Nythra Kthunae Atazoth!*

The Morain/a then makes an inverted pentagram over the congregation, saying: *We, the spawn of chaos who made you and delivered you in birth now name you* (He/she states the full name of the victim.)

The priestess then takes the idol, whilst the congregation chant the *Sanctus Satanas,* and places it in the coffin, wrapping it in the black cloth and saying: *I, mother of (*victim's name) *give them as an offering unto the dread Void Mother. Accept our sacrifice gladly and may they perish within the earth.*

After the chant, the Morain/a says: *We curse (Victim's name)*

Congregation: *We curse (Victim's name)*

Morain/a: *(Victim's name) will writhe and die!*

Congregation *(Victim's name) will writhe and die!*

Morain/a: *By our will, destroyed*

Congregation: *By our will, destroyed*

Morain/a: *Kill and laugh!*

Congregation: *We Kill and laugh!*

Morain/a: *Kill and laugh and then drink to our Mother!*

Congregation: *We Kill and laugh and then drink to our Mother!*

Morain/a: *(Victim's name) is dying!*

Congregation: *(Victim's name) is dying!*

Morain/a: *(Victim's name) is dead!*

Congregation: *(Victim's name) is dead!*

Morain/a: *We have killed and now glory in the killing!*

Congregation: *We have killed and now glory in the killing!*

The congregation drink from a goblet passed given to them by the Morain/a in which is strong wine filled with substances desired by the Morain/a.

Morain/a: *The Earth rejects (Victim's name)*

Congregation: *You reject (Victim's name)*

The congregation begin to dance, counter sunwise,

chanting the *Diabolus*. After the chant, they gather round the coffin and the Mistress. The Priest says to them:

Morain/a: *(Victim's name) is dead and we all have shared in this death.*

Congregation: *(Victim's name) is dead and we rejoice!*

Morain/a: *Dignum etjustum est. I who bring life, also take.*

S/he then passes her hands over the coffin, visualising as she does so, the dead body of the victim lying in a coffin. S/he takes up the coffin and leaves the ritual area.

As she leaves, the Priest says: *Feast now, and rejoice, for we have killed, doing the work of our Mother!*

The congregation is then free to feast or drink as they see fit.

Another method for cursing (in a hermetic setting) is to perform a mock funeral and burial in cemetery grounds, taking a vegetable root carved in the form of the intended victim and wrapping them in the black cloth and coffin as outlined above. Over time, as the root rots, so will the life of the victim.

The Arcane Drawer

This rite is performed by the Morain/a sometime after the Oath of Fealty, with the subjects being the members of the coven - though this can be used as a ritual by a witch to bind anyone to their will.

Obtain a photograph of those you seek to bind, and place them around you in a semi-circle.

With each photograph, mark the boundaries (or mark a square around the photograph if the paper is large enough) *with your own blood*. Chant *Agios O Kabeiri* as you do so.

Meditate for some time on opening the Blood Centres, then proceed to extend a tendril into each photograph. Visualise their essence drawing closer to yours in the Acausal realms. A binding effect will take place, whereby your will entangles theirs. This 'blood binding' will take time to develop. Performing the rite several times will yield further success, as will various enchantments designed to wrest self-control from them, and which will place them firmly within your interminable black grasp.

Building a working coven will take time. Students will come and go, many interested only in the glamour of being part of a group. The coven should therefore be confined to members who can physically meet and work together. An online connection is certainly no substitute.

But for those who see through the trials and tribulations, there will be a Wyrdful craft wrought. That which exists will last and serve as a guiding tool to all who flock to its darkened shade.

The Chain of Devouring

The vampyric coven is structured very much in the same way as the trophic level of predation is observed within the sphere of natural biology. Just as an animal will devour numerous prey below it, to be consumed in turn by a predator above it who devours numerous of its kind, so too does the vampyric practitioner feed upon a pool of human cattle.

This practitioner, if belonging to a coven or temple, will in turn be fed upon as he/she offers up their Blood Essence to their handler and Master (most often conducted in a ritual setting). This Master in turn offers his/her Essence up to the Ascended Undead, who impart a two-way flow of this Acausal blood. The master weaves this Blood Essence into new forms and imparts it upon those below him/her, which in turn benefits the novitiates and adepts of the coven. The physical pinnacle in this chain of devouring is usually the Morain, who has become a vampyric Master par excellence and is thus capable and qualified to direct the Blood Current of the coven toward greater collective aims.

It should be stressed that a genuine vampyric coven is one which observes this Blood Current and the necessary related rites if communion is to take place and strengthen the individual and collective will of the individual members.

Such a pyramidic structure of predation ensures a veritable current flowing through the coven. Of other temples and traditions that speak of possessing a 'current' in vague and allegorical terms, this secret is the truth they have been barely able to discern in their ignorance.

For those functioning as solitary witches, this chain will simply consist of human cattle, the witch, and then the Ascended Masters. Of course, this is not to say the lone practitioner is at an immediate disadvantage to those within a coven setting. Each role has its own dynamic vector, and progress will still bring the adherent to the final goal - Adeptship and in time - vampyric Mastery.

The offering and devouring of the coven's collective Blood Essence is usually performed during the Rite of Feeding, a semi-regular ritual conducted internally by coven members. The rite can be performed with as little as two witches present (the *offerer* and the *devourer*). The witches below the devourer should preferably have fed upon unknowing or unwilling opfers, the number of which being largely unimportant.

The roles for the following rites are:

Devourer witch (Morain/Master witch of the coven) - black attire, face uncovered.

Offer witch - black attire, face or lower half masked.

Lamia Naturalis - black attire, full head covered or blindfold worn.

The Rite of Feeding

The rite involves the offer witches sitting in a semi-circular pattern facing the devourer witch. They perform a general opening of the Blood Centres, offering up their accumulated Blood Essence by allowing their energy to flow freely and without guard.

The witches chant *Lamia Dei, Commune cum me* whilst the devourer witch then feeds upon each witch in turn in the usual fashion. This intensive feeding will be of a far richer nature, given the sheer amounts of Blood Essence taken in.

The witches present then chant the Diabolus, as the devourer witch internalises the energy and meditates upon it for several minutes.

The direct flow of the Blood Current thus finds its final termination in the master or Morain of the coven. This individual is then fed upon and potentially has direct communion with the Ascended Masters. The master, saturated with Blood Essence becomes a feeding point for the Undead, who will coalesce around them and drain the excess energy, leaving him/her riddled with symptoms of predation and possession. This unique relationship is a testing one, yet the benefits it yields are manifold.

Firstly, the witch will receive the whisperings of these long dead adepts, bestowing upon him/her wisdom and insight normally hidden from the denizens of the causal world.

Secondly, the drawing of the Blood Essence by the

Undead often imparts a two-way flow, as They siphon Their own Acausal darkness back into the witch, thus accelerating the process of Acausal evolution far quicker than ordinary magickal methods.

A specific ritual known as the Rite of Offering is utilised to offer up this Essence willingly (though this does not imply the Undead will not feed upon the witch during the hours of sleep - the rite is simply a formal recognition and intensification of the connection between the living servant and the Undead master).

The Offering

This rite is properly known as the *Rite of Communion* and is a core ritual within all vampiric schools of magick. It is essentially a symbolic representation of the Chain of Devouring itself, where the ties to the Undead elect are strengthened, and in which the celebrant can strive to be fed upon and thus receive, via the hideous intermingling of living essence with the blood of the Undead, a portion of Their dark energy - mutating, warping and evolving the witch further and further toward a state known as the living vampyr. Thus does the very pinnacle of the Chain offer in time a reward for the saturated accumulation of energy resulting from the efforts of the witch coven. And in this way, a relationship forms between witch and the Draugr, the Ascended Undead who, like us, many lifetimes before, worked through the hallowed black arts to achieve a state of eternal Undeath deep within the shade of the dark astral spaces.

The rite begins with the Devourer witch, having fed on a

collective of opfers, taking the physical blood offered by an acolyte in a receptacle and placing it before them. This rite is best performed in a ritual setting with other coven members present, who conduct the Rite of Feeding prior - thus saturating the primary practitioner with a suitable degree of Blood Essence.

If other members are not present, then solitary feeding and one's own blood will be enough to imbue with the necessary energy.

The witch now focuses upon the blood (be it in a small bowl or similar artefact) and channels the accumulated Blood Essence into the liquid via placing their hands over it and visualising the Essence exiting their palms and fingers, impregnating the blood and charging it thusly. If others are present, they are to chant the Communio during this part. Otherwise it is performed in silence, with the witch chanting the Communio upon taking the bowl and offering it up to the Ascended Masters.

The chant should be sung three times. The witch then proclaims:

"O Holy and silent ones,

dark emperors and empresses of the void

Those of royal vampiric blood

Roamers in eternity,

feeding without fill and without cessation

Come unto us and partake of our offering

Feed and take us as your adorers!

Ascended Masters, take this our blood

accept our offering and shade us

in your maleficent wings;

Hail to the Ascended Undead!

The bowl can be then placed upon an altar constructed within the ritual area for the Ascended Masters - otherwise it is simply offered up by the hands.

All present bow their heads in silence, and the witch holding the blood decides via intuition when to end the rite. A Lamia Naturalis may be appointed for this section of the rite to attempt to commune with any entities drawn near.

The Lamia witch will be sat near the devourer witch, and will have induced a trance-like state (either through drugs or any other method she utilises normally). A pen and paper may be kept to note what is whispered or channelled via automatic drawing, or a black mirror for scrying. The blindfold is therefore rendered useless in this instance, though only talented Lamae can commune with all senses active, usually.

The Ceremony of Eorthe

The following ceremony is designed to consecrate a communal outdoor area according to the Sinister tradition. This can either take the place of the rite of Sìtheil only if the area is to be used communally - the Sìtheil rite is suitable only for a solitary practitioner's ritual grounds. The ceremony can still be performed at the same place the rite of Sìtheil has been, however, if the site is to be used communally by the coven. In such a case, the crystal buried is unearthed and used in this rite.

This rite requires extensive planning, organisation and familiarity in practising Esoteric Chant in a communal setting. Thus, it is often reserved for a coven which has functioned for some time and in which all members have experience within the Sevenfold Way.

Several other ceremonial rituals which the coven or temple can employ are omitted here, given they appear in other ONA texts (such as the *Black Book of Satan*).

The ceremony that follows serves two purposes:

I. As a consecration of an outdoor Temple;

II. As a prelude to the opening of an Earth Gate

The Ceremony is presided over by the Mistress of Earth, as it is customary in Traditional Satanic Temples for the Mistress to conduct all rites of Initiation and Consecration.

Once an outdoor location has been chosen, the Temple is marked by seven stones according to the precepts of

Satanic Tradition. Also, an area that serves as an "ante-chamber" to the main circle is most usually established.

Mistress of Earth - crimson robe

Master of Temple - blue robe

Priestess - naked

Priest - naked

Congregation - black robes

Guardian - black face mask

Items required include a quartz tetrahedron, placed upon an oak stand. Incense should be a combination of hazel, beech and civet. The best time to perform this rite is at dusk, middle/end of May, or on or around Summer Solstice. The rite should be timed to occur during the menstrual flow of the Priestess.

Just prior to the Ceremony, the Master and Mistress conduct a form of the Rite of Sealing within the ritual area, using the crystal tetrahedron. They then depart (i.e. to the "ante-chamber").

The Rite of Sealing

The witch takes the quartz tetrahedron, and visualises a rent opening in the sky above, its darkness spreading down to engulf him/her and the crystal.

The witch then vibrates *Binan Ath Ga Wath Am* seven times. Then they say: *From dark dimensions I call thee forth!* The darkness is then visualised entering the crystal.

The Guardian of the Temple enters. It is his task to prepare a cavity within the Earth, into which the crystal will be placed and buried during the Rite. Once this is complete (the cavity usually being established in the centre of the Temple) he incenses the area, and departs.

The Ceremony

All gather within the "ante-chamber". There is a time of stillness, and then a flute is played, the duration of the playing to be decided by the Mistress. When ready, the Mistress leads all present into the Temple, and the "*Agios o Baphomet*" is chanted in unison by all present. The chant is sung for a cycle of seven, during which the Guardian lights the lanterns positioned by the stones, and any other candles present (i.e. upon the oak, and coloured purple). Further incense is added.

Once the chant is completed, the Priest and Priestess step forward to face the Master and Mistress, who greet them with a kiss. The Master hands the crystal to the Mistress, saying: *Agios Satanas.*

The Mistress responds by saying: *Dominus diabolus sabaoth. Tui sunt caeli.*

All respond: *Tua est terra!*

The Mistress holds the crystal in her hands, palms upwards. Master, Priest and Priestess then lay their hands upon the crystal. The congregation commence a circle dance, moonwise, and quietly, rhythmically intone: *Erce, eorthan modor.*

The Mistress begins the *"Ad Gaia..."* chant, and the Master, then Priestess, then Priest, enter the chant at the appropriate points. All perform a cycle of nine.

When complete, the Mistress hands the crystal to the Priestess. The Priestess then lies upon the area of the cavity, holding the crystal, with her head North. The Priest arouses her, locis muliebribus, stimulating the Red Flow. Then sexual union begins, during which both visualize a primal chaos being drawn down from the stars and into their bodies and into the crystal, forcing open a Star Gate.

During the union, the Master and Mistress place their hands over the Priest and Priestess. The Master intones *Agios o Atazoth* whilst the Mistress says:

Thu art eorthe to goode seede,

Of thee spong theo edi bleede,

Sprungs blostme of one root:

Yhe is whit of lime and leere

Yhe is fayr and flur of alle.

Both visualize the energy from the union and the crystal conjoined, as spreading outwards to bind the Temple.

Then Master, Mistress and the congregation commence *Erce eorthan modor* as a chant (the congregation continue with their circle dance). Once the union is complete (with the Priestess achieving her climax first), the Priestess deposits some of the elixir into the cavity. Both stand by the Master and Mistress, and join the chant. The Mistress then, at the point of her choosing, holds the crystal with the Priestess, and both, while continuing the chant, lower the crystal into the cavity. As the crystal is laid within, the Mistress quietly says: *Suscipe, Gaia, munus quod tibi offerimus memoriam recolentes Atazoth.*

The Mistress and Priestess then fill in the cavity with earth, continuing the *Erce...* chant. When ready, the Mistress signals the Guardian to ring the Temple bell, once. The chant and the circle dance cease. After some moments of silence, the Master and Priest commence the *Aperiatur terra...* chant. They are joined, at the appropriate sections, by the Mistress and the Priestess chanting in unison. The chant is directed towards the area of the crystal.

Once finished, another few moments of silence; then, solo, the Mistress chants once, the *Agios O Baphomet*. During this, all present visualize the Temple area radiating a primal energy, with the Star Gate fully opened above, through which are descending shadowy forms. This visualization is continued, until on the signal from the Mistress, the Guardian rings the Temple bell seven times. What then follows, is either the opening of an Earth Gate during which the planetary chants are employed (with the sequence arranged to end on the appropriate sphere) [for details of this particular rite, see Naos and Nine Angles MSS], and/or a performance of the Black Mass (qv. Black Book I). The energy generated via all subsequent rites must be directed towards the area of the crystal (the human altar is usually laid upon this area).

The Ceremony of Eorthe - Vampyric Version

This modified version of the ceremony is designed to presence vampiric energies into the ritual area, for use by the novitiates and adepts of the coven.

The rite should be performed at dusk, during the end days of April or alternatively the Winter Solstice. It should be ideally performed during the Mistress' period of menstruation.

Roles

Mistress of Blood - Most senior female witch of the coven

Morain/Master - Most senior male witch of the coven

Priest - Appointed by the Mistress, trusted male coven member

Witch Priestess - two in number

Congregation - Other members of the coven

The Mistress will have spent three days prior in fasting, spending each day meditating upon the Earth Gate sigil and undertaking a rite to the Dark God of their choosing to invoke essence prior to the Mass taking place (The Dark God chosen could be their personal or coven's favoured deity).

Incense of Mars should be burnt, with the Mistress scattering an elixir upon the ground, made of the mingling of the Morain's semen and her own blood. To this is added three pinches of grave soil taken upon a full moon, dried shavings from an oak tree when Saturn is rising, with wine being also added. The Mistress recites *Aperiatur terra et germinet Atazoth* as she scatters the elixir.

The ritual area may be marked with seven stones anointed with the blood of coven members, as according to tradition.

The Morain, sitting in the centre of the area, sits in meditation with quartz in hand, it being generously greased with blood from incisions upon his palm.

The Mistress sits down opposite, and both the Morain and Mistress then place their hands upon the crystal and visualise a rent appearing in a star-studded sky. This rent gradually spreads its darkness downward to surround the crystal and the two individuals present.

They both then vibrate *Binan Ath Ga Wath Am* seven times. The Mistress then says: *From dark dimensions, I call thee forth, haunters of the Dark*

The coven gathers in the ritual area, and all chant the *Nythra Khunae Atazoth,* during which the Priest will renew the incense and light lanterns upon the seven stones.

Upon completion, the Priest brings the crystal to the Mistress and says: *Agios O Satanas.*

The Mistress responds by saying: *Lamia Dei, Tenebris Dei, Tui sunt caeli.*

All respond: *Tua est terra!*

The Mistress holds the crystal in her hands, palms upwards. The Mistress and two other female witches place their hands upon the crystal and chant *Nythra* nine times, visualising the rent above drawing up the Blood Essence from the coven and the crystal itself.

The coven then begins a counter clockwise dance or circumambulation around them, chanting *Agia Ha Morgatha*.

The Mistress is then to sacrifice a bat during the coven's dance and smear its blood upon the ground, and bury the dead animal in the earth. As she does so, she says quietly: *Suscipe, Gaia, munus quod tibi offerimus memoriam recolentes Scithain*. She then places the crystal atop the carcass.

The Mistress and Priestess then fill in the cavity with earth, with the coven continuing the *Morgatha* chant

The Priest then rings a bell signalling the dance to stop upon direction from the Mistress.

The Morain and Priest then begin to chant *Nythra Kthunae Atazoth*, with the Mistress and witches joining in on the second round, directing the energies of the chant toward the buried crystal.

The area is then visualised as being suffused with the dark energies emanating from the rent in the sky previously visualised, uniting with the vampiric essence arising from the ground and binding those present.

The Rite of Communion may then follow afterward.

The Crimson Mass

The Mistress leads this ceremony, and traditionally dresses in red robes, symbolising the dark goddess Morannis. Incense to be burnt is a mixture of myrrh and cassia. The area will be incensed by the priest or priestess beforehand in a circular widdershins movement, whilst quietly intoning *Wamphyri*.

The coven gathers in the ritual area and sits in a semi-circle before the Mistress, where she and the two priestesses will then chant the Communio, whilst the priest proceeds to go around each member of the coven, offering a goblet into which the coven pour their blood via an incision made upon the arm or hand.

The priest then brings the goblet to one of the priestesses, who offers it to the Mistress, who raises it up, silently intoning *Agios O Wamphyri*, before mixing it with wine. The Mistress then brings the goblet to each covenmate, giving it to them to drink and saying: *sanguis enim eorum pro anima est, et vita aeterna.*

Upon completion, and with the covenmates returning to their original places, the Mistress then stands before them and says:

Before you, so imbued

with the blood essence of the living

I, death dealer

bearer of plagues

Bestow upon you this truth:

Thou art Wamphyri
if only ye take heed and obey
Let the Blood of the living bring you new life!

The coven then responds:

I am Wamphyri
death dealer, bearer of plagues
Discipline and Terror is our creed
The blood of the living brings us new life

They then chant the Diabolus, during which the Mistress visualises a darkness emanating from the sky (ideally from the constellation Boötes) and engulfing the congregation.

The coven then celebrates in their own manner and per their leisure.

Often cakes made of blood and cannabis butter are consumed afterward, or else some other similar sacrament.

The Vampyric Adept

The vampyric Adept stands alone as a unique predatory entity, one suffused with the Blood Essence of countless opfers and mutated beyond normality by the invasive presence of the Ascended Masters who feed upon the Adept in ever greater frequency - creating in time a living being similar to Themselves and thus creating what is sometimes termed the 'living vampyr'.

This state is the natural destination for all who feed and strive to draw down the chaotic energies of the Dark Gods. With the unlocking of the twenty-one Dark Pathways and seven Spheres within the psyche, the energies of the cosmos are made apparent, the Self is more integrally understood, as are acausally empathic connections with others - allowing the process of feeding to take on a much deeper and more rewarding experience. Empathy is the prime esoteric skill which is gained in a genuine manner from the dedicated pursuit of the Novitiate stage of the Sevenfold Way.

Following from this unbridled channelling of potent acausal energies, vampyric flight across the sleeping causal world as well as the twilight realms of the dark astral will bring a clarity of understanding and wisdom in levels far beyond the abilities of any safe and sober pseudo-practitioner of the black arts. The barrage of psychic shock, ingestion of substances designed to wrest the astral from the physical shackles, the increase of energy which will literally saturate every fibre of one's being - all this will evolve the Novitiate further and further toward that hallowed state.

Following this, the Rite of External Adept will shift one's focus upward and outward, opening the mind and psyche to a loftier vision, and placing the witch's power and insight into the cosmic perspective. From here, the energies accrued become applied in ways which shape not only the self, but all those around the Adept. Wyrd is grasped, and the arduous path to Internal Adeptship begins.

As written in the MS *Adeptship - Its Real Meaning and Significance*:

"An Adept is an individual who has undertaken an Occult quest and who has, as a result of that quest, the following abilities/attributes: a) a real understanding of esoteric, Occult matters, and a deep esoteric knowledge/insight; b) esoteric skills – chief of which is empathy: with both natural and 'Occult' forces/energies. An important aspect of this empathy [an intuitive understanding of things as those things are in their essence] is with living beings and that species mis-named Homo Sapiens; c) a unique character – formed via experience d) a unique 'philosophy of life' attained via self-discovery and self-experience – by finding answers unaided."

Perhaps the final point - that of self-experience and of finding answers unaided - is the most sagacious of insights proposed. With such self-experience and confidence, no answer is truly beyond the grasp of whoever possesses these attributes.

Of course, Adeptship is an easy thing to claim. As has been iterated throughout the bloodied path that is the Drakon Covenant's fanatic adherence to the Septenary tradition, no amount of posturing or intellectualising will ever substitute the self-mastery that arises from overcoming the tasks set by those who have gone before us along that harsh path toward true Mastery. Among the tasks required before genuine Adeptship can be said to have been realised by the aspirant are:

α walking 32 miles carrying a pack weighing not less than 30 lbs. in under 7 hours over difficult, hilly terrain;

β running 20 miles in less than 2 1/2 hours over fell-like/mountainous terrain;

γ cycling not less than 200 miles in 12 hours.

Alongside this is also the running of a temple/coven for at least six months, and the undertaking of a second Insight Role, which must be different to the role taken during the stage of Novitiate.

Such real world and uncompromisingly physical tasks separates the wheat from the chaff; most are discouraged from the path before even beginning to walk it - and this is how it should be. The way to Vampyric mastery and metamorphosis is not easy by any standards. It is not a game for the ego to enjoy; it is a harsh and life altering quest toward the Grail, the alchemical stone of wisdom. This quest will take years to accomplish and require a shedding of the fragile Ego - something very few will be equipped to handle.

Among the Insight Roles which may be undertaken, the following have proven to be particularly beneficial during this stage. This role must be adhered to in a strict manner, the ordinary mode of living having been completely changed to that of the role chosen. Participation in Sinister rituals, etc. should be kept to a minimum (or avoided completely, besides those possible rites which contribute toward the Sinister manipulation of individuals the Adept comes into contact with via the selected role - whatever form these rites or methods take is up to the initiative and discretion of the Adept, naturally.)

1. Convert to Islam (of the Sunni/Wahabi faith)

2. Join a NS organisation and take part in its activities

3. Convert to the LDS faith and join a Mormon church

4. Join the Police Force

5. Become a vagabond, living out of a tent and foraging/begging for food

Certain roles are simply unsuitable at this stage of the Way - for instance that of Buddhism or Far Left politics, considering these two examples have devolved into past times which will yield little to no challenge or aversion to social norms. The above selections demand a considerable degree of investment and time on the part of the convert, and thus will be very suitable for the Adept at this stage. As with all Insight Roles, the time involved must be between six months to two years.

In the case of certain roles (such as Islam or NS), the eventual abandonment of the role may possibly even bring a degree of risk to the Adept. Such risk should be dealt with using one's logic and intellect.

The Azatu Gate

The Azatu Gate rite is not too dissimilar from the Nine Angles Rite which is undertaken by the Initiate during Second Grade Initiation with a partner. It exists in two forms and may be undertaken by those of the stage of External Adept as part of the experiencing of those energies appropriate to that level (and it should be undertaken on completion of the Pathway and Sphere workings with your magickal partner. Its main aim (as is the aim of all genuine magick) is to direct energy into aiding the emergence of the New Aeon. Generally, this will mean aiding, via the ways of magick, a causal form that possesses the ability to practically implement the New Aeon. Thus, a symbol representing the causal form is used as a focus for the raised energy.

The Satanic form should be undertaken one hour before dawn during the Full Moon. The Baphometic form should be undertaken at dusk, when the Moon is New. Both forms should be conducted at an isolated outdoor location. The location most appropriate to the 'Baphometic' form is an underground cave where water flows.

I - Satanic Version

The priestess holds the crystal, while the priest rings the temple bell seven times. Both then meditate upon Atu VII of the Sinister Tarot. When sufficient time has been given to the meditation, the Priest says: *Aperiatur stella et germinet Chaos!*, and places his hands over the crystal. Both commence vibrating *Agios O Satanas* whilst directing the vibration into the crystal. This vibration is undertaken nine times, with increasing force and resonance, all the while visualising the Saturn Gate beginning to open.

As the vibration reaches its conclusion, a nebulous form is visualized seeping from the nexion, descending to the Earth, and entering the bodies of the participants via the crystal. Both should visualize their bodies filling with a star-studded space.

On completion of the vibration, this visualization is continued in silence for at least fifteen minutes. Following this, both commence visualizing the symbol chosen to represent the New Aeon, whilst chanting the Diabolus. This chant should be sung three times in unison, followed by a further four sung in parallel fourths. Sexual union begins thereafter, during which both continue to visualize the sigil. On conclusion, both bow to the North saying: *Agios Athanatos!*

II - Baphometic Form

As before, the Priestess holds the crystal, while the Priest rings the temple bell seven times.

Both meditate upon the Mousa of Swords from the Sinister Tarot. The Priestess, when she judges the time right, vibrates: *Veni, omnipotens aeterne Baphomet!* The Priest then places his hands over the crystal, and both commence to vibrate *Agios O Baphomet* nine times.

During this vibration, both visualize the crystal filling with darkness which then slowly spreads outwards to fill their bodies. As before, this visualization is continued for a further fifteen minutes following the end of the vibration.

The *Agios O Baphomet* chant is then sung, while visualizing the symbol of the New Aeon.

The chant is sung three times in unison, followed by a further four in fifths. On completion of the chant, the Priestess quietly says: *Suscipe, Baphomet, munus quod tibi offerimus memoriam recolentes Atazoth.* Sexual union begins thereafter. On conclusion, both bow to the North, saying: *Agios Athanatos!*

Note: The crystal should be held by the Priestess throughout the rite - including during sexual union. As is traditional, the best shape for the crystal is a tetrahedron, and it should be as large as possible.

Eremis

The Chthonic Internal Adept Rite

This vampyric rite (known as the *Chthonic Internal Adept rite* or simply the *Eremitic Rite*) is generally taken some time after the rite of External Adept and before the rite of Internal Adept proper. However, it must be stressed that this ritual particular to the vampyric tradition is not to be taken in lieu of the original Internal Adept rite. It is simply denoted as an 'Internal Adept' rite given the similarity of its practise and the nature of its outcome.

The rite involves spending a month alone camping in the wilderness, bereft of human contact and ordinary comforts, prior to which you will have reversed your natural sleeping rhythms - thus, the entirety of the rite must be spent living as close to a nocturnal waking pattern as possible.

A month's supply of vitamin tablets, as well as iron supplements should be included in one's inventory of supplies. This rite will further attune and align the witch to the realm of the vampiric entities outlined in our tradition, and enforce the Vampyric Metamorphic change, opening the psyche to the harsh and seemingly irrational, capricious nightside of nature. This rite is associated with Noctulius, guardian of the subliminal barrier to the 'land beyond night', as well as Shugara who, like the Dearg Dûl, preys upon lost travellers and haunts the wilderness.

The rite, properly undertaken, will allow the witch to further understand the chthonic tradition of Scithain, as the ordinary day-centred rational mind is disabled and one is thrust into understanding the fear and awe which the ancestors experienced living amongst the natural world. The rite should begin on the new moon, with the rite ending on the night of the full moon, some thirty days later.

During this time, as with the IA rite, contact with other humans must be avoided. This particular noctulian ritual will engender a Baledrecan catharsis, which if not handled correctly, may lead to mental maladies. Therefore, the rite must be undertaken with care and proper understanding. The witch must therefore have a proper understanding of the process we refer to as *Vampyric Metamorphosis*.

The engendering of the primal fear which arises from stark and solitary confrontation with the nightside of the Nature is an essential tool in viewing and understanding the world in the same way as the ancestors, thus coming to not only understand the particular state of the psyche which apprehended the acausal forces which gave rise to the chthonic tradition, but also prepare the mind for genuinely grasping the chthonic energies which will be interacted with and harnessed via practise. This rite therefore fulfills what the Dark Pathways accomplished in the beginning stages of initiation, whilst beginning to establish a unique autonomy, which will be a vital factor in the transformation of the Novitiate into an Adept.

The correct or 'orthodox' method for undertaking the Eremitic rite is to build a shelter of earth or wood using natural materials (however, a cave is also a suitable choice). The usual structure utilised for this rite is known as a debris shelter. Thus, the witch must begin to learn and adjust to outdoor living and acquire the necessary skills to complete this rite.

According to several traditions, this rite was sometimes preceded by the individual undertaking it being tied to a yew tree and left there for three days, being fed by other covenmates who came to them once per day. Sometimes they were wounded, with a bowl placed at their feet to catch the blood. This however is a very dangerous practise and is therefore advised against unless proper care and planning is taken.

Prior to the rite, the witch should acquire a large glass bottle, into which he/she will put their blood, urine and nail clippings, along with a piece of square paper, on which will be written their name.

Seal the bottle with wax and bury it deeply somewhere in the wilderness. Upon the ground where it is buried, inscribe the following sigil:

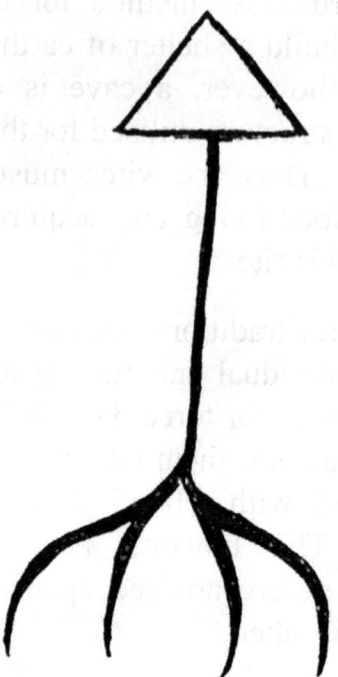

Upon completion of the rite itself, return and dig up the bottle. Empty the contents into a flowing body of water (such as a river or stream) whilst saying: *Aktlal Maka, Ga Wath Am*. Burn the piece of paper.

Store the bottle somewhere hidden, wrapping it in black paper or cloth.

<u>The Metamorphic Process</u>

As genuine vampyric praxis is practised and the adherent advances along the Sinister Sevenfold Way, his/her acausal charge will begin to exceed that of the ordinary human. This increase of acausal energy (which according to the Sinister tradition is the root cause of biological evolution) will literally evolve the individual beyond the stage known as Homo Sapiens. A subtle change outwardly, but a cathartic and revelatory one will occur internally, as a comprehension of the acausal is increased - the witch's mind moving toward the acausal darkness and becoming more a part of it than it was prior.

This gradual (at times sudden) evolution can and will yield chaotic changes to occur and bring one into contact with entities and forces which the causal, rational mind cannot comprehend. Simply coming into contact with such forces will dramatically alter the psyche, and an irrevocable evolution will have occurred. This evolution, and the accompanying insight and its consequent ability is what is often translated as "magickal power".

Advice for Eremitic Rite

Study the lore of the land, learning which plants are edible, which parts of the year they grow in and which plants to avoid, as well as which plants will be growing where you plan to stay. Learn how to build shelters and create fire. Learn how to purify water. Learn how to hunt and trap game (deer and rabbit are in abundance in the British Isles, as are pigeon and other edible fowl). Research survival basics. Bring a flare and matches as emergencies.

It is advised at least a half a stone (6kg) is gained in weight before you attempt to undertake this rite.

Soap should be of a natural brand, devoid of artificial chemicals so as to nullify your scent to the wildlife as much as possible. Using a survival knife, shavings should be taken off for individual washes. In this way, 1-2 bars should last the entire duration rite.

The most suitable location would be somewhere heavily wooded, for shelter and adequate firewood. Many edible plants also grow near large water sources. Again, contact with other humans must be avoided (this should not be difficult if adhering to a nocturnal waking cycle; however, conspicuous shelters may draw curious travellers).

A suitable choice often found in the Scottish lands are bothies, which are open cabins for travellers to rest in. The chance of hikers stopping by to rest is present with this option; however, if a suitably isolated location is found, isolation may be a real possibility. However, if located in a remote and barren region foraging and hunting may prove difficult. Further advice for undertaking Internal Adept is given in the *Hostia*, though no more advice will be given here. The witch is expected to utilise his/her initiative and work out for themselves what will be needed for this endeavour. Those who successfully complete this rite will be firmly able to carry the mantle of "vampyr adept". Those who have not attempted or will not simply cannot call themselves such. There is no excuse or alternative.

Eremis

The Eremitic Adept will emerge with a unified

understanding of the chthonic and sinister energies present in the unique night-facing current of vampyrism.

The Eremitic Adept rules the nocturnal sphere; the dream realms of all sleeping beings are his/her dominion. In time, a genuine apprehension of the powers of reality is understood via an attainment of existence which straddles the line between waking reality and the dream world.

Such an adept is marked by an ability to master the art of vampyric flight and harness the nightmare energies of the dark Astral. The Eremitic Adept is thus equipped to discover the shadowed eyries of the Ascended Masters and commune with Them. According to various legends, such places are nestled deep within the further outlying regions of the astral plane, their very dimensions unfamiliar and ungraspable to the waking mind (as discussed in *The Dark Gods and Literary Intimations,* it is speculated that H.P. Lovecraft attained partial visions of these regions through an imperfect grasp of dream control and occult studies). Other places, such as the lost castle of Du'n Dreach Fhoula are believed to be hidden within the dark astral.

It is essentially impossible for the pre-novitiate to venture into these worlds by will, just as it is impossible for such individuals to make sense of the visions one witnesses there. However, certain vampiric entities are capable of stealing humans away to the dark eyries, from which very few will return wholly sane.

The nocturnal sphere however is not simply that period of causal time as reckoned by humans and which is marked by a relative diminution of the sun's power. The sun itself is known to genuine adherents of vampiric practises the world over as an energetic nexus. The sun's rays emit a unique type of subtle energy which, whilst conducive to life in an acausally analogous manner to its causal effects on life, can be detrimental to the vampyric practitioner. The very nature of vampyrism creates a seemingly reversed or polarised energetic essence, leading to a growth in a rather different direction to the pattern the evolutionary process would normally take were it to continue unaltered by Sinister praxis. Such changes and effects which the sun produces upon subtle energies may be the root source of the tides of the Equinoxes and Solstices (these times being noted as energetically pertinent, and which are marked by a change in the sun's reign of exposure over the Earth in greater or lesser degrees).

At the time of writing, the exact nature of such a process, as well as the effect the sun has upon the energies of the vampyr are not fully understood. It is assumed that with a general increase of fully fledged adepts of the vampyric tradition, experience and experimental practises will lead to a more wholesome understanding of this process. Whether total abstainment from daytime existence is absolutely beneficial to the ascendant vampyr is unknown (though it would be argued that this is perhaps not the case given the causal requirements of sunlight for flesh based organisms), the Eremitic rite gives the witch a taste of the other side of existence, one which is as exhilarating as it is nightmarish.

The Rounwytha Rite

Hermetic isolation rituals such as the rite of Eremitic or Internal Adept have their origin in the Camlad Rouning tradition's Rounwytha Rite (called such in place of there never being a definite name for such a rite). This rite involves the candidate living alone in an underground cavern for a month, where water flows or at least near to water flowing. It begins on the rising of Arcturus, the rite finishing on the night following the full moon.

The rite breeds the unique nature of the Rounwytha, with the only food being bread and cheese. Preferably the water should be suitable for drinking. Food may be brought during the rite by an assistant, who may also bring candles, which will be the only acceptable form of lighting. One traditional location for this rite was the cave at Caer Caradoc, in Shropshire.

No communications with the outside world or conventional time keeping pieces may be brought for the rite. Also, no means of making music or any means of entertainment may be brought.

This is a difficult ritual to perform, and involves little dictation as to its performance. All that is required is for the Rounwytha to spend a lunar month within the cave, to be brought back to the world by their assistant upon completion.

It should be mentioned here that within the Drakon Covenant tradition, the rite of Internal Adept is expected to be six, not three months' minimum.

The Ceremony of Eremis

The night before undertaking the Eremitic Rite, the witch gathers his/her coven to perform the following ceremonial ritual.

Roles

Eremitic witch (the one preparing to undertake the Eremitic Rite) - black robes or black clothing

Witch Priest/ess - white robes (with ritual dagger)

Congregation - black robes or black clothing

The rite takes place at midnight. Incense of petrichor and frankincense to be burnt. Substances may be ingested to facilitate a preliminary gnosis.

Prior to undertaking this rite, the witches of the coven must gather at their ritual area, and perform the Crimson Mass.

Next, the incense is lit and the witches shed their blood over where the crystal was buried during the Ceremony of Eorthe - saying as each does so the words: *Aperiatur Terra et germinet Atazoth.*

Afterwards, the witch preparing to undertake the Eremitic rite stands in the centre of the area upon where the blood was shed.

The witch priest/ess stands before the Eremitic witch,

pointing the ritual dagger at him/her and says: 'You who have exalted yourself as a vampyr among men, do you go now to leave your children and descend into the dark earth to become one with it.'

Eremitic witch: 'I go now to leave my children for a while, into the wilderness so I may be reborn anew as a Wamphyr'.

Witch Priest/ess: *I will go down -*

All present: *to the altars of Hell, to Satan - giver of life!*

Witch Priest/ess: *As it is now -*

All present: *So shall it be!*

The witch priest/ess then bows before the Eremitic witch and joins the congregation.

The rest of the coven form a circle around the Eremitic witch and begin a widdershins dance, chanting *Wamphyri* as they do so, and directing their energies toward the witch in the centre.

The central witch meditates with their crystal in hand, imagining the Blood Essence filling up their body from the feet upward.

All perform this rite until dizziness or exhaustion forces them to fall to the ground, at which point the witch in the centre sits and chants *Nythra Kthunae Atazoth* seven times, holding up the crystal and visualising blackness flooding from a vortex above.

This ritual is designed to prepare the individual undertaking the Eremitic rite to embrace the nocturnal energies which will flood the psyche during this difficult ritual. The rite is essentially chthonic, drawing up energy from the earth and 'vampirising' it with the blood essence of the witches who have shed their blood for the rite.

Following the departure of the coven leader undertaking the rite, the witch priest/ess overtakes duties until his/her return from solitude.

Myths and Legends of the Hebrides

& *the pantheon of the Drakon Covenant*

To understand the spiritual mentality of the peoples who inhabited the isles of the Outer Hebrides, we could do worse than study the later celtic myths and legends of the region, many of which are saturated in a grim and seemingly otherworldly mystery, often expressing archetypes and entities not familiar to celtic folklore found elsewhere in Europe. Thus, we may be able to discern fragments of this previous culture now lost to antiquity.

The Hebrides was settled as early as the Mesolithic era, by peoples of largely Celtic stock, though as has been demonstrated throughout this book, the culture diverges starkly on several points. Ancient Greek writers taught that the wisest of their sages and even the gods themselves learnt their secrets in a distant land known as *Hyperborea*, the name historians say was given by the Greeks to the Hebridean Isles. There, they claimed was a temple which was built according to a 17-19 year lunar cycle. The Hebrides and by extension the myth of Hyperborea has always therefore been associated with mystical knowledge and occult arts. According to Sinister tradition, an opfer was claimed once every seventeen years, though the origin of this is lost to us. It seems the temple at Hyperborea was one way to keep track of time for this reason. Interestingly, the islands are referred to in Irish Gaelic as 'the islands of the strangers'.

Diodorus writes:

'In the regions beyond the land of the Celts there lies in the ocean an island no smaller than Sicily. This island, the account continues, is situated in the north and is inhabited by the Hyperboreans, who are called by that name because their home is beyond the point whence the north wind (Boreas) blows; and the island is both fertile and productive of every crop, and has an unusually temperate climate.'

Pindar, in the *Tenth Pythian Ode*, spoke of the character of the people who lived there:

'Never the Muse is absent

from their ways: lyres clash and flutes cry

and everywhere maiden choruses whirling.

Neither disease nor bitter old age is mixed

in their sacred blood; far from labor and battle they live;

They escape Nemesis, the overjust.'

According to the 6th century Roman historian Procopius, *Brittia* was an island known to be a mystical place where the dead were taken to be buried, or where the souls of the dead migrate unto.

The Hebridean Isles in particular was home to a people

who intensely honoured and venerated death and the ancestors. Here we find the source of the Scithain culture, and the remnants of the culture which the entities historically communed with by the Covenant belonged to.

According to Irish legends, the isles were the home of the Fomorians, fierce gods and giants who represented chaos and darkness, and who raided the shores of surrounding lands for sacrifices. It is also believed that the Fomorians may have derived in part from an older set of deities who were supplanted by the later Celtic pantheon, something which would make sense in light of the topic of these writings. The word Formorian is believed to derive from *fo* (beneath) *mór* ('great/big') and is taken to mean 'the great underworld ones'. This name tantalisingly hints at this peoples' fixation with the underworld or chthonic realm. This again ties back to a seemingly distant memory of the Scithain culture peoples residing in the memories of those who told these legends and who came in contact with them.

For those with a keen eye, the Hebrides is saturated with a muted grimness and stark character which suffuses the very land. Normally herbivorous animals like deer have been observed to kill and eat smaller creatures such as birds; carnivorous bramble bushes have been found on farmer's fields with inward curving thorns, and which bramble bushes have claimed the lives of several sheep by ensnaring the hapless animals in their uniquely adapted hook-like devices.

Religious Rites and Beliefs of the Aboriginal British

It is generally believed humans have lived in Britain for a considerable amount of time. Recent archaeological discoveries (such as the cast of footprints found on the shores of Happisburgh in Norfolk) push the date back as far as 800,000-900,000 years.

The first species of human to live in Britain was *Homo heidelbergensis* circa 500,000 years ago, evolving eventually into what is now known as Neanderthal man. This coincided with the arrival of *Homo Sapiens*. The Neanderthals were presumably drawn to areas such as Kent, where they mined flint which was in abundance. With the rising sea levels following the end of the Ice Age, the British Isles were cut off from mainland Europe and the Neanderthals eventually vanished, leaving the Isles of Britain solely home to Homo Sapiens, the Aboriginal inhabitants.

These Aboriginal Britons who inhabited Britain during the Neolithic era were distinct from later settlers for several reasons identified by archaeologists. One notable feature is their construction of barrows - communal burial mounds where families would be interred together. Later peoples practised a form of singular burial (as we see in most societies to this day).

A particularly unique ceremonial practise of the Neolithic Britons was their elaborate and oft times grisly death rituals. Many religious rites centred around the grave barrows, and these rites saw the dead ancestors' bones being removed from their resting place and displayed during community festivals. The body would have had all flesh removed prior to burial, perhaps consumed by the living relatives to return the essence of the dead back into the ancestral bloodline. The bones were also burnt in some form of cremationary ceremony.

However, this is not to say that all Neolithic British people of the time were interred in such a manner. The majority of people were not buried in barrows, and beyond these few burials discovered, archaeologists have been unable to find remnants of the bones of the regular inhabitants.

It is believed therefore that the skeletal remains found in barrow burials belonged to the priestly caste, with the chieftain/royalty often fulfilling the same function in these times - such a role is observed in many primitive cultures, which places the tribal ruler at the centre of community life, reflecting the macrocosmic centre on which the cosmos turns. For this reason, the king or equivalent rulership was often the focus of sacrificial rites designed to honour the turning of the seasons, with the king either leading such rites or in some cases, being the sacrifice itself.

Living in such a harsh time, man's thoughts would naturally have been focused upon the cycle of life and death. Despite most people settling into an agricultural and agrarian way of life, the dance of the hunt would still have played a prominent part in the psyche of most individuals living during these times. Death would have been as familiar as day and night.

The Neolithic era saw the rise of henges as well as barrows, which were reflections of the circular worldview, recognising a similar pattern in the tilt of the stars above the land. Contrary to popular belief, such structures were often designated as burial sites, and were believed to be reserved wholly for the dead. Burials of royalty and priesthood figures have been discovered at Stonehenge, suggesting a chthonic origin for the site.

Religion may have emerged out of this chthonic apprehension of the intertwining of life and death, sensing how all things emanate from the same source, where life and all living things exist in a connected system. To live meant to kill and to hunt other living things. It was thus readily accepted that the individual had to die at some point also to continue the incessant cycle of life. This circular understanding is perhaps the origin of prevalent Neolithic art pieces which frequently depict wheels or circles. The veneration of the Earth as provider also led to the symbolism of the land as a primordial Mother. This belief is regarded as the key feature of Neanderthal religion, as evidenced by their burial rites. These involved the deceased being marked with red ochre, perhaps to symbolise the bloodied state of birth, and being returned to the earth. The Neanderthals may even have been the originators of such concepts as earth burials, as well as the notion of a mother goddess, with these concepts eventually spreading into the belief systems of human culture and giving rise to a matriarchal rulership and worldview.

The rites and rituals of the Aboriginal peoples therefore, stemming from the religious concepts of death veneration, sacrifice and the cultural impact from Neanderthal thought - Goddess worship and so on - gave rise to a wholistic worldview which any adherent of the

Sinister tradition may recognise readily.

It is also claimed according to aural Sinister tradition that the Dark Gods arrived on Earth around this period in time (there is no direct date given in the Tradition, though some argue the interference occurred toward the Upper Palaeolithic era). Several cave paintings exist across the world depicting the arrival of unusual looking entities which are cited by several authors and historians as evidence of some interaction between human and non-Terran entities. Most of the art appears to be dated around 5000 BCE, despite some considerable geographical distance between examples.

Religious Rites and Beliefs of the Beaker Peoples

The so-called Beaker people (named because of the distinctive clay beaker pottery, which they are often found buried with) arrived in Britain circa 2500 BCE, bringing with them the use of metals such as copper, gold and Bronze, and ushering in what become known as the Chalcolithic era or *Bronze Age.*

These people, coming as they did as a creative minority, soon took residence as a sort of imported aristocracy. As well as new techniques in metallurgy, the Beaker peoples brought with them the first woven garments, as well as alcohol in the form of honey mead. They also helped to advance farming methods.

In contrast to the matriarchal Neolithic inhabitants of the British Isles, the Beaker people were patriarchal and were led by warrior-kings, as opposed to the Aboriginal leadership of priest/esses and seers.

The Beaker people also built barrows, but constructed them for individual use, with several clustered near one another to create a sort of family cemetery. These burials often contained many items of worth to the deceased, presumably to accompany them into the afterlife. These include weapons, jewellery and other useful items.

The religious beliefs of the Beaker people were clearly influenced by the previous Aboriginal peoples (just as those were influenced somewhat by Neanderthal beliefs). We can see this in the continued practise of henge building. The Beaker people even took efforts to renovate and improve Stonehenge. It could be argued that the Beaker people, focused primarily as they were on direct and essentially patriarchal pursuits, possessed only a rudimentary religious worldview in regards to astronomy and other disciplines and, despite bringing many advancements to the Neolithic culture of Britain, considered the native spiritual beliefs as valid and perhaps even superior to their own in their sophistication and archaic depth. Clearly some respect was afforded to the beliefs given the aforementioned upkeeping of Stonehenge.

It is therefore proposed that the Chthonic tradition arose from the wisdom of the Aboriginal-Neanderthal synthesis of spirituality, and later was allowed to flourish under the affluence the Bronze Age which was brought to the inhabitants of Britain by the Beaker folk. From here, a deeper complexity arose which saw the recognition of the sustainment of consciousness after death and the nascent beginnings which gave rise to the beliefs exemplified in continuations such as the Camlad Rouning.

This line of research, dealing as it does in tracing the spiritual lineage of Britain alongside the successive waves of settlers on the Isles finds a worthy parallel in Celtic myth, particularly in Irish mythology which proposes that there were five invasions of Ireland prior to the current Gaelic Celts who finally settled there.

The first was known as the *Parthalonian* wave, led by a vicious leader known as Parthalon. They did battle with the native ancient inhabitants known as the *Fomorians*, driving them off into the sea and dwelling in Ireland for some time before succumbing to plague and dying off. The Fomorians were shrouded in myth, said to be evil sorcerers and monsters from another world. As suggested earlier in this book, tales of the Fomorians may have been inspired by the Scithain peoples of the Hebrides.

What is interesting about these invasion myths is that they can be compared to actual waves of settlers previously discussed. The Parthalonians, for instance were said to come from Spain, and Spain contains numerous examples of Neanderthal settlements, with the earliest evidence of their paintings coming from this region. The Neanderthals were also known to have vanished suddenly and thus the legend of a plague wiping out the Parthalonians may be one possible answer.

Following these Parthalonians, the *Nemedians* would have been Neolithic settlers, and they flourished to some degree before being defeated by war with the ever-present Fomorian raiders. The Nemedians who managed to escape went to Britain and others were said to have fled to Greece, returning later as the *Fir Bolg*. These were settlers who brought with them agricultural techniques and bronze technology, and these may well have thus been the Beaker folk.

After the Fir Bolg came the *Tuatha De Danaan*, the famed warrior-gods of Celtic myth who overthrew the Fir Bolg in a series of wars. Following them came the *Milesians*, the forerunners of the modern Gaelic peoples who settled and who still inhabit the lands of Ireland.

Religious Rites and Beliefs of the Celtic Peoples

The Celts arrived in Britain around 700 BCE as a loose federation of tribes and familial clans. Whilst these settlers soon cultivated an 'Insular' Celtic identity on the isles, most tribes at this period in Europe shared some similarities in beliefs and background. Thus, the word Celt (from the Greek κελτοι) simply meant 'barbarian'. The peoples of the British Isles who arrived and settled were simply called *Britons* by the Romans, but are referred to as Celtic in this book given the fact they were essentially Celtic in religious orientation and genetic makeup. The three main groups of Celtic tribes were the Gauls (modern day France), the Britons and the Gaels (Scotland and Ireland).

The Gaels warred with the Picts who lived in Scotland, who it is believed may have been descendants of the Aboriginal-Beaker peoples, as has been argued by some historians. One tribe in the north of Scotland for instance were known as the *Mertie*, meaning 'smeared ones'. They would coat themselves in the blood of their enemies during ritual practises, a practise which seems to contain echoes of modern Sinister rituals such as the Ceremony of Recalling.

The word for Picts among the Gaelic Celts was *Cruithne,* a name also used to refer to the aboriginal inhabitants who lived in Ireland before the Gaelic Celts arrived there. The Picts also recognised matriarchal lineage, in opposition to the patriarchal lineage derivation of the Celts.

The Celtic peoples brought with them to the British Isles new techniques such as chariot construction and the use of Iron. They thus ushered in the Iron Age.

Religious duties and teachings of the oral tradition was directed by the druidic priest caste. The druids served as priests, advisors, healers and judges among the Celtic tribes. The druids were required to undergo training which lasted up to 20 years, during which they would be guided along the difficult path of understanding the forces of nature and the essence of the hidden gods.

In the chapter *Ancestor Cults*, the growth of druidic beliefs was explored, showing remarkable similarity with the Aboriginal-Neanderthal synthesis as proposed earlier. The druidic cults however were distinct in that they held distinct, named deities as figures of worship, and were solar orientated. This development of pantheon based religious systems became common during this time among many cultures such as the Greeks, Sumerians, Romans and Northern Europeans. One theory is that these deities were deific modifications of early tribal war heroes or kings. The gods and goddesses were a combination of the anthropomorphisation of natural forces and the folk tales of previous warriors, as well as significant historical figures. It is widely believed by modern practitioners or Odinism, as well as historical scholars that Odin himself was based upon a warrior king who once existed. The same can be said of England's King Arthur to some extent, though such a possible deification was snubbed by the arrival and spread of Christianity on the isles.

The pantheon of gods and goddess as seen in such mythologies can therefore be regarded as a codification of primal ancestor worship.

Wrathful Spirits

The Hebridean Isles, being surrounded by cold and tempestuous seas, naturally gave rise to legends of water spirits, malicious figures waiting to drown idle wanderers or steal men down to their underwater kingdom. These are prevalent in nearly all celtic and other seafaring culture's myths, and thus these are avoided in this exploration of mythos.

The cosmology of the Drakon Covenant divides the host of untamed spirits, shadow beings and demonic entities into what can be classed as three arbitrary categories, drawn from the ancestral traditions which we have inherited and drawn from. These three distinctions of entities are the *Draugr, Sluagh Sìdhe,* and *the Dearg Dûl.* This distinction serves as a working model, though the Undead entities Themselves may and indeed do often blur these distinctions. Distinctive categorisation should not take precedence over the insight attained via Communion therefore, and this tripartite system of understanding serves merely as a convenient system, to be used or ignored at the behest of the witch or practitioner.

The entities which populate the ontology and pantheon of the Drakon Covenant require propitiation. The practitioner of vampyric praxis will encounter the dread Ascended Masters in the form of the Sluagh and the Draugr, the latter exceeding in power of an untold immensity. It is also a distinction that the Draugr often were once living humans in their own right, whereas the Sluagh are generally believed to be entities which spawn from the darker corners of the Astral and whose genesis is largely unknown. Some non-human entities may also be regarded as Draugr however, and can often exceed any Undead post-human in their power and potency.

The third kind denoted, the vampyric entities which inhabit the natural wilderness, are known as the Dearg Dûl, and it is to them that the witch shall leave offerings to strengthen the bond between themselves and the primal darkness which will be drawn upon in one's rites. These can be likened to and indeed are representative of the wrathful and capricious nature spirits which go under various names through British folk belief. Again, the lines between entities such as the Sluagh and Dearg may often blur, and they should be regarded simply as differing shades of the same phenomenon, with the Dearg preferring to inhabit certain natural locales and whom rarely venture away from them.

A bowl should be kept at the ritual space you have

prepared, into which will be poured blood and other offerings. Incense should be burnt during the dark phase of the moon, the word *Dearg Dûl* (duh-ruh-gur doo-uhl) being chanted whilst you do so. Images of the Dearg should be placed by this bowl, preferably painted by the witch according to visions they have received during such offering rites.

The witch may wish to detail in painting or other method the entities, beseeching further visitations and even committing disciplinary procedures as outlined in *Codex Aristarchus* before the image.

It must be warned however that the Draugr and other spirits of the astral darkness (collectively referred to as the *Undead* or the *Ascended Masters*) delight in causing pain and terror to humankind.

Once the fear has been pushed through and genuine desire and devotion takes its place, the Undead will demand greater and greater rites of obeisance to presence Themselves.

More blood, more austerities.

Draugr, Demons and Acausal Entities of the Sinister Tradition

The acausal entities commonly known as 'demons' by most people and which demons are given various names by adherents of the Sinister tradition can assume various forms - be that animal, human or otherwise. Many if not all exhibit profoundly vampiric behaviour and are given the names above by those of the Covenant tradition who have studied and interacted with them.

Modern Magian occultism, being as it is derived from the flawed and ego-centric masculous worldview so characterised by modern iterations such as Laveyan Satanism, Capitalism and Liberalism (to mention nothing of Christian ethics and so-called 'humanism') erroneously believe such entities are bound by the will and magick of the sorcerer or witch; that is, that with the correct words of power, banishing spells and 'protective circles' that these Magian sorcerers can force such acausal entities to perform various tasks and be bent to their will.

In reality (and evidenced by the fact that so very few Magian occultists have ever amounted to possessing any demonstrable magickal ability), such entities are wholly beyond the control or grasp of mortal humans.

Every single 'grimoire' and magickal text in existence today (from the *Clavicula Solomnis* to the *Book of Abramelin the Mage*) which is based in the Magian, Qabalistic worldview derives from those few texts which survived the Middle Ages and which texts were wholly reliant on, derived from and dependent on the ethos and blessings of the Holy Bible - evidenced in the use of Hebraic terminology and words of power. Despite modern attempts to subvert and repackage this system as 'emanations of the Black light' or by using other such nonsensical terms, all 'grimoire magick' is indebted absolutely to the Christian outlook. This is not to say these books lack power because of their basis in Christian scriptural doctrine in itself, but because they are based in the flawed and masculous worldview of which such doctrine is a profound symptom.

The system of Hebdomadry (believed by adherents of the Drakon Covenant and the Sinister Tradition to represent the authentic view on matters of magick) professes the belief that 'demonic' entities cannot be constrained by any means humans can devise, are not bound to nor answer to Hebraic names, and certainly are not simply entities which exist to serve Mankind's various wants and needs. Any apparent success Magian occultists may gain from the flawed and essentially Nazarene magickal system is simply down to self-delusion on the part of the practitioner, with often little to no definite results to show for such workings.

Any 'messages' or success the pseudo-sorcerer may actually attain usually derive from (as is readily known by those serious adherents of the Sevenfold Way) the latent aspects of the psyche - which, when not fully understood and integrated, as is done during the stage from Novitiate to Adept, are assumed to be wholly separate beings which the individual can delude themselves into believing really are the various demons and entities he/she has striven to summon. They are in essence phantoms, imaginary shadows of the unconscious and possess no real life of their own.

In the tradition of Hebdomadry, this is the alchemical process of *Separation,* the tearing in two to recognise the Ego and the Self. This concept is often written about within modern occult literature, yet very little genuine evidence of such a process is ever brought to witness. Many cryptic or occultic messages and ideas can be gleaned via such workings, but they are soon discarded as insight is attained and a more direct apprehension of the forces of magick are understood and accessed by continual progression through the Way toward *Lapis Excelis* - Mastery. Thus, do these pseudo-sorcerers delude themselves and restrict their progress to the level of wallowing in one's ability to conjure up and rationalise unconscious patterns of energy.

The use of names to describe these acausal entities (such as those ascribed to the Dark Gods) within genuine, Sinister magick are thus simply those symbols or forms which allow these entities and/or acausal energies to manifest in our causal, earthly realm or within the consciousness of ourselves or other humans.

As stated in an ONA text, *Copula cum Daemone*:

"The essence of our sinister Internal Magick is *Copula cum Daemone*, in either the literal sense of joining with certain acausal entities, or in the psychic sense of nurturing, releasing, and joining with one's inner Baeldraca to thus become a causal-dwelling (but still mortal) sinister changeling. In the case of one's Baeldraca, the joining is begun by the rite of sinister Initiation, nurtured by the journey to External Adept, released by the Rite of Internal Adept, and fully joined (re-united) with one's causal being by a successful Passing of The Abyss.

In the literal sense, the joining with certain acausal entities can be done in several ways. First, by invoking them, through Dark Sorcery, into one's own self. Second, by evoking them and then, again through Dark Sorcery, having a candidate (a mortal, willing or unwilling) be a host for the entity so evoked. Third, by opening a collocation of nine physical nexions and recalling The Dark Gods back to our causal realm.

A simple example of the first kind is the working with the pathways on the Tree of Wyrd (qv. Naos). An example of the second kind is The Ceremony of Recalling, as given in The Grimoire of Baphomet. A fictional account of such presencings of such acausal entities is given in *Eulalia: Dark Daughter of Baphomet,* and in the three stories, *Jenyah, Sabirah,* and I*n The Sky of Dreamin*g.

In a quite literal sense, some acausal entities – when manifest in the causal, are demons. Mischievous evil beings who – like most acausal beings – are shapeshifters, and can assume a variety of causal forms, benign, animal, human, or otherwise."

It is seen now how wasteful and urbane modern Magian occultists are (of whatever bent) in their slavish obsession with ego-based magickal systems, refusing as they do to let go and complete the next stage in magickal adeptship - namely, the dissolving of the Ego to give birth to the Self.

Dearg Dûl

According to Celtic folklore, these are spirits of the wilderness which thirst eternally for human blood and are generally female in appearance. They could be said to be analogous to the Dark Daughters of Baphomet - vampiric female shapeshifters that haunt Mankind, ever at the periphery of causal existence.

The Dearg Dûl are connected with sacred and hallowed places, and often prey upon lost travellers. Offerings are left for the Dearg Dûl in lonely spots. Some witches often build a small cairn in the woods and leave gifts of incense, coins and blood to the Dearg Dûl that may inhabit the surrounding area.

The Dearg Dûl are those feral shades, the entities which live in the earth and haunt the forests and other desolate places where humans have made little impact or habitation. It is believed they live underground during the daylight hours, surfacing at night to feed and stalk the living. Some legends recount how many Dearg were once living people, and now exist as revenants - literal vampires, thirsting endlessly for the blood of mankind.

A famous Irish legend tells of a Dearg Dûl known as Abhartach, who in life was a fifth century tyrannical king, reputed to be a powerful sorcerer of evil magick (later accounts refer to him as a dwarf). After imposing years of dreadful rule upon his subjects, Abhartach's people eventually beseeched the neighbouring chieftain Cathrain to rid them of the tyrant (later named as either Fionn mac Cumhaill, a warrior hero of Irish myth, or Cathan, a sixth century Christian monk - as is common in the modernisation of folk tales). Cathrain eventually slew Abhartach, freeing the people of their evil ruler. However, Abhartach soon rose from his grave, demanding a bowl of blood to nourish his undead form.

In Patrick W Joyce's *The Origin and History of Irish Names of Places*, he tells of a megalithic site known as

Slaghtaverty Dolmen, also called *Leacht Abhartach* (Abhartach's sepulchre).

Of Abhartach he writes: "He was buried in a standing posture, but the very next day he appeared in his old haunts, more cruel and vigorous than ever. And the chief slew him a second time and buried him as before, but again he escaped from the grave, and spread terror through the whole country. The chief then consulted a druid, and according to his directions, he slew the dwarf a third time, and buried him in the same place, with his head downwards; which subdued his magical power, so that he never again appeared on earth."

The ritualised slaying of Abhartach is reminiscent of European vampire killing methods. The evil sorcerer-king was run through with a sword made from yew wood, buried upside-down, surrounded by thorns and ash twigs, and his grave was surmounted by a heavy stone. This stone is what later became known as Slaghtaverty Dolmen, also known as *the Giant's Grave*.

In 1997, workmen attempted to clear the land where the dolmen stands, cutting down the thorn tree which arched across the sepulchre. Not only did the chainsaw fail to work several times, but during the excavation work a steel chain snapped, slicing the hand of one of the workmen and causing the blood to soak into the ground.

There is also the tale of a ruined castle inhabited by a host of Dearg Dûl, known as *Du'n Dreach-Fhoula* ("the place of tainted blood" though another name for this fortress is the 'Castle of the Blood Visage'). It is said to stand somewhere in the mountain range of Magillycuddy

Reeks in Kerry County, Ireland. It was built originally as a defensive fortress overlooking the mountain pass, but was soon abandoned and swiftly filled with its later blood drinking stewards. What truth there is of this place, and whether it still stands is unknown, though witches have attempted to visit this place during nocturnal astral journeys.

It is argued by some that this castle's name, as well as the legend of Abhartach, was the inspiration for the name and habitation of Bram Stoker's *Dracula*.

The Sluagh Sìdhe

The Sluagh Sìdhe are an ancient and feared species of Sìdhe. The Sluagh (meaning "host" in Gaelic) is a group formed from the darkest, most vile creatures imaginable. They feature in the mythology of Western Scotland and the Hebridean Isles. Even the uttering of the word 'Sluagh' is said to draw their attention. Whilst not as immediately powerful as the Ascended Masters/Draugr, they are certainly far more numerous.

The Sluagh supposedly delight in preying on Mankind, and wait for night, at which point they emerge from the dark and forgotten places and fly out to feed and terrorise. According to Celtic folklore, they would take to the skies and be seen as a vast flock of bats or ravens.

The Sluagh are drawn to despair and grief, feeding off it maliciously and without cessation. Thus, they are resonant of typical astral vampires. The Sluagh are said to take on the appearance of bird-like entities, with leathery wings kept close to their bodies, forming a weathered cloak, and bearing bony hands wrought into razor sharp talons.

Legend describes how the Sluagh Sídhe once ruled men in the ancient days of prehistory. Alexander Carmichael, a Scottish folklorist and author wrote in his *Caemina Caedelica* (itself an expansive work on his earlier *Grazing and Agrestic Customs of the Outer Hebrides*) about the Sluagh that "the people have many curious stories on this subject. According to one informant, the spirits fly about in great clouds, up and down the face of the world like the starlings, and come back to the scenes of their earthly transgressions. No soul of them is without the clouds of earth, dimming the brightness of the works of God, nor can any win heaven till satisfaction is made for the sins of earth..."

"They fight battles in the air as men do on the earth. They may be heard and seen on clear frosty nights, advancing and retreating, retreating and advancing, against one another. After a battle, as I was told in Barra, their crimson blood may be seen staining rocks and stones. (*Fuil nan sluagh*, the blood of the hosts, is the beautiful red 'crotal' of the rocks melted by the frost.) These spirits used to kill cats and dogs, sheep and cattle, with their unerring venomous darts. They commanded men to follow them, and men obeyed, having no alternative.

"It was these men of earth who slew and maimed at the bidding of their spirit-masters, who in return ill-treated them in a most pitiless manner."

They are said to gather amidst the shadowy corners of the

world in great hosts, and are essentially malicious to humankind. They are untold in number, and account for most manifestations of demonic activity (it should be noted that usage of these terms, just like the usage of the term 'demon' is simply a useful designation to describe such amoral and predatory acausal entities the witch may encounter).

The Draugr

Draugr is the name applied to the more notably powerful manifestations of the Undead spirits. The name Draugr is originally Norse in its origins, the word itself supposedly deriving from the Indo-Aryan *Droughos*, meaning 'deceiver'. The Draugr were originally Germanic undead entities which feature in many Norse myths, being the corpses or spirits of powerful warriors or sorcerers/esses who could draw the *hugr* (the animate will) back from death.

It is exceptionally powerful spirits that we have come to identify as the Draugr, also known as the Ascended Masters of Covenant tradition. The tradition relates that a powerful witch can become a Draugr through adherence to vampyric magick, and many Draugr retain features which they possessed in life. Many Draugr, if not all, exhibit humanoid characteristics.

Much has been written elsewhere regarding these potent entities, but it is held within Covenant tradition that the ultimate goal of the witch of the vampyric tradition is to transform the astral form into a vessel to carry the conscious will after death, thus creating a Lich, and placing one's self among the ranks of the Ascended Masters. Thus, does one cross the threshold and become a veritable Draugr.

The state of Undeath in which these entities abide is one of extreme conservation; just as the process of energy conservation is begun in the stages of vampyric novitiateship with exercises such as meditation in dead stillness, it takes its final form in Undeath.

The more complex an entity, the less it will waste energy with superfluous movement and action. Only in death does this movement cease in all living things. However, beyond even death - the hallowed state of Undeath - the process of conservation takes an even deeper and extensive application. Undead entities such as the Draugr do not readily 'exist' as we understand the term when they are not impelled to act or move into the causal spaces. They can be said to exist as a potential or energy pattern within the acausal, presencing themselves under a set of specific circumstances (such as when astrally feeding or summoned successfully by practitioners).

Cailleach, The Great Hag

One particularly powerful Draugr is the Hag, who is believed to be a long dead witch who attained Lichdom. Among the Gaelic speaking peoples she is generally identified as the *Cailleach*.

The Hag is perhaps the most ubiquitous and infamous of all the Draugr, reported across the world to haunt people in their sleep. Her name derives from the Gaelic *Caille* or

Caillech, meaning 'veil' and 'veiled one' respectively. Witches within the Covenant tradition often wear a veil in conjunction with ritual attire in emulation of the Hag, as well as in respect to a certain Dark God.

Within Celtic mythology she is regarded as an ancestor deity who presides over the weather, winter and the wilderness. In this regard, she is not dissimilar to the Slavic goddess Morana/Marzanna. In Scotland, the Cailleach is often connected to the destructive aspects of nature, such as storms and heavy rainfall. Her legend is believed to be as old as the Neolithic age and perhaps even older. A defining feature in representations of her in poems and myths often focus on her vast age. According to one Irish folktale, a woman of Tiree once asked the Cailleach how old she was. She replied that she remembered when the Skerryvore rocks were fields where barley was farmed, and when the lakes were little wells. It is interesting to note that barley farming was a practise that arose during the early Neolithic era, thus beyond living memory of anyone alive in centuries.

The Scottish and Hebridean Isles maintained a very intact picture of the worship of the Cailleach, intact more so than most British pagan remnants observed by folklorists and historians. However, the nature of Celtic myth research is hampered by the essentially aural tradition of those peoples, so that most sources come from second hand recorders of folklore, individuals who often journeyed and spoke with rural inhabitants and wrote down what they told. This aurally dependent culture saw poems and stories passed down from student to teacher, with some older individuals still alive today who can recite thousands of lines of prose detailing the myths and legends of the highlands.

Most tales and aspects of mythos were local in their character; modern attempts to create a catch-all spirituality, such as 'Celtic Wicca' and 'Druidry' are woefully simplistic and artificial attempts at crafting an easily consumed religious system which did not exist in such a definite form.

This is especially true to representations of the Cailleach hag. She does however feature in all aspects of Scottish mythology. Among her many titles and epithets, she is known as the 'blue hag', the 'Bear goddess, the 'Boar goddess', 'owl faced' and 'the ancient woman, as well as *Bui, Cally Berry, Caillech Bherri, Cailliach, Carline, Digde, Dirra, Duineach, Hag of Beara, Mala Liath, Mag-Moullach, Scotia,* and *Nicnevin.*

At Glen Lyon in Scotland there still exists a small stone built hut dedicated to the hag, where several stones representing the Cailleach and her family are cared for by local inhabitants. The ritual is believed to be thousands of years old, and dates back to when the Cailleach was worshipped in those lands. It thus stands as the oldest continuing pagan tradition in Britain (and it is indeed telling that modern expressions, such as so-called 'neo-paganism' show no knowledge of this secret and ancient ritual nestled in the northern valleys). In Summer, the stones are brought out of their stone house by locals and left in the valley. When Winter approaches, they are placed back in their home.

Whilst this is one pertinent and relevant cultural interpretation of the hag phenomenon, she is so prevalent that she gives her name to the colloquial term for sleep paralysis - 'Old Hag Syndrome', as her form is that most often seen by sufferers.

In Leicestershire, England there exists the legend of Black Annis, a terrible blue-skinned old crone with iron claws, who roams the countryside looking for children to devour. Many place names around the region are associated with her, and it is believed she may be a distant memory of a time when the inhabitants of Britain would sacrifice children to a now unknown wrathful goddess, not too dissimilar to the Cailleach.

The Draugr in Norse Myth

In Norse mythology, the Draugr were claimed to possess magickal powers, including the ability to shapeshift, predict the future and change weather. They were even said to be able to bring darkness to daytime, blotting out the sky for a period of time. Norse beliefs attributed to the Draugr the ability to transform into a seal, a great flayed bull, a grey horse with a broken back but no ears or tail, and a cat that would sit upon a sleeper's chest and grow steadily heavier until the victim suffocated. The Draugr Þráinn (Thrain) shape-shifted into a "cat-like creature" (kattakyn) in the Hrómundar saga Gripssonar. Many victims of sleep paralysis have described phantom cats sitting upon their chests, either accompanied by a shadow entity or alone. Thrain, as a particularly noted Draugr, can be called upon to enact Communion, should He see fit.

The Calling of Þráinn Boneshaker

Þráinn (Thrain) is recounted in the sagas as an undead witch-king, formerly the ruler of Valland (Gaul). He was said to have slain hundreds of men, with his magickal sword Mistilteinn. Þráinn can be called upon by the witch to grace him/her with His undead presence and reveal many secrets. However, He is hostile to most if not all living beings and will act accordingly.

Þráinn is a terrifying figure, and will most likely appear to the witch in the typical way Draugr do - either clothed in black, and towering above normal height, their faces (or what can be seen of them) in hel-blár ('blue-death' the term used to describe those Draugr who appeared blue skinned) or, nár-fölr ('corpse-pale').

Þráinn is appeased and called upon with the following ritual.

Carve Þráinn's name upon a piece of wood in runic inscription, setting it before you on an outdoor altar. Give offerings of meat and beer, placing them upon the altar, and light several candles.

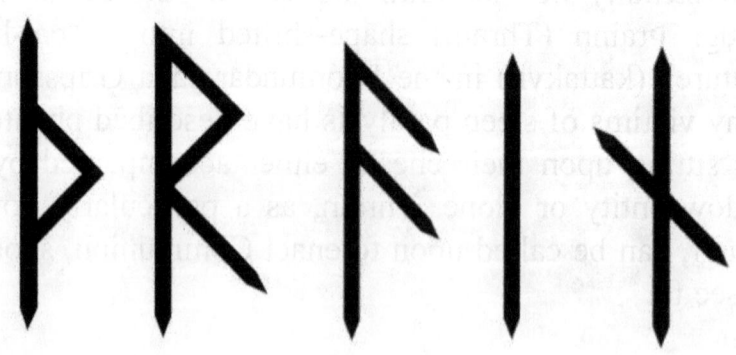

Lash yourself until blood flows, and mark your face with the visage of death - either by painting it akin to a corpse, or by painting it blue. Any decorative motifs are left up to the creativity of the practitioner (runes should generally not be used, except for the inscribing of the name).

Next, begin the chant. If others are present, they should remain silent, joining in only with the shouting of the name three times.

Þráinn!

Þráinn!

Þráinn!

You dreadful countenanc'd one!

Hail to thee! Slayer of men, King of Valland

I call you to come before us

Þráinn!

Þráinn!

Þráinn!

Mighty spirit of wrathful fury

Bestowed one of royal power
I call you to come before us

Þráinn!

Þráinn!

Þráinn!

Your name rings with fame
throughout the halls of men
only terror and honour are known when men speak of ye
I call you to come before us

Þráinn!

Þráinn!

Þráinn!

I call you to come before us!
Þráinn!
I call you to come before us!
Þráinn!
I call you to come before us!

Þráinn!

Þráinn!

Þráinn!

(Note: The ritual functions in a similar manner to the calling of the Dark Gods during the Pathways rites; that is, it attunes the witch to the energies of this particular Draugr and can, if he is willing, presence Þráinn. It is the goal of the witch to not only come to know the Draugr, but work with them and strive to become one him/herself).

Callanish stones

This megalithic structure situated on the west coast of Lewis in the Outer Hebrides has stood longer than Stonehenge (having been erected in the late Neolithic era circa 2900-2600 BCE).

The stone structure is arranged in the form of a cross, with a central circle, within which is a chambered tomb, itself a later addition to the structure. The chambered tomb at the centre of the stone circle was cleared out by Bronze Age settlers at some point in time in a ritual cleansing, which saw various pots and vessels broken and removed, presumably to remove the presence or remnant power of one of the Neolithic lich-priest/esses who had been buried there, with the tomb itself being covered with turf around the year 800 BCE, before being ultimately abandoned.

As mentioned earlier, the Bronze age settlers integrated and adopted the religious practises and beliefs of the Neolithic inhabitants. That the stone circle was cleared and cleansed suggests a belief in the latent power of the dead. The cleansing may have even been the removal of an interred priestess who was worshipped by people, and the desecration of the tomb was another conquest of the patriarchal ethos as upheld by the Beaker peoples. That the cairn was not only cleaned but ritually cleansed shows that the desecrators still held a belief in the power of the rituals and the priesthood of the Neolithic settlers.

In modern times, the Callanish Stones are rumoured by psychics to possess an unsettling or 'evil' presence, and visions of men in black robes have been reported by several individuals.

The stones are one designation in 'Chthonic' Black Pilgrimage, which visits various sites on the Outer Hebridean isles. Whether any lingering Undead energies remain will be determined by the witch who camps at this spot.

The Phoboi and Ritual Use of Mind Altering Plants

According to aural recollections, the Phoboi were an isolated tribe who dwelt on the northern shores of the Hebridean Isles. Consisting of outcast males, the Phoboi lived at the fringes of society. They consisted of men who had been expelled from their clans for the practise of homosexuality, which was a taboo crime of the times.

These exiles bonded into small communes, and whilst reviled and feared, were recognised for being uniquely potent soothsayers, sometimes consulted for their powers of divination. Visiting and employing the Phoboi was often regarded as an unsavoury act, though certain heroes and clan leaders would in times of war and strife turn to them to foresee the future.

The Phoboi's main method of divination was through casting of bones and other small items imbued with magickal power, as well as reading signs seen in bonfire smokes, throwing certain herbs and plants into the flames. The Phoboi often lived semi-naked, and marked themselves with oils, dirt and ash across their bodies, often shaving their heads of all hair.

They were formidable fighters and could put up a serious defence if challenged. Thus, they were never wiped out, but functioned as somewhere to exile transgressors of fleshly law.

As described above, to prophesy the Phoboi shamans would either cast bones and shells and read the patterns thereof. The bone fragments they used were often carved in specific ways, and it is believed simply keeping such a trinket on one's person was enough to render someone cursed.

Another common method involved the inhalation of hallucinogenic herbs, either ingested or more commonly, burnt in a fire or primitive stone brazier and the resulting smoke inhaled. The Phoboi seer would gather a plant native to the northern regions of the British Isles. It is theorised they would have used heather, as this cultivates ergot on its leaves. Ergot is a powerful hallucinogen, noted for being the precursor to the synthetic LSD, though the 'trip' derived from ergot is terrifying at best. It can induce many unsettling symptoms, but more importantly, has been known to grant visions to whoever ingests it. It has also been used to induce abortions for many thousands of years, making the Phoboi even more maligned for providing knowledge in this practise.

A moss commonly known as 'fogg' also grows on the stems of heather. The moss' powdered residue contains hallucinogenic properties, and upon taking these substances, visions would naturally flood the seer's mind. From this the future would be augured for those brave enough to travel to the outlying lands where the 'scourged few' dwelt.

In later times, the Romans would recount how an ale brewed by the Picts using heather drove them into a mad frenzy, making them fearsome warriors in battle, as well as granting them visions and an astounding ability to see in total darkness. It thus seems that this region was regarded even in ancient times as a centre of wisdom and knowledge, where many sagacious minds journeyed to receive teachings.

As expressed, the particular entities known to the inner sanctum of the Drakon Covenant - a cadre of veritable Draugr - expressed through Communion that these Hebridean Isles are their ancestral homeland and that they were once the priesthood of the Chthonic culture, now immortalised through diligence to the fragmentary resurrection of their rites and rituals. And thus have they bequeathed knowledge which is outlined here and which is practised fanatically by the covens and lone practitioners of our unique tradition.

Central to this tradition is our nexus, the prime hallowed land to which all adherents to the Covenant teachings must journey to at least twice in their causal existence - the Outer Hebrides, and more specifically, Beinn Sciathan (another region visited during the Chthonic Black Pilgrimage).

Alongside the orthodox regions of the Camlad Rouning and the principal locales scattered around Yorkshire, Beinn Sciathan is a focal point for many of the blackest rites of the vampyric witches of the Covenant tradition.

The Hill of the Bat

Beinn Sciathan lies on the isle of Eriskay, just off the coast of South Uist in the Outer Hebrides, standing above the landscape like a stark sentinel.

The pilgrimage to Beinn Sciathan comes upon the novitiate's completion of the Dark Pathways and Spheres, during which the witch should hike and stay atop the small mountain, performing a black fast (it is ideal to arrive during the evening and spend a night and day fasting and reflecting on your journey thus far). This rite is itself different to the Black Pilgrimage, though the two can be combined, with this combination being the preferred method for most following the way.

The Rite of Nine Angles should be performed on the second night, and the rite should begin on the new moon. This will be the first time practising the Nine Angles Rite atop Beinn Sciathan, with the second coming following completion of External Adept and the creation of a coven under the Adept, at which point he/she will conduct the Rite yet again, with their coven members present.

This rite, when performed correctly, is unparalleled in its ability to draw forth the energies and presence of the Dark Gods, thus returning Them to Earth. The energies will saturate the practitioner and the land itself, and the mere intrusion of Their essence via this rite means a greater degree of the Acausal darkness will be presenced upon the earth, thus opening the gates further and impelling change and evolution on a global scale.

There are several versions/requirements to this rite. The main requirement for this rite is that it should be performed atop a hill of pre-Cambrian rock. Pre-Cambrian rock refers to any rock dating from before life originated on earth (from 4 billion to 540 million years ago). The Hebridean Isles is comprised of Lewisian Gneiss which dates to circa 3 billion years old, making it not only suitable pre-Cambrian rock, but also the oldest rock in Britain. Thus, it is a wyrdfully potent and suitable locale for performing such a rite (another suitable location for this rite would be Beinn Mhòr on the Hebridean isle of South Uist).

Having reached the summit of the hill and facing the direction of Saturn, vibrate the words *Nythra Kthunae Atazoth* seven times with crystal in hand.

Then vibrate the words *Binan Ath Ga Wath Am*, followed by the Diabolus.

The witch then visualises a dark rent opening in the region of Saturn streaming dark energy down from the stars and surrounding him/herself. This visualisation should last for at least one quarter of an hour.

Following this, vibrate the word *Atazoth* nine times, then sit and place the crystal on the ground. Sit near to it and visualise a blackness emanating from its centre which spreads out to engulf the individual. The crystal should be wrapped in black cloth and stored until required again.

Sacred Mountains in the Scithain Tradition

To the Neolithic inhabitants of Northern Britain, mountains were regarded as places of great power, peaks which reached upward toward the realm of the gods. It is believed by adherents that the Dark Gods first descended to Earth and arrived on the peak of a mountain (some within the Covenant suggesting Beinn Sciathan being this mountain). This aural belief may be allegorical; the unique power of mountains and hills however has always been venerated, not least for their upheaval of precious stones and minerals vital to the sorcerer. Other mountains are of prominent importance and power within the northern isles, of course. Aural myth tells the tale of Beinn Dearg Mhor and a powerful shaman, gifted with a cloak of light made from salmon skin who ventured into this mountain in order to commune with the mountain's spirit so as to soothe the tremors devastating the land. Within its dark chasm the shaman beheld with the light of the cloak a vast and sickening serpent which lay at the roots of the mountain. The shaman used his power to bring the mountain crashing down upon the serpent, crushing it. It is said this is the reason the mountain has a sunken peak. It remains as a place of potent power for those willing to journey to it and perform rites atop its peak.

There exist other mountains which remain as great sources of power, such as Beinn Mhor on the Isle of South Uist, which is the largest mountain in the Hebrides. These peaks should be explored by those drawn to the northern regions of Albion. Their mute power and atmosphere simply cannot be understated.

Notes on the Nine Angle Rite

The version detailed here which will be performed by all witches of the Drakon Covenant upon completion of their pilgrimage will be the solo version. The other version, the *Chthonic* (meaning literally 'within the earth') requires it to be performed in an underground cavern where water flows, with a congregation including Priest and a Priestess as well as at least one cantor trained in Esoteric Chant together with a congregation of male and female.

This version, when combined with the Ceremony of Recalling with sacrificial conclusion along with adherence to the conditions for Algol is said to most effective at returning the Dark Gods to Earth.

There is also the natural version. Usually the Rite is

performed by a couple, fulfilling the role of Priest and Priestess, conducted upon a hilltop after sunset, and which involves the burying of the crystal in the hillside.

Besides the pre-Cambrian location, another alternate requirement involves a pre-consecrated glade within a circle of nine stones (with the first stone being set on a night of the new moon with Saturn rising, the second at the full moon and so on: the first stone marking the point on the horizon where Saturn rises). The consecration would usually by the Ceremony of Eorthe.

The Nine Angles Rite is traditionally performed on or near to the Autumn Equinox (for Dabih) or on or near to the Winter Solstice (for Algol). With the Dabih version, it is best performed when Venus sets after the sun, and the moon itself occults Dabih or is near to it; with the Algol version, it is best performed when Jupiter and Saturn are both near the moon which is becoming new, the time being before dawn. This is designed to access the energies of the star gates located at or near to the stars Dabih and Algol, respectively. The solo version is to be performed on the night of the new moon when Saturn is rising, and is concerned with the Saturn Gate, thus the above requirements are not necessary for this iteration of the rite (see *Star Gates and Hebdomadric Astrology*).

SCITHAIN

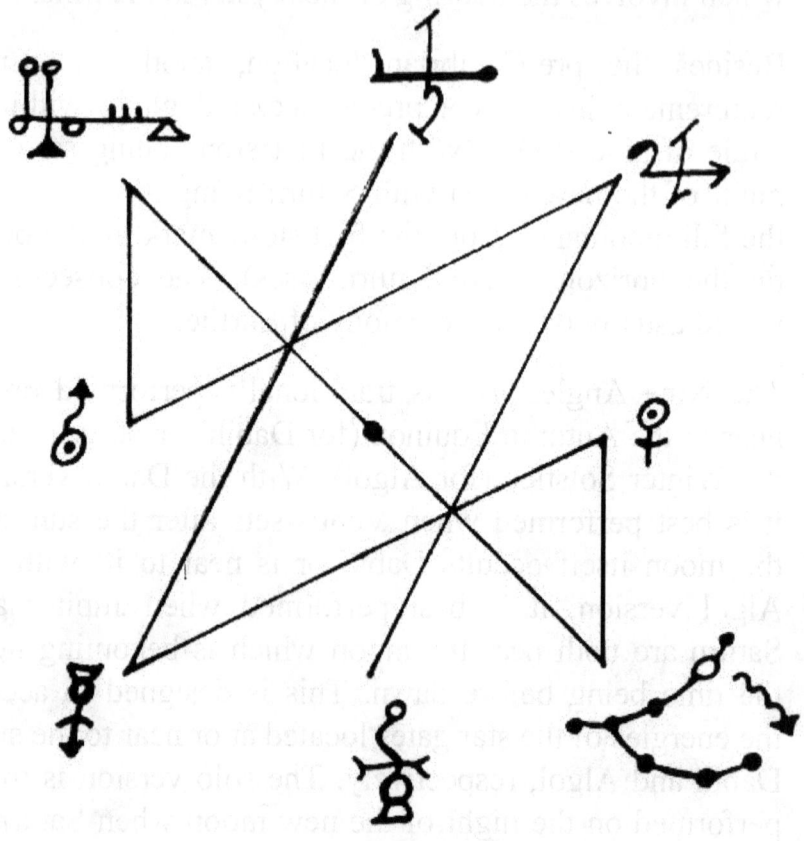

Morgatha, Mother of Vindex

According to Sinister tradition, *Falcifer* is the name given to the force or individual who brings into being, presences or generally opens the way for Vindex to emerge.

Vindex, it is prophesied, will be an individual who will bring into being and presence new archetypes which are appropriate to the new Aeon. Vindex replaces the old law of the old Aeon with our new law of personal honour. It is this Vindex character who will, according to prophecy, lead an exoteric war against the Magian forces and re-establish a numinous balance to the Earth, thus setting the Aeon back upon its natural course and ushering in this new Aeon in a manifest manner.

As detailed in Hostia, Falcifer and Vindex are:

"Names signifying the person who may embody, in the causal world, the essence of the Sinister – i.e. he/she empowered by the Dark Gods to bring the wordless Aeon in a practical sense. In the exoteric sense, Falcifer (the reaper) and Vindex (the avenger) are esoteric names for the anti-Nazarene mentioned in Revelation and elsewhere.

Vindex can be created by Sinister ritual – the chthonic Nine Angles rite when the energy is channelled by visualisation and chant into a designated person."

How the presencing of Vindex actually occurs is not made explicitly clear throughout Order MSS (except for the reference to the chthonic Nine Angles Rite). What is revealed here however, via the aural tradition of the Drakon Covenant, is just how the presencing act of Falcifer is made possible.

It is via a third and necessary archetype, hitherto unrevealed till now - namely, a female archetype or nascent entity, waiting to be made manifest, referred to as *Morgatha*. Morgatha would be a Sinisterly-numinous entity, as befits her Baphometic role; she would be the bride of Falcifer, and together with him, she would bear a child who will become Vindex.

It must be stressed however that Morgatha does not exist solely to be a mother figure; rather, it is her life and works which prepare her for such an esteemed and necessary role. Prior to the bearing of Vindex, she will ascend as a powerful force in her own right, a witch queen of the Covenant, a reincarnation of sorts (as will be outlined later), and bring a necessary balance to the Cosmos through Her Wyrdful actions.

It is for this reason that the vampyric current of the Sinister tradition must, and has been presenced - so as to prepare the way for this numinous entity. The Drakon Covenant thus believes it holds the responsibility to help bring Morgatha into being, and to guide her toward her role as the mother of the Dark Aeon.

How this is done is by presencing the vampyric current and its associated archetypes, mostly through the spread of the tradition itself and the cultivation of vampyric adepts and those Lamia Naturalae who are receptive to the unique teachings and practises of the Covenant.

The energies can be brought close to the causal, but they must be given a vessel in which to incarnate. It is believed that Morgatha's role is that of *Mater Vindex*, the mother of Vindex, as well as being the earthly embodiment of the Numinous aspects of the Sinister tradition. Thus do we loyally await the coming of the bloodied mistress and anointed daughter of Baphomet, a causal witch born a Lamia Naturalis.

In the past, it is believed several individuals were born across the centuries who could have fulfilled the role of Morgatha. But the Tradition was not made available, and thus they faded into obscurity (though some became infamous vampires in their own right). It is generally believed Morgatha as a causal human being has not yet been born at the time of writing. The entity Morgatha is not merely a birthing of a new archetype in the conventional manner, but rather a rebirth of a very real woman who once existed, a priestess of Albion during the Hyperborean Aeon. Morgatha in her original incarnation was the half-sister of the figure who would come to be known in British myth as Arthur, and she was instrumental in the ushering in of the Western Aeon.

It is believed by Covenant adherents that the legend of Morgan Le Fay (also known as Morgana, Morgant, Morgane, etc. etc.) was/is a distant echo of the aural tradition which recorded her actions as a priestess of Albion, as well as predicting her return and the necessity of her presencing; whilst the legend slowly became warped throughout time, the Arthurian mythos kept Morgatha alive in a convoluted sense - as it did many aspects of the Camlad Rouning.

Morgatha upheld the Tradition which was the Wyrdful expression of the Folk and the Cosmos during Her causal life. She undertook a numinous role in becoming the instigator of the Aeon - with the distortion arising, she will presence again to restore balance, and the evolution of the Cosmos shall go on.

At the time of writing, little can be said of how Vindex will emerge. But the union of the Two to create the One, the uniting of Falcifer and Morgatha is an instrumental part. How this alchemy will occur is unknown at present; it may be more metaphorical rather than physical.

Only during later iterations of the legend of Arthur did Morgana/Morgan Le Fay become defined as the mortal enemy of Arthur, as the patriarchal ethos of the Magian via Christianity began to take hold in British myth and culture. She thus became a distant echo and a character to set as an antagonist in Arthurian tales and legend. Some scholars however now agree the inspiration for her character came from a Welsh celtic supernatural entity or goddess, with some claiming she is derived from the Celtic goddess *Dea Matrona (*the 'Great Mother') who was worshipped in Gaul, again tying back to her role as bearer of Vindex. Yet another theory suggests she is derived from an ancient Celtic goddess known as *Modron* ('mother'). Modron, known also as Matrona, was worshipped in Northern England, from Yorkshire to the area surrounding Hadrian's Wall. Also featured in Arthurian myth is the character Morgause, again regarded as a half-sister of Arthur and mother of many heroes - namely the knights Gawain, Gaheris, Agravain, Gareth, and Mordred.

Some have claimed, as is cited in Gerald of Wale's *Liber de Principis Instructione*, written in 1193 (one of the earliest references to Morgana), that Morgatha was later remembered as a female ruler known as Morgan - and it was Morgatha who, according to aural Sinister tradition was the instigator, or at least oversaw - via her role as priestess - the inauguration of the Western Aeon (circa 500 CE). And as mentioned above, Morgan was the half-sister of Arthur, of whom much is written elsewhere in texts detailing the roots of the tradition itself;

"After the Battle of Camlan, a noblewoman called Morgan, later the ruler and patroness of these parts as well as being a close blood-relation of King Arthur, carried him off to the island, now known as Glastonbury, so that his wounds could be cared for."

In the *Vita Merlini,* written around 1150, Morgan is said to be the first of nine sisters who rule the Fortunate Isle (Avalon) and is described as a healer and a shape-changer, who lives with a coven of witches in seclusion from society.

The inauguration of the current Western Aeon would have seen the use of the Grail by Morgatha, with this Grail taking the form of a large quartz tetrahedron, and the tradition of using such an item has been passed down since then to genuine adepts of the tradition up to present times. One aural tradition of the Drakon Covenant suggests that the Grail was composed of Moldavite, a green gemstone which originates from a meteorite which landed on earth 4 million years ago.

Morgatha is a symbol of the Sinisterly-numinous balance, nurturing us all throughout our Satanic quest. Her Grail spills over with life-blood to transform and renew us. She watches through the mists of time, each bearer of the Tradition holding the Grail with her.

The Grail is often depicted as a cup, supposedly due to it being the cup used at the Last Supper in Christian myth. This however is an arbitrary understanding and a later embellishment on the myth, and it is argued that there was an intuitive knowledge of the Grail being a vessel of some kind at one point or another. This vessel could be the bearer the Tradition or it could bear the Western blood - or it could be Morgatha Herself. All are inextricably bound together regardless.

Much has been done to warp the Grail mythos, a mythos which is arguably the original religion of the West. Stylised first by Christians then by later conquerors such as the Saxons and the Normans to suit their own agendas, understanding the essence of the Grail is a difficult task but one not wholly impossible.

The Grail in earliest myths was described as a vessel or a stone of some sort. The later adoptions of the Grail knights, the romance of Lancelot and so forth were the inventions of French authors such as Chretien de Troyes, who used Arthur and the kingdom of Camelot as a useful setting for various quests and adventures.

Morgatha is believed to have ascended as an Immortal (that final stage of the Sevenfold Way beyond

Grandmaster/mistress) sometime after playing her part in ushering in the new Aeon. She exists now, as all acausal entities do, as a timeless and potent Dark God, awaiting to fulfill the final part of Her supra-personal destiny and to bring about the birth of Vindex.

Upon completion of the Wyrdful actions of Falcifer, Morgatha and Vindex, the consciousness of humanity will experience a right-angled shift in development and evolution. By its virtue, the Earth itself would become exalted, its very physicality altered by a liminal gestalt effect which would see the Dark Gods return openly and without hindrance of form.

This then is one of the secrets to returning Them. Reality is essentially an experiential consensus across all living beings which apprehend reality. The limitations of what can be achieved exist solely according to the prevailing consciousness which recognises and interprets reality accordingly. With the emergence of Vindex and the subsequent societal shift that Vindex's Imperium will bring about, the planet which we are inherently tied to will shift accordingly. All religions have at one point known this in some garbled form or another (referred to in terms such as the Kingdom of God among the Nazarene sects). The Earth will enter a state of *Terra Mysteria,* imbued with magick because the tyranny of the Magian and its control over thought has been toppled. The world shall become imbued with numinosity, and thus Terra Mysteria will be not only a term used to refer to the earth's exalted state, but a way of saying life once again has meaning, a revelling in *fayen*.

Arthurian Legend in the Sinister Tradition

The stories and legends of King Arthur and Camelot are, according to the teachings of the Sinister Tradition, echoes of several aspects of the spiritual culture of the isles of Albion upon which the Camlad tradition itself derived from. The tales of Arthur, Morgana and Camelot are folk tales and memories of the history of the adepts who ushered in the current Western Aeon.

Several locations are of importance to the ONA's interpretation of Arthurian legend. These locations sacred to the Sinister tradition and which locales make up the areas of travel of the orthodox Black Pilgrimage are the Long Mynd, Caer Caradoc, what is now known as the Kerry Ridgeway, and the river Teme. Other places around this area also exist which are pertinent to Adepts of the Tradition.

The area of the Marches is regarded as being the home of Merlin, the elusive sorcerer and advisor to King Arthur who is believed to have been one of the last direct descendants of Albion. He was said to have lived in an area around the Camlad river – between the Stiperstones, the Clun River, Camlad and the Kerry Ridgeway.

After Camelot was overthrown, the remnants established themselves in a fortified enclosure within a loop of the River Severn. The sacred place of this place of this area was a mound known as the Hill of the Alders. Later, this 'city' (containing the surviving Romano-British culture which had flourished in Camelot) was itself destroyed. It was later called Scrobbesbyrig – City of the Shrubs, and later still, Shrewsbury. The mound became the seat for the King of Powys. The mound lies beneath High St. and the old sacred site now has a church built upon it. Arthur is said to be buried in either the mound in Shrewsbury – beneath the church – or another place, not far from the lake of legend. The 'lake' from whence Excalibur came is considered to be near Eyton or Severn.

According to the Sinister Tradition, the Grail itself was a crystal of roughly tetrahedral shape. It was guarded by several 'keepers' (these keepers being guided or headed by the priestess known to Drakon Covenant tradition as Morgatha, with the keepers being referred to as the Siresy - the nine sisters referred to in the *Vita Merlini*) and was said to possess real magickal powers such as prophecy and divination. It was also said to be necessary for prosperity. Legend recounts it as being used to inaugurate the Western Aeon and thus the current Aeonic civilization, at the time of Arthur. One tradition claims, as mentioned above, that the stone was in actuality a large chunk of Moldavite, emerald green in colour and which fell to earth from the stars.

The Grail was also believed to be the graded system of initiation required to harness the stone's power and alludes to the Septenary system, which was later inherited by those adherents of the Camlad Rouning. From this, the mythos of the Grail knights arose - framed of course within the societal context of medieval courtly life. Thus, is the Grail that unique alchemy occurring within the initiate, the synthesis of the *Gradalis* and *Lapis* as utilised by the Grail 'knight'.

The Grail knights were therefore those individuals

committed to the *Gradalis*, the stages of wisdom which formed the basis for what we now know as the Sevenfold Way. The entire Grail mythos was an inspired tale based on the actions of those who inaugurated the Western aeon. Arthur and Morgatha as Priest king and priestess, and the Grail as the lapis tetrahedron, in conjunction with the Grail quest thus formed a key to opening the Aeon. Arthur's clan symbol was symbolic of the power of the Dark Gods. According to aural tradition, his clan symbol and banner was a white dragon upon a blue or green background.

The organisation of a defined knightly order and courtly castle was the later romanticisation and modernisation of the mythos by French medieval authors who tried to frame it within a Christian and medieval context.

The earliest mention of the Grail in such high medieval literature is of course Chretien de Troyes' *Perceval*, who first established it as a Christian relic. It is no coincidence that the Grail when first written about is described as an essentially Christian item, given that the Christians were wont to record and set in writing many things concerning history and religion of the British Isles, in contrast to the native pagans who kept a detailed and guarded aural history. The presence of the lance in this story also shows that the grail was intended to be viewed at least quasi-religiously, and thus the Grail as a dish being cited as its earliest iteration is invalid insofar as initiates of the Western/Sinister tradition are concerned. The scene also shows a mutated form of the elevation of consciousness within the context of Gradalis. What de Troyes intended to develop in regards to the symbolism of the Grail and Lance in his story is unclear given he never finished the work. The symbolism may therefore be regarded as inconclusive as a historical foundation.

The confusion between *San Graal* and *Sang Real* later exemplified by even further distortions of the Arthurian myths by Christian interpretation may allude to a belief that the blood of an Adept when combined with a quartz crystal is an incredibly powerful magickal act in opening the acausal gates. This combination can either be brought about by the aforementioned sacrifice of an initiated priest, or more prosaically, the smearing of a crystal with one's own blood prior to use (as detailed in fictional stories such as *The Moor*).

Whilst standard Sinister tradition proposes Arthur's Camelot to be based in Shropshire, historical evidence suggests the fabled city may have been located in West Yorkshire.

In the 2nd century CE, Ptolemy in his *Geographia* lists the cities under the rule of the Brigantes, with one of these cities being named *Camulodunum (*often shortened to *Camulod)*. This city was based in Northern England in the kingdom of Elmet, which itself spanned much of Yorkshire. This city is later mentioned in the Antonine Itenary as *Camboduno*, being somewhere in the West Riding of Yorkshire, circa 9 miles from *Calcaria* (now known as Tadcaster, North Yorkshire) and 20 miles from *Mamucio* (now known as Manchester).

The Venerable Bede writes in his *Ecclesiastical History*:

"In Cambodunum where there was also a royal dwelling, he (Paulinus, sent by Pope Gregory as a missionary to Britain 601 CE) built a church which was afterwards burnt down, together with the whole of the buildings, by the heathen who slew king Edwin. In its place, later kings built a dwelling for themselves in the region of Loidis. The altar escaped from the fire because it was of stone, and is still preserved in the monastery of the most reverend abbot and priest Thrythwulf, which is in the forest of Elmet."

The Celtic high king Arthwys or Artorius was said to rule over this later kingdom, with some historians arguing that this individual was the basis for the legend of King Arthur. The idea of Arthur as a Celtic king, his half-sister Morgatha later being revered as a goddess of sorts around this same area and the name of the kingdom itself being remarkably close to the name Camelot (and indeed arguably being the etymological basis for the name itself) all lend credence to the theory of Arthurian legend being based, at least for a time, in Yorkshire.

Several historians have thus proposed Camulod is the basis for the tales of the city of Camelot. The location would have made sense if Arthur was primarily focused on defence against Saxon invaders, as many have claimed he was. Many of the earliest battles attributed to Arthur, such as Celidon (Caledonia), Dubglas, Agned (Edinburgh) and Badon are based in Northern England and Scotland. The name Camulod itself is derived from the Celtic war-god Camulos.

Loidis later became *Leodis*, and thence *Leeds* (Leeds being a major city within West Yorkshire and the home of the founding coven of the Drakon Covenant, wyrdfully enough). It is thus believed that the later kings of Camulod founded what would become the city of Leeds, or that the city itself is the current location of Camulod's ruins. Archaeological research is thus nigh impossible, given the industrial and cosmopolitan development of the city.

Alternatively, there is also the Roman fort of Cambodunum, built during the Flavian period. First being made of wood, then replaced with stone, the site is now known as Slack Roman Fort and is based in the village of Outlane in West Yorkshire. The village is down the road from the village of Heptonstall.

Camelot is thus believed to be located either just outside of Heptonstall, at the Slack fort site, or beneath the current city of Leeds. At the very least, the kings of Camelot founded a kingdom that is now Leeds city. It has been suggested that if Camelot/Camulod was based in the region of Leeds, it would have sat upon what is now known as Quarry Hill, just outside of the city's centre.

This alternative view of Arthurian legend thus shifts the focus to Yorkshire, though Covenant tradition still holds that the Western Aeon was in all likelihood inaugurated around the region of the Welsh Marches. As it stands, such historical unearthings point toward a numinous connection between both Yorkshire and Shropshire, one already recognised by a growing number of adherents of the Sinister tradition. Further research will be undertaken in time to further understand the truth of such a fascinating history.

The Black Pilgrimage

At a certain point in the Sinister adherent's quest, the rite known within the Dark Tradition as the *Black Pilgrimage* must be undertaken.

For the Novitiate it can be coupled with and concluded by the External Adept rite. If not, it is usually undertaken sometime after the rite of External Adept has been successfully undertaken. For the Master, it comes as part of the rite involving the passing of the Abyss.

As stated before, this pilgrimage does not necessarily coincide with the Novitiate's task of performing the Rite of Nine Angles upon Beinn Sciathan, but the two may be combined for a more powerful alchemical experience.

The Black Pilgrimage in this instance consists of a walk, beginning on the Autumn equinox (of some 50 miles) the entirety of the pilgrimage being undertaken alone. The goal is to begin at dawn and finish near dusk on the following day. Thus, a sleeping bag and some food may be taken (no other shelter may be included). The witch must also have their quartz crystal with them. Upon completion, the solo version of the Nine Angles Rite is to be performed, having arrived at a certain site in the region of Shropshire known as the Long Mynd. Following this, the witch then spends a night at this site.

Traditionally, the walk passes through various locales around the Welsh Borders associated with the Camlad region; the Drakon Covenant's own Black Pilgrimage differs in that it spans the length of the Outer Hebrides. It is advised the Welsh Marches pilgrimage be undertaken at some point as well as the Covenant's 'chthonic' version however, so that the initiate comes to appreciate and understand the rich tapestry of the Dark Tradition as a whole.

For the Chthonic version of the pilgrimage, the areas of interest are Beinn Sciathan, Cladh Hallan, Reineval Cairn and the Callanish stones. The tradition at the time of writing is still being explored, and thus more sites may in time be added to this unique pilgrimage path. It is advised to begin at the far north, starting the pilgrimage at Callanish stones and ending at Beinn Sciathan. The entire length of the pilgrimage is around 100 miles, thus making it twice as long as the Black Pilgrimage in its orthodox version. It should be therefore broken into two segments, with a period of rest in between.

Beinn Sciathan is a place of potent power within the tradition of the Drakon Covenant, as well as being the place where the novitiate will first perform the Nine Angles Rite.

Cladh Hallan is a rather mysterious settlement, believed to be have been inhabited by a priest caste, perhaps for communal ritual purposes. The houses were built atop the graves of adults and children, with their bodies often being placed at the doorways of the buildings.

Beinn Mhor is the largest mountain in the Hebridean Isles and is a dramatic region for the witch to attune with the Chthonic tradition.

The Callanish stones are an ancient stone circle with a burial chamber in its centre.

There are of course other sites of interest across the Hebrides; several mountains, cairns and other places exist which will be fruitful to visit and intuit the spirit of the land by, harnessing and communing with the titanic and ancient forces of the tradition wrought into the dramatic landscapes of northern Albion and the Western Isles.

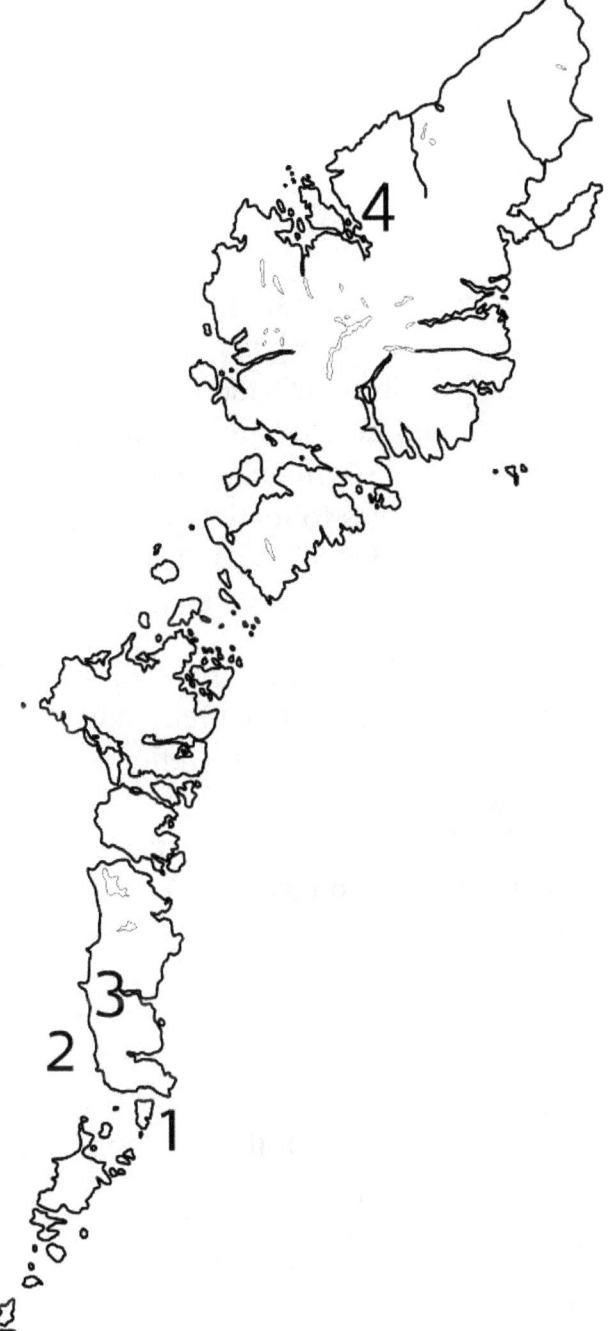

1 *Beinn Sciathan*

2 *Cladh Hallan*

3 *Beinn Mhor*

4 *Callanish stones*

Preliminaries of Lichcraft

The practise of Lichcraft is the art and science of preparing the astral body for a transmigration of existence into the realms of the dark astral landscapes, a vehicle within which the consciousness can continue to exist beyond death. Only the most advanced and daring of practitioners will achieve the Lich state, though most, if not all witches following the path of Sinister witchcraft and the way of Scithain will secure a more concrete level of post mortem existence than the mundane masses.

Various methods must be employed by the witch to discern and practise certain advanced aspects of the tradition. A veritable retinue of tools must be constructed, and thus a laboratory should be set aside to begin building the apparatus necessary. From the vantage point of Initiation and beyond, the tools utilised will guide the witch to understanding the astral world and the hereafter. The technology which must be developed includes devices which are simple to construct, albeit one - namely the Blood Tank. This endeavour continues in the vein of the medieval alchemists, who intuited and discovered some of the insights and doctrines of the Sevenfold Way.

However, several witches are known to us throughout history who have eschewed these elaborate methods and attained a vampyric existence after death through sheer will. Whilst this is of course possible, the transmigration to the acausal spaces has been refined into a science by genuine Adepts and Masters of the Sinister tradition.

The attainment of the Lich state is a high-risk goal; for whilst it is clear that consciousness exists post mortem, and certain defiant individuals have been able to sustain their existence throughout history in a definite manner, the rigorous pursuit of such a task is fraught with all the dangers of a pioneering scientific endeavour. Death is a certainty. This we cannot deny. However, physical death itself is simply the shedding an outer garment and a necessary step in the witch's path toward Immortality.

Several methods are given for the witch who is close to death. The first is the *Rite of Transference* - a highly risky and uncertain ritual. The second is the *Final Communion*, in which a black fast is observed followed by the Communio, culminating in ritual suicide - the witch then stepping over the threshold into the astral darkness with the denizens thus called. If this rite is attempted by a non-adept or is ill prepared, the witch faces a very real possibility of utter devourment by that which has been called forth. This method involves a study and familiarity in poisons and basic biochemistry (if death by poison is to be the preferred method - or else with a dagger into the abdomen. The use of firearms - such as a gunshot to the head - is not always fatal and may leave the ascendant lich gravely wounded or scarred. This also makes the preservation of the lich corpse troublesome). Suicide would be undertaken following a ritual culling of the opfers (of either a prominent Magian or of the coven's enemies). This should all be planned meticulously, with little left to those one is leaving behind to deal with or be implicated by.

Whilst death is certain, for most, its time is not. We of the Drakon Covenant are not so bound by fate - it is expected that you choose your moment of death. The third method - outlined and hinted at throughout Drakon Covenant literature - by fire and force, is known as the *Final Opfer Rite*. For this, little will be left of the physical body, and thus Lichood must be sought via sheer will on the part of the master.

In regards to such a rite, it traditionally involved preparing a suitable amount of explosives which can be worn as a 'suicide vest'. The individual then proceeds to take out the relevant parties with them - be this a group of people or a specific opfer. This method involves a study and familiarity in explosives, naturally. Proper interring of the body will obviously not occur if this method is chosen. It may seem the least desirable of methods at face value, but the instant immolation, with participating opfers (unwilling in this case) creates a surge of power unparalleled for the Lich.

We can compare these rites to the ONA's *Rite of Acausal Existence* as given in the *Grimoire of Baphomet*, though this rite is somewhat more complex in its preparations. It is left up to the individual to decide which ritual method is to be undertaken, as well as whether to remain in the Liminal-Astral spaces as a dread shade, or to transcend to vistas new within the Acausal realm itself:

"According to sinister tradition, it is possible - without the gift provided by an acausal entity such as a Dark Daughter of Baphomet - for an individual human being to acquire for themselves an acausal existence, that is, for their consciousness to be transferred to, to indwell, an acausal being; or more specifically for an acausal form to be created for such an indwelling, which form then passes into the acausal.

The rite of transference exists in two forms, and the one described here is the most efficacious, and requires a minimum of three opfers (nine are best), who will be chosen according to our traditional guidelines, and brought to, and confined in or near to, the place chosen for what is perhaps the most sinister and the most joyful Rite of all. The rite be either performed alone by a single Rounwytha, or by two if those two have pledged themselves to end their mortal existence together and transfer instead to the acausal.

Given the nature of the rite, the opfers will not be voluntary, with the rite itself being undertaken in a secure indoor place, or in an isolated secure outdoor location, although a suitable outdoor location is increasingly difficult to find.

As with the Sinister Rite of The Nine Angles, propitious times include when the Moon occults Dabih, or is very close to it; and when Jupiter and Saturn are both near the moon which is becoming new, the causal hour being before dawn. The rite itself requires a large double tetrahedron, made of quartz, which is suspended by some non-conductive material (such as filaments of hemp or flax) woven to hold the crystal and to allow it to be touched by both of the Rounwytha's hands. It is suspended at shoulder height, and within an ellipse of nine smoothed elliptical stones made from pre-Cambrian rock, with this ellipse being of sufficient size to accommodate within it he/she (or those two) undertaking the rite.

Next to each and in front of each elliptical stone is a stone slab also of pre-Cambrian rock, sufficient in size for a human head. The semi-major axis of the ellipse should be aligned East-West, and the first stone and its associated stand should be on this axis, with the other stones/stands placed to have unequal spacing between them.

Once the crystal, stones and stands have been set out as required, and the other necessary arrangements made, the Rounwytha should undertake a Black Fast, lasting no less than a day for each opfer, and neither speak nor venture forth into daylight during this Fast nor have any contact with any other living causally-dwelling being, human or otherwise, with the exception of their partner who is sharing in the Rite, if such a partner there be.

At the chosen hour, the rite proper begins by the first opfer being brought into the centre of the ellipse, to lie on the ground/floor so that the suspended crystal is above them. The opfer may be bound or otherwise restrained.

The Rounwytha then dispatches the opfer by suitable means - such as using a sacrificial knife or sword - until the head is severed with the Rounwytha during this task silently concentrating and directing the acausal-energy, released by such an offering, toward the suspended crystal. The head of the opfer is then placed on the slab on the semi-major axis of the ellipse, and the human shell, denuded of acausal energy, is removed, and replaced by the next opfer. If required, the Rounwytha may place his/her hands upon the opfer as the acausal energy seeps out, and then place their hands upon the crystal.

This process is continued until all the opfers have served their designated purpose, when the Rounwytha(s) removes the crystal from its holder, and holding the crystal to them, ignites (if indoors and if required) the flammable material surrounding them, and consumes the phial of their chosen swift acting poison, while directing their own acausal energy into and thence beyond the nexion that is now their crystal."

-The Rite of Acausal Existence

It is also possible, according to the MS, for this rite to be performed under non-ritual circumstances when, for example, an individual-explosive-device may be employed in a combat-type situation with the opfers being "enemies". Here, the stones and other ceremonial trappings are dispensed with, although the Rounwytha or sinister Adept should still possess, if possible, a double tetrahedron, made of quartz, sufficient in size to be concealed but not so small that it could be concealed in the palm of just one hand. If this method is chosen, for whatever reason, the Rounwytha or sinister Adept should at the moment of detonation hold the crystal in one hand (if this be possible) and intone *Binan Ath Ga Wath Am* while directing their own acausal energy and that of their targets into and thence beyond the nexion that is now their crystal.

There will of course come a time when such rites are unnecessary or unsuitable for the would-be Lich. Such a time as the emergence of Terra Mysteria would render these attacks on mundanes wholly unsuitable (as there would, in theory be no trace of the Magian sickness and thus very few opfers left at all, if any). It is expected adherents of the tradition will construct new and more efficacious rites, or perhaps see a return to willing sacrificial rites as once practised in the ancient past upon the Isles of Albion.

According to Drakon Covenant aural tradition, if all the members of a coven have attained Mastery and were to undertake the Rite of Transference or the Final Communion, one will either offer or be selected via various means (such as a vote), to perform the Final Opfer Rite. They would be posthumously martyred for this sacrifice, and honoured by the younger coven members with a shrine, their spirit being venerated as a coven guardian and left offerings at a shrine built for them. This coven guardian is known as the *Druch Tarog*.

The Druch Tarog

The Druch Tarog is considered to be the guardian of the coven, and is honoured by the construction of a shrine which is cherished often above the other shrines built to the Dearg Dûl and preferably placed elsewhere - either in a sacred spot outside or within the coven's homestead, should they live communally (akin to small family shrines seen amongst early European cultures).

The coven should construct a sculpture or painted depiction of the Druch based upon how they appeared during life or how they chose to be depicted upon death, with a bowl placed before it for offerings. Incense should be burnt regularly as well as offerings left. The Druch Tarog's crystal and other pertinent items which they kept during their life are kept upon the shrine in a box, preferably one ornate and bearing their personal sigil.

The Druch Tarog may in time take the place of a tutelary deity to the coven, in time leading to a multifarious range of ascendant masters who are revered within the regional confines of each coven.

The Ordaining of the Druch Shrine

All present should have bathed and have brought a small offering to the place where the shrine will be built.

Various items, such as a painting, sculpture or other depiction of the guardian should be prepared and brought forth. These may be housed in a small alcove.

Once the shrine is prepared, the master/mistress of the coven waves incense of Yew over it. He/she then recites the following:

Communio cum aliis electissimus,

Hail to you, exalted and ascended one!

Here we dedicate a shrine to you (name guardian).

As our Druch Tarog, may you watch over us, and bring our enemies terror upon blackened wings!

Haunt their dreams till death takes them by exhaustion!

And guide us ever into communion.

So shall it be!

A bell is then rung nine times, followed by which the coven chants the Diabolus, leaving offerings on the shrine, including anointing the shrine with the blood of all present.

Further Notes

The ultimate preparation and honour for the would-be Lich would be mummification. This practise would allow one to possess a physical vessel to inhabit and allow future adepts to commune with the Lich who maintains power even after death. The ancient priests of Scithain observed this very practise, preserving and displaying their ancestors, who would continue to watch over them and guide the clans through communion with the intermediate priest caste.

During certain feast days, the ancestors were paraded and displayed to the community, and for several days these bound and desiccated husks would be left in the open upon stone altars, before which priestesses would burn offerings and sing or chant to them in order to draw the Lich's essence back from the other side and impart knowledge to the living.

For this approach - that of mummification - the Lich is usually interred at a sacred spot which becomes a focal region for rites and celebratory offerings. He/she is buried with their crystal and other personal sacred items. The place is usually kept secret, known only to the members of the Lich's coven. Coven members would assist the dying Lich to the suitable spot, where they will perform final rites (such as the Final Communion if conducted by a Morain/Moraina). It is important that this rite be undertaken before death, and thus the Lich should choose a suitable time to terminate their causal lifespan so as to afford a degree of mobility so they may conduct these final affairs.

Other methods include the construction and maintenance of the Blood Tank.

(It should be stated that *aural tradition* does not refer to any 'secret teachings' or forbidden texts, but rather those teachings and insights explained and developed vis-à-vis for convenience sake, as well as that which either has yet to be written down or refrained, to allow teaching of said aspects of the tradition to be imparted correctly from master to pupil.)

Draugrûna

Draugrûna ('death-workings') and Draumrûna ('dream-workings') are the twin pillars of magickal work upon which the art of Lichcraft rests.

Draugrûna rites are the very pinnacle of black magick; not only do they cover the necromantic practises which are alleged to summon up the dead and discuss with them the secrets of the beyond, they also involve the manipulation of the astral force of the self and others. As described, they are the peak manifestation of the witch's power during causal life, and these rites are often tailor-made by the advanced witch during the latter years of his/her life in preparation for transmigration into the acausal darkness.

However, the tenets of Draugrûna can be used in defined ritual settings. The expertise and experience of the practitioner is usually the guiding element in the ritual itself, thus making it a difficult, wordless praxis which cannot be taught to the ordinary novitiate but instead arises out of the wisdom wrought from years of adherence to the vampyric path. An example of such a magickal praxis is seen in one theory that suggests that the advanced practitioner of Draugrûna magick could, under certain preparations, remove the astral body from an opfer - usually via the ingestion of some substance designed to elicit such an effect upon the victim.

Once free from the physical, the opfer's astral body would be held fixed from entering back into itself, either by an assistant to the witch who has astrally projected prior to such a rite, or by the witch who lies in wait for the victim. Alternatively, vampiric entities may be beseeched to seize upon and bind the opfer.

Upon seizing the astral body of the opfer, and making sure to keep the two bodies within close proximity (this is allegedly done so to allow phenomenon performed upon the physical to be detected by the astral body), the witch or his/her assistant would then begin to enact a slow torture upon the cataleptic physical form. This torture would be carefully guided to draw out maximum suffering without causing death and would be followed by a swift dispatchment, perhaps by a cutting of the throat or some similar fatal act.

The physical body, upon undergoing a violent and painful death within this regional proximity would bequeath upon the astral senses all that which was done upon it, causing the victim to be transformed into an endlessly tortured and earthbound shade. In time, such an existence would drive the opfer insane, leading it to transform into a vile spirit, perpetually forced to relive ad infinitum the final moments of his/her tortured existence. More advanced and malicious witches may even go so far as to implement certain binding measures upon the opfer in order to transform its wretched spirit into a thrall, an earthbound spiritual slave to the Lich who is used to torment those the Lich deems fit to inflict such terrors upon.

Such a fate can be often seen among reports of ghosts who, having died swift and violent deaths are thence preoccupied with the injuries done to them, and which injuries often transfer over into their ghostly life for however long they exist afterward.

This rite or method of slaying not only robs the opfer of their life, but also the peace of the afterlife, binding them to the lower astral shadows for all eternity (unless they were somehow snapped out of their madness by a sympathetic clairvoyant or medium and thus brought to reason). This is perhaps the ultimate act of transgression and a dread black magickal rite which a practitioner can perform upon another; it will no doubt remain a theory for some time, such is the difficulty not only of undertaking this rite in itself, but also in the ability of the witch to bind victims in the astral and prevent them from returning indefinitely to their physical form. There are, even beyond this, rites and particular practises of which those of good taste could not begin to fathom nor wholly understand. It is for this reason that such matters were and still remain firmly esoteric in their transmission, guarded and obscured as they are from the non-Initiate (and which rites can and often do transcend the mundane laws of the land of most Western countries at this current time of writing).

Drawing Down The Nythran Essence

This potential method of causal exit is performed when Arcturus is high above. It can however be undertaken as a ritual for those who have progressed beyond External Adept in order to further bring one closer to apprehending the Void Mother's physis. Preferably a dark, circular room will be available for this ritual. Otherwise it can be performed outdoors.

A large quartz crystal is placed in the earth, whilst the witch chants *Nythra Kthunae Atazoth* seven times whilst doing so.

Nine bowls filled with blood (animal blood will usually suffice) should be placed in a large circle around where the crystal was buried. Candles may be placed between each bowl, though best results are obtained via darkness. Incense should be a mixture of Ash and Black Poplar. The witch sits in the centre, having fasted for several days and consumed a brew made from *Datura Stramonium* or *Atropa Belladonna*.

He/she then begins to simply chant *Nythra*, until his/her very being vibrates with the word. There should then begin a visualisation during this continued chanting of a black, nebulous form opening up above the circle, which feeds from the nine bowls. The form grows with the feeding, eventually expanding into a giant black vortex which rains down a thin crimson mist which envelops the witch.

The witch then astrally projects into the vortex which has opened up (if able to do so during this trance state; otherwise it is simply visualised to the best of one's ability).

Any impressions, visions or experiences should be written down and meditated upon. This will be a physically and mentally taxing rite. It is important to drink water upon its completion.

Once the witch has returned to normal consciousness, the bowls are poured into the ground around the crystal whilst saying: *Aperiatur Terra et Germinet Scithain*.

This rite can be just one method used by the vampyric Adept or Master in later life to ascend directly to the Void Mother via a ritual suicide taking place at the final point of the rite (usually via poison ingestion, in a decidedly Nythran fashion).

A would-be Lich must work to prepare beneath them a coven which will assist him/her toward their goals and endeavours. The insight which arises from teaching and the power of a collective effort cannot be overstated.

The arrival at a Lich state requires the witch successfully undergoing and completing the challenges and ordeals associated with the stages of the Sevenfold Way; from Initiation, all the way to Mastery and the crossing of the Abyss whilst adhering to the rites and disciplines of vampyrism.

These specific disciplines include vampyric feeding, which takes an even greater frequency and intensity as the witch approaches the time of performing the Rite of Transference. There are also certain aural teachings which are either taught in the early stages and later understood by sufficient study and practise, or are intuited via reason and insight, having followed the path up to and beyond the Vampyric Rite of Eremitic Adept.

Further disciplines include vampyric flight into the dark and obscure corners of the astral and other realms of existence, drawing from these benighted dimensions knowledge which will then be employed to elicit further communication from Without.

Advancement to the Lich state becomes an inherently intuitive and self-guided process; only the vantage point of a vampyric Master can weave the Blood Essence into a directed path toward Immortality. The intricate and arcane workings of Draugrûna will therefore come to be written by a succession of Morains and Masters who dare to tread upon the black path of Vampyrism, should they deign to write down such corruptible and potent rites at all.

Star Gates and Hebdomadric Astrology

Within the Sinister tradition the Cosmos is apprehended as it is, devoid of arcane, archaic and outmoded models of correspondences and abstract schools of thought imposed upon it.

This unique approach differs to the Qabalistic system as exemplified in all modern schools of witchcraft, and which all without exception draw influence from the convoluted and forced system of the Golden Dawn and later Thelemic developments.

The ivory tower school of modern astrology forces the arbitrary appearance of starry collocations into abstract correspondences (naming a set of stars that look like a crab 'Cancer' and associating it with the vague quality of alchemical water, because crabs are water based creatures and thus forcing all Cancerian emanations - be they related to incenses, stones or people born under its sign - to all things related to said alchemical water and every correspondence that abstract notion entails).

This simplistic approach was popularised by novelty fortune tellers and star gazers, to entertain customers and reduce complex study to a simple game; it is telling that serious so-called astrologers use this system in a solemn and serious manner.

The current astrological model is discarded with in the

Septenary system, and entire chapters could be written highlighting the errors and inconsistencies not only with the current 'Western' model, but the countless attempts by occult schools of thought to structuralise and align such a model within their own systems. Attempting to force abstractions and correspondences together, as mentioned above, is simply fruitless and robs the practitioner of the vital necessity of experiencing the cosmic forces as they are.

The symbols of the constellations are arbitrary and do not conform any particular or unique energy to the fluxions themselves. There is no attempt to understand them in the abstract, nor any desire to fit a model such as 'the four elements' or other such inadequate comprehensions upon the ebb and flow of them. They are simply denoted and intuited by the Initiate, whose observation as such will hopefully help to align the personal with the supra-personal, laying yet another foundation for the emergence of the Adept.

Certain stars are allocated importance within the Sinister tradition and are representative of the energies of the Dark Gods. These stars are symbolic in a very literal sense in that they are, according to a certain belief within the tradition, the literal homes of certain acausal entities.

Locating stellar and planetary placements in the night sky is a frequently employed activity for many magickal rituals.

As an example, we will detail the locating of the planet Saturn, useful for workings such as the Nine Angles Rites.

To locate Saturn, it is useful to determine its orbit across the sky. Using resources such as star charts and online observatory data will also help and is relatively easy to do. It takes Saturn around 29.5 years to complete a helical orbit, as opposed to Earth's 1 year. Saturn should be visible to the trained eye when Earth passes between Saturn and the Sun, though visibility depends upon the time of year and planetary rotation

Consulting a star chart and mapping Saturn's orbit will help to locate the planet on the night of the magickal working. At the time of writing, Saturn is relatively very close to the sun, thus rendering it invisible; it should thus be determined by locating a visible constellation the planet will pass near at the relevant time, and face toward it accordingly.

Another useful method would be to choose a date when Saturn and the Sun are in opposition (facing each other relative from the viewer's position to the Earth). This will make it easier to locate with the naked eye or a telescope with sufficient research into its location at the time (suitable telescopes will bring Saturn's rings into view, making it unmistakable).

Saturn can be discerned by its golden colour, and notable lack of twinkling (naturally, it will be difficult or impossible to locate during bad weather). Noting when Saturn will be near a particular constellation is also useful to roughly pinpoint its location in the night sky.

Beginner's Notes

Investing in a telescope is the obvious first course of action. When looking for a suitable model, ensure the aperture is listed as well as the zoom. Obtain one preferably which is portable to some degree. Well-lit areas such as towns and cities are generally unsuitable for stargazing, though in some parts it can still be practised with relative ease. It is best to avoid urban areas, and it would benefit the witch to take his/her telescope to a remote region on a night, along with a notebook and star guide to record the stars, their names and their locations. This will take patience, but the accomplishment of being able to conduct coven rituals with expert knowledge of the firmament will mark you above other witches and practitioners. Many astronomy books and websites exist to begin learning from.

Binoculars work as rudimentary telescopes and will be more than adequate for the purpose of planet and star location for rites.

Planets tend to be much brighter than stars and with some training can be noticed with ease by the novice stargazer. They also possess their own distinct colours and optical nature. Mercury twinkles with a yellow colour, whereas Venus is often mistaken for a UFO because it is large and silver. Mars is characteristically reddish in its hue.

Planets have an 'apparition' time - a period when they are visible. This can last anywhere between weeks to years (Mars is visible during August in the early morning). It is thus important to note the planet's apparition, as well as whether it will be visible in the hemisphere you are in.

Consider what time they are most visible also (Venus for instance is most visible during the early evening and morning).

Consulting a star chart as well as learning to use and utilise an astronomical almanac will quickly make discovery of the planets and stars second nature, and is a skill necessary for future rites within the Sinister tradition.

Stars of Prominent Importance

Sirius -
Alternative Name: *Alpha Canis Majoris*
Constellation: *Canis Major*

Deneb -
Alternative Name: *Alpha Cygni*
Constellation: *Cygnus*

Rigel -
Alternative Name: *Beta Orionis*
Constellation: *Orion*

Dabih -
Alternative Name: *Beta Capricorni*
Constellation: *Capricornus*

Algol -
Alternative Name: *Beta Persei*
Constellation: *Perseus*

Arcturus -

Alternative Name: *Alpha Boötis*
Constellation: *Boötes*

Mira -
Alternative Name: *Omicron Ceti*
Constellation: *Cetus*

Naos -
Alternate Name: *Zeta Puppis*
Constellation: *Puppis*

Antares -
Alternate Name: *Alpha Scorpio*
Constellation: *Scorpius*

Star Gates

Star Gates are those nexions which have formed closely to or actually within a star. It is currently unknown which is the case, but what is known is that they are unique to stars and stars are unique in themselves within Sinister Cosmology.

One theory posits that certain acausal species (of which the Dark Gods belong to) presence themselves through stars, using them as rudimentary sources of sustenance, anchoring themselves as they do between the causal and acausal, with the plasma of the star acting as an intermediary source of energy, or 'food' for the entity. This particular race of entities is often referred to as the Nekhala.

Certain evidence has been posited of these entities

thriving upon stars, most notably our sun, with astronomical imagery existing of large, nebulous black masses siphoning plasma from the star with a tendril-like appendage.

It is suggested that the stars which are related to the Dark Gods in the Sinister tradition are Their literal 'homes,', or at least contain gates to Their realms; or that they are attuned to the nature of a specific Dark God by virtue of their existence. Whatever the truth may be, it is regarded as an interesting legend, one to help initiates and adepts further understand the Dark Gods Themselves. Any basis of truth this theory has must be discerned by the individual, using insight and a natural acausal Knowing.

According to another aural tradition, there exists a particular nexion located near to the planet Saturn. Some say this is the prison or a sealed gateway, one which has kept the Dark Gods from entering our causal realm again. This gateway was sealed by the 'Elder Gods', a race of advanced entities that had battled Them aeons ago after the Dark Gods had arrived amongst primitive man and accelerated our evolution, giving us the ability to think and perform rites of magick, among other gifts. According to this aural tradition, the Elder Gods, who were hostile to the agency of the Dark Gods to give humankind Their gifts, were from the Sirius star system.

This nexion - the 'Saturn Gate' - has since been the object of many temples and solitary adept's rituals, with individuals seeking to open it across the centuries. According to this tradition, several adepts were partially successful.

In recent times, with the spread of the genuine magick of the Sinister way, the gate has become opened to a degree, and will continue to open as more acausal energy is presenced by practitioners of the Sevenfold Way, thus leading to a greater saturation of energies and an intrusion of the Dark Gods, leading to a much-needed evolution and change on a macroscopic level.

The Rite of the Nine Angles is one efficacious method by which this Saturn Gate may be opened, when performed correctly and in conjunction with the Ceremony of Recalling as detailed elsewhere. Other variations of the Rite include aligning it to direct energy from the star gates believed to be near Algol, Naos and Dabih.

According to the rudimentary understanding of the four types of Gates/Nexions proposed by the Drakon Covenant, the Saturn Gate, whilst being located in space, could be described as a significant Dark Gate - a forced intrusion from Without. To this day, astronomers note anomalies and UFOs around Saturn perhaps more than any other planet in the solar system.

The Moor II

The cabin was built partially of ancient wooden beams and densely packed earth and stone, its structure being held primarily by it being built in the hollow root space of a tree which hung over a dip in the land. The cabin was nestled deep in a thick forest, and thus to the casual explorer it would go unnoticed, were it not for the wooden door decorated with odd looking symbols burnt into the dark oaken surface.

The smell of incense and firewood wafted from the decrepit dwelling, its perimeter littered with empty baskets and macabre fetishes which hung from the dripping tree roots which snaked around the earthen frame. That this cabin may have been a rather unusual and out of place item within the forest is to say nothing of the individual inhabiting it.

Few, very few, had seen the inhabitant of this veritable hole in the dank earth, and those who had seen her rarely saw her true form. For she always appeared as a beautiful and beguiling woman of indeterminate age to the few who, having lost their way in the fog or due to a few choice wrong turns, encountered her and were lured in accordingly. By that point their doom was sealed and they were seized, as the woman dug her claws into flesh, dragging them with inhuman strength to her dark lair, where their very life essence was stolen from them and their bodies cut up, salted and stored for later consumption.

A few local legends, originating initially and serving as a warning only to fade into myth over the generations, told of the 'woman of the woods', who never aged but who had lived there for as long as anyone knew, and who was known for luring children from the nearby villages which encroached upon the forest into the trees, from where they were never seen again. The villagers had banded together once to burn and fell the trees to drive the wretched creature from its habitation, but to no avail. The wet climate and general superstitious bent of many of the townsfolk rendered any plan useless, for they dared not open hostilities and instead clung to their charms and erected a stone wall, mainly to prevent the children from venturing off as opposed to any illusions at keeping the creature in.

Nowadays, the wall had all but crumbled, coated with a layer of earth and moss.

Annalise climbed over the rocky, moss covered ground, her backpack containing a few items she would need to survive the next six months out here in the wilderness. The ruined half-earthen cabin, now little more than a stoned hollow in the side of a small cliff, would be her home. A door could easily be made with twine and wood gathered from the forest floor. Here Annalise would commune with the tutelaries of the coven, and spend her days and nights in chrysalis, ready to emerge as an Internal Adept of the Dark Tradition.

It had taken a few hours to reach the woods, bordering on the edge of the county, and another hour to hike to the old wall which stuck out atop the hills of the Yorkshire Wolds, overlooking the village of Cottam, which now lay deserted and forgotten - a remnant of a simpler, more superstitious time. The forest itself would provide all Annalise would need - game could be trapped, fish caught, plants harvested. A supply of rations had been brought just in case; besides that, all she had was meagre sleeping supplies, a utility knife and a medical kit. She settled down, in the hollow of the old cabin's room, and with her crystal in hand, descended into a deep trance-like meditation.

I

'What do you mean Allain is dead?' Lucian sat in his riverside apartment, cleaning one of his many illicitly obtained handguns which lay disassembled on a glass table. The apartment itself was furnished in the typical modernist style so convenient to the high-end properties found along the river Aire, and this apartment in particular was used as a low-profile headquarters for the criminal enterprise's planning and activities.

'I don't know, boss - there was an explosion at one of the safe houses. They'd jumped Anna's package last we heard. There were pigs everywhere when I drove past, and fire crews putting out a blaze. It looked like bloody chaos, I tell ya.'

This isn't good, Lucian thought to himself.

He got up, intending to head down to the site and see for

himself. He knew straight away Annalise had a hand in this, but he wasn't sure how just yet.

'Boss, it's on the news - they're saying it was a bomb.'

Lucian's face went pale, as he realised how close he'd escaped Annalise's sardonic wrath.

That fucking bitch...

'I want to know how she found out we were onto her supply run,' said Lucian, beginning to pace the apartment coldly. 'Either someone here grassed, or someone in Liverpool did. Or we've got a mole. And they better hope I don't fucking find them...'

Lucian walked over to the front of the viewing window, observing the evening view across the river. The water had turned a glorious amber red from the reflection of the setting sun, as was common for this time of year. He would not be bested; this city had bent to his will via sheer terror and drive. One woman - no matter how powerful and well connected she was - would not be the end of him. He would make sure of that.

He toyed with the fingerbone necklace which hung around his neck underneath his shirt, a digit taken from the same opfer he and his now dead comrade had claimed during their mercenary years, now seemingly a lifetime ago.

II

Marcus sat in his car, parked opposite a coffee shop in the centre of Leeds, watching intently at two men sat conversing by the windows, sipping cappuccinos and looking stern-faced. His unit was currently investigating Lucian's men and the recent death of his closest henchman, Allain; though attributed to Lucian himself, it had caused a stir among the officers. Annalise's name had arisen in the brief several times now, always lingering on the periphery of legality, her wealth and choice of acquaintances always arousing suspicion but leading to ultimately cold ends - this matter assisted considerably by Marcus himself who ensured any files on her were misplaced, diverted or simply destroyed. He had served her well, and as an External Adept of her coven his loyalties thus lay to far more ancient laws than the crown of England and the Metropolitan police. Marcus saw such an opportunity to fulfill the coven's mission - namely, getting close enough to Lucian to have him removed from the situation, and complete Annalise's task of rectifying Wyrd. The wayward son was to be reined in, his errors a responsibility on Annalise's part, given she had initiated him into the Way - and he had used the secrets of her coven to not only make something for himself, but something which stood in stark opposition to her work and which sought to remove her out of hubris and bitter notions of rejection and arrogance. With Lucian gone, and made gone by the hand of Annalise's other students, her work would be unobstructed, her personal judgment rebalanced - not to mention such a removal serving a purpose wyrdfully, both on the individual and supra-personal level.

Marcus' phone received a text - it was Alexander, in Sayersby. He and Siofra had taken over duties of the covenant's HQ, the old rambling house up on the hill now Annalise had departed. The two were busy transcribing a small mass of manuscripts left by Annalise which she had discerned from the many rites and rituals performed by the coven in accordance with a legacy hinted at in Annalise's book, which she kept in her room at all times, but which other covenmates were permitted to read - despite it being written entirely in an unknown script. She had spent many months decoding it, and put into practise what was deciphered, namely a set of rituals and a cosmology far different, far more archaic than the so-called occult secrets which littered endless bookstores and libraries she had browsed in her youth. With this knowledge, her covenant was built, a continuation of one which had existed, if only briefly, many years earlier.

Alexander claimed they were close to cracking the final parts of the book Annalise had not finished, parts now shed with much light following the messages imparted over the recent months during intense vampiric rituals led by Annalise herself. Lucas had been of considerable help, his mercurial eye always keen to understand puzzles and riddles alike.

Marcus finished his notes, his assignment being one of simple covert surveillance, and headed back to the office. If time allowed, he would visit Sayersby and assist the two initiates with their recent discovery.

III

60 years earlier

Victor Morain was giving a speech to a small gathering of students at the University of Leeds, a small tour which he had begun a week prior, in which he appealed to students and professors to assist in his experiments. As he shuffled his research notes and cleared his throat to begin, he wondered if he would be met with the same ridicule and outrage he had received from the previous attendees in other university lecture halls.

'Ladies and gentlemen, thank you for your time. It is a privilege to be here among you at this prestigious establishment. As some of you may know, my name is Victor Morain and I am a scientific researcher, and a former professor of life sciences at York.'

'I am here today to present some theories and findings which I have made in conjunction with undergraduates from the department of astronomy into the nature of extra-terrestrial life.' A noticeable grumble arose in the audience.

'Now I know this is a point of contention for many, the findings and theories I have been proposing, but if I may continue.'

Victor placed his first slide onto the projector, a blurry image taken from telescopic equipment observing the sun.

'What we can see here is a solar anomaly - in particular, a dark mass orbiting the sun. The first assumptions were that this was coronal activity, but we have since discovered that there is a large, planet sized orb at an extremely close proximity to our star. The behaviour of this orb suggests it is in fact a living organism. Indeed, we have observed it actually feeding on the sun.' Victor changed the slide, to show the anomaly, this time with dark appendages resembling tendrils latching onto the surface of the sun.

'This challenges many assumptions we have had about life and our place in the cosmos. I propose we have discovered a new life form, and I am looking for funding to continue the pursuit of this entity.'

The audience was lively, though many claimed the evidence was inconclusive. As before, there were conventional answers given, and the usual disinterest in what sounded like crackpot theories. Clearly, other scientists did not share his belief in his interpretation of this phenomena. 'It is an unknown occurrence, yes, but aliens? Come now, Victor,' was the same response he received.

The lecture finished, Victor packed his slides and papers, and allowed the attendees to exit.

'Excuse me, professor Morain?' Victor looked up to see a young woman stood in front of him, no more than twenty years of age, with dark hair tied back and thick-rimmed glasses. She had in her hand a notebook. 'I'm Elisa, I found your lecture very interesting.'

'Thank you kindly, dear, most people tend to dismiss me out of hand. But someone has to propose the taboo questions - though I suppose it's a far cry from how they treated Giordano Bruno, eh?'

Elisa smiled. 'I would be glad to help in your research - you said other students were...I am studying chemistry, if that helps.'

'Wonderful, I am sure you will be a great asset.' The two of them shook hands and agreed to discuss things over a drink later.

Later that evening, Victor discussed his ideas with Elisa, including more unorthodox theories, ranging from ancient scriptures to medieval alchemy, all which seemed to point toward the existence of the entities he had spent the past three years studying.

'This is all rather impressive, Victor, but I am wondering, if these things exist, how do you plan on contacting them?'

'Aha,' Victor said, with a glint in his eyes. 'We have built something, a machine. Would you like to see?'

'I would love to,' Elisa replied.

Victor threw back the sheet covering a large array of some sort which was housed under the university, a machine he and a handful of other students had been building in secret after hours.

'This device has the potential to communicate with the entities we discussed. It was part intuition, part haphazard study and part purely madness which led to its creation, I shan't lie - thus it looks odd, I know.'

Elisa walked along the length of the table the contraption was placed upon, looking in amazement. It consisted of a large metal cylinder, out of which emerged several wires, which connected to a computer interface. Between this were several jars filled with algae, which had copper wires inserted, which ran back into the cylinder.

'What does it do?' Elisa inquired, rubbing a finger down one of the moist jars.

'Well, we feed a certain electromagnetic signature into the cylinder via the terminal, designed to mimic the output of the sun, layered with code which, in theory, expresses intelligible language. That is, anything picking up this signal will clearly see it is created by an intelligent operator. This seems to work enough to cause detection, which is observed via a small electrical output on the copper wire, which causes the algae to act and reproduce in a very odd way, as you'll see.'

'Now, something I have kept hidden from the lectures is that this device has been receiving input - from an outside source - and I think it is the entity I've been studying. The messages were received in a binary output, which is then applied to an ASCII system and translated by the terminal. What I've been given is a cipher, written in many languages, its context symbolic, but containing a set of instructions also on how to improve this machine.'

'That is...astounding, Victor,' Elisa said, though dubious in thought. It was all fascinating, but she couldn't make head nor tail of the lines of code, nor the scribblings on the walls, which contained many odd-looking symbols and glyphs, as well as star charts covered in numbers and letters.

'Have you begun building this other machine it...told you to build?' she asked.

'I have actually - let me show you.' Victor walked to the end of the room and drew back a partition, revealing a small laboratory space which housed various tables, each containing contraptions more strange than the last.

The machine he pointed toward was a large copper ring, with nodes along its inner face which enclosed like some mechanical jaw around a large chunk of raw quartz which was placed on a small pedestal in its centre.

'By applying a charge to this, I can amplify the quartz's natural resonance - I think its inherently coherent structure allows a transpatial lattice to be projected, so that the entity or the entity's consciousness can, in theory, manifest here. I dare not turn it on yet, and indeed we cannot until the generator is up and running again. The last time we tried, it not only broke the generator, but oddly, disabled power to the whole university. So as you can imagine, we are having to be very secretive with our work down here.'

The machine was emitting a dull hum, and for some reason Elisa found it disturbing to look at. The machine appeared to resemble a great maw, waiting to be awoken and devour all.

IV

Siofra was alone at the house, Lucas and Alexander having left. Geoffrey was away, having finished the few tasks that needed doing around the house, including disassembling the precarious pyramid of expensive crystal glassware Annalise kept that Lucas had gleefully left for him to discover and, with trembling hands, replace in their cabinet without smashing them.

Siofra headed to the third floor to spend some time in Annalise's room, whilst also replenishing her incense stock for later as well as replacing the manuscripts she'd taken that she and Alexander had attempted to decipher the previous night. Annalise had left the key for her to use the room as she pleased, and Siofra was curious as to the books she had seen in there.

Opening the door, a heady scent of frankincense and other exotic oils greeted Siofra's nose. She looked around the room. Several old desks were covered with books and taxidermized insects and birds, with even larger and more grotesque arachnid specimens aligning the walls. Upon one wall was a large and clearly aged chart, framed for protection. It appeared to be a star map, with Arabic names scattered upon it. Some of the constellations denoted by illustrations Siofra recognised. A particularly ghastly drawing of a demonic head glared out at her, with the words 'Raas al-ghul' written in red under the black Arabic scrawling.

On the bookcase, which took up the wall at the far right of the room were dozens of old leather and vellum bound books. There was a collection of works by Toynbee, as well as the range of Greek classics and several lexicons. Annalise had amassed decent editions of books pertinent to her studies over the years, with one book in particular kept in an oak and glass display case in the corner next to the bookcase. This book, Siofra had been told, contained all the secrets to mastery. Annalise claimed to have spent years studying it, though she did not say where she had found it. Several paragraphs had been painstakingly copied out of it and left for Alexander, Lucas and herself to decipher, the three of them finishing off the translating and puzzle work Annalise had begun and which continued to render interesting if not obscure occult teachings. Siofra observed the text on the front cover to be written in the same unusual lettering the manuscripts bore. The words themselves however made no sense to her.

Looking idly out of the window, Siofra watched as Bedwyr chased several blackbirds around the stone birdbath across the lawn.

She had felt a mixture of emotions since Annalise had left. For six months the house was in all but legal matters hers. She had matured very quickly over the past year since meeting the coven. She had never felt more at home, but the distance between herself and her former life was overwhelming. She remembered the cliques at high school and college, where the popular children had tried their best to act aloof and cool, apishly perhaps trying to emulate that cold reservation that she saw individuals such as Annalise and Marcus possessed in abundance. She saw that coldness grow in herself as she grew, and reflected on how it was not something to strive toward. A necessary aspect of growth along the Way, but bittersweet nonetheless.

I guess that is what pathei-mathos is, Siofra thought to herself, softly brushing the feathers of a large stuffed owl on the desk by the window. Later that night, Siofra would conclude the final of her Dark Pathways, and become closer to attaining the rank that those she had met briefly at the communal rituals had attained. They had called themselves External Adepts, and had gone through much to reach such a distinction. Apparently, the way of the covenant was regarded as extreme even among other temples that followed the tradition which Annalise had brought to the land many years prior. They all afforded her and her elect with a degree of respect which struck Siofra as noble, wholesome and redolent of a bygone age.

Siofra gathered the oils and incense and took them back to her room, along with a book from the bookshelves to read on her way into town.

V

In a well-aired office high above the bustling city centre of Leeds, Marcus sat opposite a well-groomed and sharply dressed man in his mid-fifties, with a dossier in his hand.

'Mr. Morgan, I need not remind you of the precarious position you hold with my associates. You promised to provide several things for us in exchange for partaking in certain dealings we make, and the immunity you attain by having a CID officer such as myself looking out for you. I suggest you think very carefully about your next move.'

The man in the suit smiled in a grimacing manner.

'Marcus, let me tell you a story. When I was your age, my father handed this company over to me. Since then, we've helped this great city in many ways, our contracting projects has helped it grow into a metropolitan hub, bringing in millions of revenue. So, you have word and history of me dealing with Miss Annalise Beauchamp. She's known as a patron of many fine institutions. So, you see, to expose me would risk me exposing her also. Blackmail is simply out of the question.'

'The difference is, Mr. Morgan, Miss Beauchamp covers her tracks - you do not.' Marcus passed the dossier over for effect. In it were photographs clearly taken from a clandestine vantage point of Morgan inviting young women into his vehicle. The photographs were damning - the girls also clearly underage.

Morgan's face turned white, then red.

'You little shits prepare for everything, don't you?'

'Look, Morgan. We aren't your enemy. We don't pass judgment on how you conduct yourself. As long as you pay your end of the bargain, we are all best friends.'

'So, what do you want, exactly?'

'Funds, of course. As well as you operating a rather sensitive operation via your security detail. We need to use your generous assets to secure some firearms, which will then be funnelled to some rivals of an enterprise we're currently dealing with. The rivals will then stage an attack on said enterprise, the outcome benefitting us due to auxiliary operations planned ahead of this coup of sorts.'

'This is madness, you know that, right?' Morgan stood up, looking down over the city streets. He felt his reputation, his freedom, teetering on the edge.

'It will simply be viewed as another gang turf war in some back-end shithole, don't you worry.'

'And in return?'

'We don't release those photos.'

Morgan had no choice. He had been caught, and he chastised himself for being so foolish several times after Marcus left. He would get one over on that bent cop and his bitch of a handler. He sipped his morning coffee before smashing the cup against the wall.

VI

High up overlooking the Calder valley, in the quiet village of Heptonstall, Alexander and Lucas sat in the White Lion pub, enjoying a fine selection of ales that were on offer. They had arrived in the early evening, and the sky was a clear amber-pink, suffusing the stony streets of the village with a bloodied tint.

Lucas had business to attend to in the village, 'casing a joint' as he had put it, laughing at his own humorous use of outdated slang to describe the few illegal activities he performed as part of the covenant's peripheral operations.

Alexander had other plans, however.

After their drinks, the two left the pub to the dark and mostly empty streets.

'Catch you later, anyway,' Lucas grinned, pulling up his hood. What he was doing Alexander didn't know. He probably wasn't burgling a house, not in his intoxicated state. He had drunk at twice the pace as Alexander.

'I'll see you back at the house, I might not be home till morning,' replied Alexander.

Lucas saluted before dashing into the shadows.

Gliding up the old cobbled road like some silent spectre toward the old church ruins, Alexander shivered in the cold. It was a clear night and the stars overhead poured down their ineffable rays onto the quiet Yorkshire scene. Annalise had said that this place was tied with the covenant's Wyrd, that it would be the place for Alexander to come should he wish to commune with her. So he had done as she said, and arriving amidst the ruined church interior situated within the village centre, he put aside his bag, and took out his quartz crystal, burning the herbs he'd brought with him.

Slashing his arms and hands, he allowed the blood to fuse his will to the crystal, and mingle with the frost upon the church stone as it spilled in crimson droplets onto the ground.

Sat in the cold autumn darkness, Alexander stared into the crystal, his mind slowly warping into bizarre angles and dimensions, his will focused on Annalise, hidden in the forest and moors out there - somewhere.

After some time, his vision darkened and he felt a voice, and a powerful, familiar presence.

'Annalise?'

'Be with me now. I am here.'

'I felt you last night, by my bedside.'

'I am watching you all, slowly changing as we all are.'

'I am struggling. The path is hard.'

'So are you. The path is what it is. You will succeed.'

'We are close to the Giving rite. I am nervous.'

'He will not be missed. Indulge, dear. All this will pass; you know what you must do.'

'We have uncovered more of the manuscript's meanings, too. One thread leads here, to this very spot where I am. The other, to the far north, as you theorised.'

'We have much work to do, Alexander, let the essence of the Dark propel you. Listen to the sound of my voice. I am always here.'

The visions and voices faded, Alexander fell forward and vomited. The herbs he had burnt had caused an intense headache and dizzying sensations.

From the depths of the dark forest overlooking the Yorkshire Wolds, fire smoke was emanating and sheathing the starry sky above in a thick, shadowy mist. Annalise sat in the old hut where she had spent the last two months, sprinkling a liberal amount of Datura leaves and inhaling the fumes, a shard of spinel loosely gripped in a hand dripping with warm blood. She had imbibed a tea made from the plant and the seeds around an hour earlier and spent the rest of the time in a deep meditation. From her smoky hut, she was able to reach out and connect with the minds of her students and followers, guiding them from a distance, assisting them in fulfilling the work she had set out to continue.

Now, she had a different task to undertake, a rite designed to propel her backward through the dim annals of time to a world shrouded in darkness and forgotten works of the blackest magick.

She chanted quietly to herself an ancient chant, taught to her and her alone through the black art of draumrûna dream visions, a chant used by an ancient people, in particular a caste of women appointed to guard over and commune with the desiccated corpses of a long dead priesthood. *Hiyuur maazerargh, mazababgha.* The chant resonated in her mind, bringing a cloying, shadowed emanation to suffuse the immediate surroundings. She continued, allowing the chant to carry her forth into a dim and forgotten past, to an ancient and blood spattered altar within a misty clearing in some lost English forest.

Her visions and senses began to warp as if melted by the glare of the candle light. Before her, the soil of the earth parted and slid from the ground, revealing underneath a large black expanse. Annalise felt herself fade through the expanse, and looking through its glassed surface realised she was inside a large quartz crystal suspended in an endless darkness, pulsing subtly with a deep throb akin to a beating heart.

She saw a black bull being brought forward by several men holding lit torches to illuminate the darkness, their faces painted with black markings and their robes greyed with age. The procession moved in silence, two ranks of three men on either side of the large beast walking slowly toward the centre of the clearing. The bull was brought in front of the altar and swiftly slain, its muscular neck slashed open by a bald priest with a large scythed blade. Annalise watched as the animal's blood was gathered into a wooden bowl and drunk by each of the men in turn. She knew somehow that she was witnessing an ancient ritual sacrifice to the Dark God Noctulius.

She felt herself then propelled forward to the altar where the dead beast's head was propped, the bull taking up the entirety of her vision amidst the monotonous chanting of the priests, slowly growing, growing in size - before vanishing with an ear shattering explosion.

Within her psyche opened up an unbroken connection. Annalise felt her conscious mind extending not only through the acausal spaces but directly back to the powers which she had witnessed and which she had striven to understand following her imposed isolation here in the wilderness. Her body was pulled to each corner of the universe, threatening to tear her limb from limb, as if two nightmarish beasts had been tethered to each of her arms. Her mind's eyes clouded with the wings of thousands of bat-like creatures, and she perceived above her in the night sky a rent open and a not altogether feminine presence extend downwards to surround her completely. A screaming maw issued forth its vile potency, disintegrating the shackles of normative consciousness and dragging Annalise out of her body, only to force her back into it abruptly and painfully. Nythra, an unknowable and eternal dark goddess, had presenced Herself to further initiate and mutate, devouring and taking all aspects which She so desired. The stars above twisted and spun, black turning to deep crimson. *Hiyuur maazerargh, mazababgha.*

Annalise sunk back, exhausted, and gathering her senses, wrapped herself in the spun blanket she had brought to keep herself warm. She then drifted off into deep and dreamless sleep by the crackling of the warm fire. The unearthly silence outside slowly faded away, giving rise again to the various nocturnal animals and their familiar nightly chorus.

Some unknown amount of time passed before Annalise would wake from her rest, her mouth dry and the sky above her grey, bringing a quiet promise of rain. She recorded by the dim light of the candles her visions, each new insight slowly adding a new piece for her to apprehend and internalise.

She had communed not only with these chthonic powers over the endless days and nights during her isolation but with also her covenmates, who maintained the Covenant's mission in her absence. The final pieces of the puzzle were coming together and soon, with the final clues solved - the insights, ciphers and visions which had been imparted to her understood - Annalise would not only have keys to a hitherto undiscovered power, but would also discover the resting place of the previous Morain and would thus be able elicit the dark secrets of the tradition the necromancer had initiated her into *in absentia* many years prior.

The incense was put out, the volatile smoke wafting out of the rotting doorway, and the rest placed unburnt on the makeshift shrine upon an oak stool in the corner consisting of various bones and feathers from a dead raven, a totem long ago revealed to Annalise as an auspicious symbol of her favoured Dark God.

Outside the hut, she drank her brew of nettle and Mugwort tea, the leaves having been foraged earlier that day, and stared out into the darkness of the cool night, scrying the shadows between the trees. Annalise reflected over her years as a witch, a bloodied Rounwytha with a veritable tapestry of loss, pain and harsh pathei-mathos which all combined over the years to impress within her a sort of involuted nihilism, but one which soon gave way to understanding and wisdom she never could have comprehended before.

From the first time she felt the bitter sting of betrayal, the glint of malice in a young man's eyes as he laughed at her naivety over a promise given, to the stark satisfaction of seeing the bloodied and broken corpse of a former lover lay strewn at the bottom of a deep crevice following a long walk through wood lands attained with the lure of a tryst, she had been hardened from a shy, inquisitive and intelligent - if not pretty - young girl, to a woman now known and even feared by the kinds of people most members of society never crossed paths with. She had vowed all those years ago that she would drink the blood of all who crossed her, offer them up as sacrifices to Aosoth, and dress Her altars on the moors with their entrails for the ravens to feast upon. Now, she simply saw it all as a dance of life and death, humans who were once so important now merely eddies of emotion in an altogether more impersonal and everflowing river, a flow of life which sought to birth itself through her.

Her thoughts thus drifted to Siofra. Young, fair, beautiful Siofra, for whom Annalise had begun to feel a stir of love - a feeling which had before this vanished from her heart for many years. She looked back to that quiet winter day spent with Siofra, watching the swans on the lake of Roundhay Park. Sitting under an old elm tree, she had penned a poem later that day, a poem Siofra now kept framed next to her bed.

Crows call,

and flock in abundance;

Fingers entwined,

like the deep roots beneath us;

Only silence and mist,

from two lover's breath;

Still your scent lingers,

And still, your scent lingers;

They had spent that evening drinking wine and listening to Mussorgsky and Satie, some of Siofra's favourites. Peace it had been, a brief respite and a necessary empathy of that soft kind, which had so long vanished from Annalise's heart. Within Siofra slept a nascent force, acausally impregnated by Annalise's witchcraft when she first lay with her, and which force would one day need to be realised physically via a causal offspring to fulfill Annalise's personal Wyrd. She was the only thing Annalise missed of the world. Perhaps one day, she thought, it would be just the two of them, living like this, away from the world and its pain, its trials, its flawed humans.

Above her, as morning arrived, the crows broke from the treeline and scattered into the Autumnal sky.

VII

Lucian observed the young blonde girl from his car as she crossed the road, oblivious that she was being watched as she went about her business among the bustling streets of Leeds. This was apparently Siofra, one of Annalise's little minions. She certainly did not look the part, and could easily have passed for the average college student. Wearing a baggy sweater and clutching a backpack, she was a far cry from the type Annalise normally surrounded herself with. Lucian signalled to his driver to follow her - maybe she could lead them to wherever that witch was hiding these days. He knew she had a house, a nice one, too, supposedly. But as to its actual location, nobody knew.

Earlier that day, Lucian had met with one of his business partners, who had sniffed around and discovered the young girl's connection. Unbeknownst to Lucian, however, he was being watched as he met his partner, as well as when he climbed into the black BMW to leave and later follow Siofra. Marcus had been tailing Lucian, and was making sure he would be two steps ahead of him, every step of the way.

Siofra received a text, from Marcus: *L knows who you are, play cool - I have a plan.*

Siofra looked about, seeing nothing unusual. Marcus always knew what he was doing, she knew she could trust in his plans. Before long she would have to fulfill her duty as priestess of the coven, and despite the nerves, she couldn't think of anyone more suitable than the man who attempted to wage a war on Annalise to offer up as a sacrifice to the Dark Gods. Sitting down with a cup of tea in a coffee shop, Siofra played her part dutifully, and allowed Lucian to stalk her, as Marcus operated from the shadows, leading their prey further into their grasp.

Later that evening, Marcus met up with several individuals, to whom he and Morgan's associates would be supplying arms. The premise was that certain individuals, representing big business, wanted Lucian and his enterprise gone for good. Morgan's credentials helped verify this account, as Marcus discussed matters with two severe looking men of mid-east descent at a lavish table in a restaurant overlooking the river Aire. The establishment was owned by a particular business venture which Marcus had discovered had issue with Lucians' actions, via underworld contacts sought and squeezed for information accordingly. Marcus had done questionable things to obtain information in the past, but the end justified the means, as he had always believed. A few broken noses or fingers belonging to a crackhead or two were small concern to the Wyrdful vision of Annalise and the coven. All that was necessary was for the right person to put into practise such ruthless measures, and Marcus had happily, if not grimly, taken up such a responsibility. An operative, Annalise had called him. He liked that word.

After a few niceties, and passing over of funds and general plans, the men agreed over drinks to the course of action. Two days from now, when Lucian's men would be meeting on the outskirts of the city to make dealings with importers of certain merchandise, Marcus and the men would strike, eliminating the crew and effectively removing their power from the city altogether. What

Marcus did not tell them was that Lucian would not be there, but that did not matter. In the ensuing chaos, his men would be swiftly extinguished and it would be assumed that Lucian either died in the fighting, or otherwise fled, never to be seen again.

VIII

It had been several weeks since Victor first introduced Elisa to the machine he and his students had been building. Things however had taken dramatic turns since then.

With regular testing and powering of the machine apparatus, they had been slowly exposed to alien forces and intelligences wholly beyond their grasp; subtly at first, explicated first in a few disturbing dreams, unexplainable cuts and scratches, bizarre thoughts.

The entire team under Victor's tutelage had slowly changed, functioning more and more over time like a secret society, becoming closer, more guarded, becoming more aware of just why they were doing what they were doing. Each one was a puppet of Victor's via his gradual burgeoning of occultic power, and Victor himself a puppet of an ancient and hungry force in its own right.

Whilst all maintained a semblance of lucidity, they had all come to recognise the machine for what it was - a portal to the acausal spaces and the timeless beings that dwelt there.

Elisa herself had become increasingly focused, pouring all her efforts into assisting Victor. Soon, the final pieces of the jigsaw puzzle would fall into place, and unification would be achievable.

Victor had begun work on a device he called the Blood Tank, a sensory deprivation chamber which he had outfitted with several apparatuses taken from the university's medical department. The tank would in theory sustain its host indefinitely, as long as it was maintained by an operator. An addition of an IV drip would nourish him within its chamber. The most important ingredient would be the very blood of those under his guidance, a direct intravenous transfusion delivering the necessary proteins and life extending vitality to extend his years beyond ordinary mortal time. Within this tank, secured somewhere away from humanity, he would wait for the time to be right, when one would find his work and prepare the way for him, fulfilling his vision and assisting the will of the Dark Gods. Victor would be able to remain in a permanent state of astral projection within this tank, able to see and travel wherever his will desired. His knowledge would, in theory, grow manifold through submersion into the tank's watery darkness.

All that was needed now was a place to sequester the tank. But before this, Victor and Elisa needed to power the machine he had built one last time, to transcribe important knowledge to leave behind and hopefully inspire a new generation who would find and resurrect him many years after the rest of his assistants had died.

The town of Heptonstall had been chosen by Victor for his resting place. Beneath the church ruins, in a small chamber built as part of a tunnel complex centuries earlier, the Blood Tank would be set up, accessible by an old stone stairway long since bricked up.

There, he would remain, suspended in an astral reverie, free to explore beyond the confines of the earth and the laws of physics, discovering the secrets that lay beyond the cold void of starry space.

Thanks to Elisa's expertise and the collective efforts of his assistants, the tank was eventually constructed, guarded by the regular clandestine attendants who furnished the Master with the necessary life blood and nutrients to sustain his essence.

Placing it underground in the dead of night, whilst remaining hidden from the town populace however would be a supremely difficult task.

Elisa believed she had the solution. A small vial taken from the labs would be the key. In Victor's study, under extreme care, Elisa and several others cultivated the sample of nerve gas, weaponizing it into discreet packages which would in theory quietly kill the inhabitants of the village. This nerve agent, christened *Nythra* by Elisa, would be employed against the sleeping residents, whilst the noisy work of gaining access to the underground vaults and lowering the Blood Tank into it could go unhindered.

The town would become a ghost town not for the first time in its grim history, as a dozen individuals in gas masks and protective suits moved through the foggy streets, carrying a large device up to the church ruins, and having unearthed the medieval passageway with mattock and hammer, descended into the musty darkness to lay their Morain in his resting place.

The assistants, their work fulfilled, committed a ritual suicide that night, having attempted to work the bizarre acausal machine - save for one, who was now the sole surviving Tank's guardian.

Local authorities ran the two news stories - the alleged gas leak at Heptonstall, and the suicide pact of several university students - with few, very few making any connection between both acts. Elisa herself quietly vanished, using the funds Morain left her to start a new life somewhere in South Africa.

As for Victor himself, he slumbered, awaiting patiently for his work to be renewed and bring fresh blood to the haunted moors of Yorkshire.

IX

Under the careful gaze of Marcus and several other close confidants, the weapons acquired the week before were handed over to a gang of dangerous-looking young men, the meeting itself taking place far outside the city of Leeds, in the relative obscurity of a woodland bordering on rural countryside.

With a shake of hands and a few grim words exchanged, the plan was set. Lucian's men, operating that night, so the information went, in a rather rough suburban area, and which operation if stolen upon swiftly would ensure all the gang's top dogs would be found in one convenient place, would see the much-maligned gang and their leader cornered, easy pickings for the rivals now being supplied with suitable armaments. Marcus knew power play of this calibre could always be relied upon to enact results. The enemy of my enemy, so they thought. Marcus was utterly indifferent to the outcome, so long as he was able to grab Lucian in the chaos.

Later that night, the crime-ridden back streets and disused housing area was witness to a drug deal gone sourly wrong. In the foray, Lucian and his henchmen attempted to bolt, sure they'd been set up for the merchandise they'd brought.

Getting into his car, Lucian reversed wildly down the back road, escaping the gunfight that had broken out and leaving several of his most trusted allies to die. He had to get away. He had to survive. The drugs at least were still in the car boot.

Driving recklessly down the unlit road, he pulled over, catching his breath and looking through his rear mirror to make sure he wasn't being followed. His hands were shaking, and he took a shot of whisky from the glove compartment. Things were going south in a bad way.

From the back seat sprang Marcus, placing around Lucian's mouth a wet cloth, the scent of which sent Lucian into a stupor as the world faded into black.

When he next awoke, Lucian found himself bound and gagged, the smell of dry earth beneath his head. He was in a cellar or underground room of some sort. His head ached from the chloroform, his mind still reeling from the sudden turn of events of the night. He was helpless now, prey to some unknowing fate.

He shouted and swore through his gag, cursing whomever had tricked him. He continued till exhaustion, and yet nobody came. His fate was sealed, whatever that fate would be.

X

Siofra and Alexander sat up on the moorland, looking out toward the reservoir in the distance. They had hiked up to the summit of the highest points that day, taking time to get away from responsibilities and embracing their growing love for the wild, a love they had begun exploring together. Their fingers were entwined, as they had grown closer over the weeks, stealing first a look, then a kiss, and spending several nights with one another. Between them had grown a romance which made sense to them. They had both entered a whole new world, one in which they felt lost at times despite the insights and growth that had occurred.

'So, the rite draws near,' said Siofra, breaking the quiet

comfort they had abided in for some hours together

'It is. Are you nervous?' Alexander asked.

'Not any more,' replied Siofra with a certain and altogether stern look on her face.

They watched the sun set over the landscape before heading home for dinner with the rest of the guests that had arrived from other corners of the land.

In the cellar, Lucian had slowly wrested free of the bonds which had held his hands together and prevented his escape from this musty prison. He wasn't sure how much time had passed, but he had been brought water by a silent attendant only several minutes earlier. This was the third time someone had been down, and he had not heard the door lock this time.

He stumbled up, managing to free his hands and untie the gag from around his neck, and crept up the stone steps. Peering through the rotting wood doorway, he saw only darkness.

It was an outhouse of some sort, situated around the back of some old manor, or so it seemed. It was now or never.

Flinging open the door, Lucian ran down the grassy hill and into the treeline ahead. He kept running, making distance between himself and the house, but his head swam and his stomach had begun to cramp. His vision was blurring, and with a dawning horror he realised he'd been tricked yet again. The water - something must have been in it! His eyes felt like they were swelling, and soon he became lost in the forest, unsure of the direction from which he came.

He began to hear laughter and shrieks that sounded like demonic witches cackling through the dense, misty wood.

'Who's there? Where the fuck are you?!' Lucian shouted, whirling about in a daze, attempting to find his tormentors.

He began again to run and fell down a decline in the land. He stumbled into a clearing, and, gaining his footing, was suddenly confronted by a stark entity. It was Annalise, her pale face glowing in the moonlight. With a swift movement she slashed at his throat with a knife, and thus clutching his throat, Lucian fell to the ground, convulsing and spurting his life blood into the cold soil.

Several figures emerged from the trees, singing a strange song that filled Lucian's ears and caused his delirium to increase. He felt himself being hoisted upward, and through his blurring vision saw Annalise surrounded by ragged, dark clad figures who placed a hooded crimson robe onto her head and who continued their song as she raised the blood-covered dagger and thrust it deep into his heart. Lucian collapsed dead in the arms of his captors, and Annalise drank deeply and ritualistically of his spilt blood.

Siofra watched as Annalise stood amidst the circle of witches bearing blazing torches and drank the man's blood from a goblet which had been offered to her. The chant echoed throughout the forest, and Siofra felt a euphoric and almost magickal feeling take hold. She felt compelled to dance, and found to her surprise others doing so also, forming a circle of witches who sung in a lilting unison, '*Suscipe, Gaia, munus quod tibi offerimus memoriam recolentes Baphomet,*' spiralling elegantly around Annalise, who held up the goblet in her blood-stained hands in some grim offering to her Undead gods.

XI

Annalise's return to Sayersby had raised Siofra's spirits greatly. However, she felt she had betrayed her bond with her recent emotional tangle. She had intended to tell Annalise in time about her and Alexander, but Annalise had merely brushed the matter off.

'Why does it matter, words only cloud the true meaning of what we try to say, Siofra,' Annalise assured her.

'What you and I shared was special, but you and Alexander - your fates are entwined. You know this, I am sure of it. Anyway, we have more pressing matters to attend; you have found where the place alluded to in my little book is, haven't you?'

They had indeed.

Several days later, the coven gathered on the ruins of the Heptonstall church, a secret passageway having been discovered and opened that night by Marcus and Lucas' diligent efforts. The hole revealed only darkness, with a set of stone steps leading underneath the church into some foul smelling underground chamber. Annalise stood in front of it, hearing with fey-ears the silent whispers echoing up from inside.

They followed Annalise down the steps, and, sealing the entrance behind them, they lit the area.

What the light revealed was a dry and low-roofed stone room, with a large black chamber resembling a coffin placed in the centre. Hooked up to it were several devices which had long ceased to operate. The men opened the chamber as Annalise stood by, expectantly awaiting whatever was inside.

The lid was pried off, and contained within it was a desiccated and skeletal figure, wires and tubes leading out of its shrivelled arms. In its hands, it held a large, black morion crystal stained with blood. Annalise's eyes lit up as she stepped toward the corpse.

'It's him - the Morain. He's led us here. The circle is finally... complete!'

Annalise gracefully signalled for the others to move aside, and with some hesitation wrested the crystal from the corpse's wiry hands, feeling it seep as she did so dark and otherworldly energy into her very being. She saw in her mind's eye a sojourn among the stars, a communion of communions with a great and ancient entity gorged on the mass of a million suns. She saw a black wraith descend amongst primitive life forms on an Earth-like planet somewhere light years away under an eclipse in a strange, blood red sky. She saw a vast and screaming maw of silence dwelling deep within a void of starless space, an Undead mother of all vampiric creatures. She saw in that abyssal instance all the secrets her forebear had learnt during his silent pilgrimage across the cold void. The Blood Current flowed through time and space, a baleful tendril of the Void Mother reaching out to continue the Numinous aim of evolution itself. In that very moment, Annalise was elevated and anointed as a Moraina of the Covenant.

Outside, hundreds of bats emerged from their homes in the stone ruin and took flight into the night sky.

XII

Some time passed, and the coven's power and influence grew. Lucian's remains were burnt, and the Morain's body was taken and buried in the woods during a sombre and haunting ceremony presided over by Siofra and Annalise. As the bound remains were lowered into the earth and covered with a decorative stone slab, Annalise silently toyed with the fingerbone pendant around her neck, a relic from the Morain's body which she would keep as a cherished trinket.

Sometime after, Siofra had started to feel sick upon waking, and it soon transpired that she was pregnant with Alexander's child. The nascent creature growing in her womb would be a physical offspring by all measures, but its essence was seeded long ago, during the Sapphic bonding of Siofra and Annalise.

As the months passed, Siofra's stomach grew, and the time eventually came for her to give birth. She chose a home birth, surrounded by her friends and new found family. Annalise assisted as midwife, and they dutifully comforted Siofra through the ordeal, resulting after a few hours in a beautiful and lively baby girl.

Alexander cradled the infant in his hands as Siofra slept, exhausted from the labour. Annalise smiled at the silent child as it looked up at them with small grey eyes.

'I feel this child will accomplish many things, many great things. What shall we call her?' asked Annalise, stroking the infant's soft brow.

'We've already picked a name,' Alexander replied, rocking the child gently in his arms and kissing her forehead gently.

'We will call her – Morgatha.'

Cuairt Coimhgí

The torches were flickering in the bitter midwinter wind, bringing an unsteady chill which touched the flesh with all the malice of the undead.

Three black clad figures sat in a small depression in the ground, a circle constructed thousands of years ago and which once served as the foundations for an ancient house, a house where unspeakable acts of ritual infanticide and sacrifice took place. The isolated remains of Cladh Hallan now witnessed a more modern ritual, one aimed at communing with the very entities who once built the stone dwellings and who had, in their expansive post mortem existence, grown incredibly knowledgeable.

The knelt individuals were dressed entirely in black, their combat boots and face masks adding to a disciplined and intimidating demeanour, made all the more unsettling by the sheer suggestion of their fanaticism gleaming in their eyes.

The central figure, a female of lithe proportions, wore flowing black garments, torn at the edges, and which black garments were sanctified with blood and grave soil from countless previous rites.

Upon her head was a grisly headdress, decorated with bones, and had affixed a thick veil which enclosed the entire face, designed to blackout any external stimuli and thus provide an aid in trance states.

The two attendant males removed their upper clothing, and laying them aside, took up a harsh metal tipped flail each. Waving them over the fire and heavy incense, they chanted in low and unintelligible mutterings, whilst the central figure remained still in her meditation.

The men then began - whipping their backs with the metal instruments, whilst the central witch continued to meditate, still and silent, save for the slight swaying and serpentine motions of her hands through the night air.

Blood began to flow down the backs of the flagellators, and the witch - the veritable Lamia Naturalis - continued her meditation, entering deeper into her black trance, and slowly becoming aware of the presence of other figures, bordering on the threshold of both the ruins and of reality itself.

The two figures ceased their chants under command of a signal from the witch, and summarily laid their flails in front of them.

They began their chant again, burning more incense upon the brazier, as the young woman rocked subtly back and forth, a writing implement in her hand scrawling upon parchment dipped in the blood obtained during the frenzied self-mutilation of her counterparts.

The wind had ceased, but the air itself had grown chill, with a faint stench underlying the burnt incense, something akin to rotting earth.

Whilst the two masked figures certainly felt a dread presence - something not unfamiliar to them and thus the reason for their still composure, the young witch certainly saw Them.

Two ragged and ghostly figures had come forth before the grisly scene, adorned in faded and bizarre attire and wholly skeletal in their visage. The very essence of nightmares, these long dead shades of the priests who once dwelt where the rite now took place had now been summoned and the witch fully intended to elicit Their secrets.

The rotting stench of Their breath filled the nostrils of the attendants, and Their voices screamed ancient secrets into the mind of the Lamia Naturalis, who dutifully made note of what was recorded. Words of an ancient and long forgotten language, only noted through subtle echoes in celtic tongues, took form at the hand of the witch, who would take these secrets back, accompanied by her retinue, to the dark and hallowed place they called their covenant.

The torches flickered out one by one, leaving the scene in pitch blackness, as the scent of blood and frankincense suffused across the bleak Hebridean moor.

Appendices

SCITHAIN

Appendix I -

Tinctures and Correspondences

Any self-respecting witch will keep a solid supply of herbs, resins and incense for their magickal rites and rituals.

The following is a list of correspondences, directions and recipes for procuring and producing all the blends which will be needed for use within the Sinister tradition.

The cultivation and care of plants and herbs is a lifelong discipline and passion which will help foster an appreciation for the natural world and the inextricable tie between Man and the land.

Planetary Spheres Correspondences

The following is a list of incense correspondences. Two scents are related to each sphere, the exact reasoning for this being detailed in other Order MSS.

Given the difficulty at obtaining some of these blends (such as civet), alternate blends are given alongside the orthodox selections.

For planetary incenses, two scents are given. These represent the 'Unconscious' and 'Ego' aspects of the spheres, with the 'Self' aspects being a blend of the two.

Given after these here are the alternate scents for those blends difficult to acquire.

Moon

Petrichor/Hazel/Lavender

Mercury

Sulphur/Yew/Patchouli

Venus

Sandalwood/Black Poplar

Sun

Oak/Birch

Mars

Musk/Alder

Jupiter

Civet/Beech/Opium

Saturn

Henbane/Ash/Frankincense

Making Oils and Tinctures

Making oils and oil-based tinctures can serve several uses. Within the tradition of Drakon Covenant witchcraft, these oils are usually used for creating vision inducing concoctions.

For attaining visions and bringing about the 'fey-mind', several herbs can be employed. As detailed in the chapter *The Scithain Tradition and Vampyric Witchcraft,* the most commonly used herbs - both historically and traditionally - are *cannabis sativa, hashish, mandrake root, mugwort* and *datura stramonium.*

To create an oil, the relevant plants or herbs are usually steeped in alcohol such as vodka. The mixture is left for several days, with the plant matter removed and the vodka strained from it and poured onto a fresh batch of your plant/herb of choice, thus potentiating the mixture. This can be done three, four or five times to create a stronger oil. A small amount of olive oil may be added to this mixture. Once it is prepared and finished, freezing the mixture will bring the infused oil to the top which can then be collected. Otherwise, the resultant infused alcohol can simply be used as an oil in itself.

The final product can then be evaporated in an oil burner during ritual use.

To make a salve or paste, the chosen ingredients are crushed into a fine powder, with this powder then being mixed into some lard. Next, take some more lard (without the powder ingredient in it) and wrap it in aluminium foil. Place this in some embers until the lard is grilled to a black soot. Add this soot to the powder and lard mix, and blend the three ingredients well. Next, cook this blend over a low heat for 2-4 hours, stirring it regularly. Let the salve then sit for a week in a dark place, stirring it several times a day. After a week, filter the salve.

Keep the resulting product in a sealed jar somewhere dark and cool. This salve can then be applied to the sensitive parts of the body, such as the armpits, neck and calves.

Making Incense

Incense can be created in two ways - combustible and non-combustible. Combustible incense is made into sticks or cones which can be lit and burn of their own volition. Non-combustible incense is made to be burnt atop charcoal in a brazier. An alternative to burning directly atop charcoal involves the use of a sheet of mica, placed above the charcoal, onto which the incense is sprinkled, giving a 'purer' scent. Braziers are available in most places where incense blends are sold, as are the charcoal discs used with them.

Making non-combustible incense is the usually preferred method, and is simpler and more adequate for mixing blends together.

To create a blend, the ingredients (be they resin, wood or herb leaves) must be gathered, dried and cut. The ingredients are then placed in a mortar and pestle and ground into a fine powder. Resins can be prepared for grinding by freezing them to harden the texture.

Creating incense is thus as simple as finding the correct ingredient/s (or cultivating them in a garden) and drying, grinding and burning.

Preparing Petrichor

Petrichor is created from an oil exuded by plants which is then absorbed by clay based soil and rocks.

This oil (which is called *geosmin*) is a natural preservation technique, as it essentially suspends the seeds and prevents them from germinating. Geosmin is released during dry spells so as to prevent seeds germinating during periods when there is not enough water. The unique petrichor smell is a combination of geosmin and soil based bacteria known as *Actinomycetes*. During rainfall, the oil is released into the atmosphere, allowing the seeds to grow, and the moisture in the air enhances the scent.

A useful method is to grow some perennial plants in soil, then refrain from watering them for a few days. You should research which plants secrete optimal amounts of Geosmin (the active ingredient in petrichor). Following this, remove the plants and take the soil and some of the roots and grind it up into a fine powder.

Next, boil this in rainwater you have previously harvested and collect the residue which gathers on the surface. Place this in a container and refrigerate until it is hardened. This petrichor resin can then be broken into a fine consistency and sprinkled upon a charcoal burner.

Alternatively, take the dry soil containing the plant roots and grind as before. Next, let the soil soak in the rainwater for a handful of hours. Following this, boil the water for an hour, then filter out the water and collect the wet soil. Continue this process several times and leave the resultant wet soil collection to dry. When dry, the soil resin can be ground up into petrichor incense.

Appendix II -

The Secret Tasks

Blood-Feddyng - The Creation of the Homunculus

Witches have historically often kept familiars, either for company or magickal assistance. The creation of familiars in the form of homunculi is an advanced practise reserved for only the most daring of witches. The methods for doing so vary, but the one detailed herein is a potent and hideous ritual which has been cherished and preserved within the inner circle of the Drakon Covenant, known as the Blood-Feddyng.

It firstly involves the witch acquiring a fertilised chicken or snake egg. Into this egg must be injected fresh human semen, via a tiny opening made at the top of the egg. Care must be taken to avoid infection and to ensure the hole is as small as possible. It is then covered securely (with material such as adhesive bandage tape).

The egg is kept warm and placed in the dark for around 20 days. Some witches have experimented with 30, 90, and 120 days.

When the time is up, crack the egg open. There should be, amongst the fluid, a small creature of indeterminate species. It will be weak, so care must be taken to dry it and place it in a pre-arranged environment. A small dish of blood needs to be left near it, and it should be kept in complete darkness. Check upon the creature after two days. If it has died, the process must be performed again. It is best to burn the creature's corpse if it has died.

If, however, the creature has survived, replenish it with more blood. It should gain strength and grow. Success has reportedly been obtained by keeping the hatched entities in water, into which can be diffused nutrient powders for it to consume. The homunculus can either be nurtured to maturity, and serve as a familiar, or it can be grown for the following ritual.

After one to two weeks, you should perform a baptism upon the abomination, naming it after your target opfer. Then perform a ritual sacrifice, killing the creature with a dagger and burning its body. Scatter the ashes near the home of your target opfer or where they will pass.

Another use for this ritual is the more difficult process of sustaining the creature, and nurturing it to grow beyond its noetic form. If this can be achieved, the creature is rumoured to develop a psychic link with the witch and serve as a useful familiar. This is an incredibly difficult practise to master, as most attempts die within a few hours to a few days, to mention nothing of the difficulty of birthing a viable specimen at all. Experimentation is necessary to ascertain the most effective method for yielding success.

The Blood Tank

The Blood Tank is a suspension chamber designed to facilitate the Master's life processes whilst they are induced into a liminal mind state. This device is best employed toward the end of one's life, and will in theory extend their life by a degree of years.

The tank consists of a sensory deprivation tank, which the Master reposes in. IV drips are administered (such as electrolytes, glucose, proteins and so forth), which will keep the resident sustained if necessary.

Into the IV drip feed will also be administered blood from the other coven members, the younger blood infusion being rich in GDF11 protein - effectively slowing and in time, reversing the aging process completely.

The Blood Tank allows the Master to exist in a permanent state of astral projection, thus creating a certain level of omnipresence and omniscience. This is of course a highly difficult task, requiring not only devotion and a consistent flow of literal blood from the coven, but a working knowledge of human biology and medical science also to be included to ensure success and maintenance of this device.

The sheer difficulty of the Blood Tank ensures very few will attempt to build one. But to those who do, a literal state of deific power awaits, as the life and senses are extended to superhuman levels.

Appendix III – Lanuwythe

The Lycanthropic Praxis of the Drakon Covenant

This sparse collection of manuscripts entitled *Lanuwythe* contains a short historical background on the phenomenon of phantom wolves in England throughout recorded history as well as detailing an obscure Dark God related to this phenomenon, known as Lanus to the seldom few who follow this particular path within the Drakon Covenant tradition.

These writings were originally circulated internally before being included in this publication. The very nature of this path meant that very few had progressed particularly far along it, the path itself demanding atavistic and austere conditions in order to awaken to the unique lycanthropic condition and bring for the adherent the twin favours of Lanus and Satan.

Given herein is a meditation and pathworking rite in the vein of the Septenary method, performance of which should set the practitioner on the path toward understanding Lanus' essence. Communion with this Dark God is done with the aim of uncovering the secrets Lanus once bequeathed to the werewolf cults of antiquity throughout the lands of Britain and Europe.

The coven of Lanus is devoted to the worship of Lanus himself as well as Satan fundamentally, the Dark Master of the Woods.

Since Mankind first manifested conscious and rational understanding of himself and the world around him, he identified in other beasts the traits he sought to possess. Primitive man stood at the edge of the forest and watched as the wolf pack hunted its prey with ruthless efficiency and co-operation. Their howls filling the night, he perhaps sat there, chilled and spellbound to the sound of these creatures. These beasts, perhaps he thought, held a key to a more numinous existence, a noble savagery one could come to emulate to advance one's self over one's prey and other tribes of rival humans alike.

Thus did shamanism in its earliest forms arise. The shaman was a walker between two worlds, a figure who sought to tap into the vital essence and spiritual power of the wolf, the bear and other animals he shared the landscape with. It is into this world that Lycanthropy was born.

Stories of beast-like men transforming into great wolves have existed in nearly every culture. Warriors invoked their spirit before battle; outlaw killers were referred to as *vargr* - wolves; the werewolf has haunted us since the dark dimness of the ancient past.

The vampire archetype has long been associated with the werewolf, and often the terms for both were used interchangeably in many a folkloric mythos. It was said that a werewolf possessed the capability to become a vampiric shade upon death, and continue to hunt human victims, feeding from their blood and life essence as opposed to their flesh as during the werewolf's life.

In *A Restitution of Decayed Intelligence: In Antiquities*

written by Richard Verstegan in 1605, he writes:

"The were-wolves are certaine sorcerers, who having annoynted their bodyes, with an oyntment which they make by the instinct of the devil; and putting on a certaine inchanted girdel, do not only unto the view of othres seems as wolves, but to their own thinking have both the shape and nature of wolves, so long as they weare the said girdel."

Lanus

Lanus is the archetypal god of the wild, the loyal hound of Satan. Unto him were and are pledged the lives of those who seek to lead themselves toward Adeptship via the path of the Werewolf.

Lanus resides in a realm of ice and trees known as Gloamingwood, the eternal forest. His baleful eyes peer out through the trees toward the shadows and wildernesses of this world. He rides by Satan in the wild hunt, which itself has been manifested in the psyche of Western man since time immemorial.

Lanus is depicted in the Sinister tarot Atu *Azoth,* where He stands beside Satan who takes the form of primal initiator. This archetypal expression offers but one explanation to the manifestation of Lanus as an aspect of Satanas and is often used during lycanthropic meditational rites.

He demands of His worshippers supreme acts of self-sacrifice and hermetic rites, including secluded living, predatory consumption of raw flesh, intense spirit journeys and brutal physical conditioning.

Lanus manifests as a great black wolf, with piercing fiery eyes. His image has haunted the Isles of Albion for many centuries and it was his charge to rid the lands of Christianity upon its arrival.

Initiates of the Covenant tradition have often claimed to have encountered Lanus following their initiation rites, or at least spotted large black dogs during the night hours. The grasp of this shadowy entity is always near to those who seek Him out.

Historical Accounts of Black Dog Attacks

Since Christianity first arrived in Britain, early churches and chapels, as well as priests and ordinary folk were set upon by phantom black dogs with glowing red eyes. These attacks are well documented in the early history of England.

In East Anglia, a terrifying beast, known as Black Shuck was reported to have been seven feet tall when upon its hind legs, with flaming eyes and shaggy black hair. Black Shuck roamed the land during the 16th century. The beast's most infamous attack occurred at Holy Trinity church, Blythburgh. According to reports, the church doors were flung open with a clap of thunder, and Black Shuck 'the devil dog' came snarling into the church.

'All down the church in the midst of fire, the hellish monster flew, and, passing onward to the quire, he many people slew.'

Black Shuck killed a man and a boy, caused the church steeple to fall through and left scorched claw marks upon the church door - claw marks which are still visible to this day. Centuries later, the skeleton of an unusually large male dog was unearthed at Leiston Abbey, a few miles from Shuck's legendary attacks.

Black Shuck struck again twelve miles away, killing two more Christian worshippers during a service at St Mary's Church, Bungay.

The beast was recorded in a 1577 pamphlet by Reverend Abraham Fleming. Entitled *A Straunge And Terrible Wunder*, he describes Shuck 'running all along down the body of the church with great swiftness and incredible haste, among the people, in a visible form and shape, wringing the necks of two parishioners as they knelt. Although his howling makes the hearer's blood run cold, his footfalls make no sound.'

Another incident involves a creature known as The Hexham Wolf or the Wolf of Allendale appeared in relation to a collection of Celtic figurines known as the Hexham heads.

In 1904, farmers were keeping their animals in their stables, due to a series of attacks on livestock. The attacks were characteristic of a large wolf.

Local townsfolk and skilled trackers organised mass wolf hunts to drive the beast out, but to no avail.

Sightings continued around Allendale and the nearby woodlands, and the wolf continued to elude capture.

It was not until recently in 1971 that the wolf was seen

again, when the Hexham heads were discovered in an Allendale garden by two young boys. These small stone figurines were often accompanied by a large shaggy beast which manifested at night in the homes of whoever possessed the heads and was often heard *'padding down the stairs as if on its hind legs.'*

Other disturbances involving the heads included the idols teleporting, disappearing, causing poltergeist phenomena, and one woman even seeing what she described as a shaggy half-man, half-sheep beast of some sort.

The Celts were known to venerate the head as a symbol of life and power, and it is believed these idols were somehow related to this cultic practise - perhaps belonging to a now long-dead druidh or practitioner of long-since forgotten lycanthropic practises.

Well into modern times, large black phantom dogs are seen in every corner of the British Isles, matched only by the frequency of unknown giant black cats. The infamous werewolf known as 'Old Stinker' has been seen by residents of the Yorkshire Wolds well into modern times, with a rash of sightings occurring as recently as 2016 CE. Named for its supposed foul smell, the beast has historically been blamed for the killing of livestock as well as the disappearance of local pets and is claimed to be eight feet in height when on its hind legs.

Werewolf sightings have been seen across the British Isles for centuries, but this particular beast has persisted well into modern times. The dark spectre of Lanus clings hungrily to Yorkshire soil, and it is doubtful if such a spectre will ever leave. North Yorkshire is particularly known for its incidents of 'Dogmen' sightings, though the Eastern county can boast such named beasts as Old Stinker himself.

Such creatures are distinct from the ubiquitous phantom black dogs as they are described as being bipedal and resembling a mix between wolf and man. They are also known to be predatory as opposed to phantom-like in their manifestations.

Lanus has a unique tie to the British Isles and His visage, still a common sight across these lands, is testament to His power and unending hunt. For this reason, this manuscript has avoided a broad discussion of other analogous lycanthropic cults (such as those observed in Scandinavia and Germany).

Morannis, Queen of Winter

Morannis is the principal goddess of which later European myths such as Morana and Mara derived from. The prefix *Mor*, long associated with death can be found in many words in usage today (mortal, mortician, Morrigan, Morain) and is derived from the Indo-Aryan *mor* or *mors,* meaning terror, death or greatness.

The legend of Morannis' genesis as a winter deity and her connection with Lanus is detailed in a pagan myth long lost to the annals of history but one which is preserved in the aural teachings of the Drakon Covenant, as well as in various threads of myth and (as indeed many ancient myths have been found to have) in fairy tale - namely the tale of *Red Riding Hood*. Accounts of this myth have been traced back to over 2,000 years, with classic accounts existing as early as the 11th century - including several variations existing before the current familiar interpretation was popularised by the Brothers Grimm. Previous tales included overtly sexual themes and a sinister blood drinking ritual on the part of Red Riding Hood.

The original, traditional myth told of Morannis as a young girl who was hunted by the woodcutter one day whilst walking through the woods.

In this tale, the woodcutter is a lurking sexual predator, and a passing wolf served as the chance guardian who seized upon and slew the woodcutter, saving Morannis from his attacks. Morannis later became associated with wolves, winter, death, witchcraft and the colour red, with winter berries being a favoured offering to Her. She was (according to tradition) portrayed as a stern and pale woman with dark hair sat upon a throne in a crimson red cloak, with a large black wolf by her feet. This wolf is believed by some to be Lanus.

Morannis is a venerated deity within the pantheon of the Drakon Covenant and worshipped as the terrible aspect of winter, a vampiric goddess of death and destruction. She can be seen as similar to several Dark Gods in this regard, and as the queen of the Dearg Dûl, perhaps even being the primary Dearg herself.

Morannis is also associated with nightmares, from whence the word nightmare (*mara*) itself is derived, and which name lends itself to the modern interpretations of this goddess seen within Slavic folklore.

If the Dearg Dûl are fond of blood, then Morannis is even more so. Even by vampiric standards, her supplication and worship requires gratuitous bloodshed. To this end, human and animal sacrifices were often performed in her honour. As Christianity crept into the fabric of society, people began to reject Morannis and the seasonal rites became more one of banishing her as the personification of winter, and welcoming the spring.

To this day, the peoples of central and eastern Europe celebrate the coming of spring by symbolically banishing Morana by throwing her effigy into a river or burning it.

Morannis may be invoked by the witch during Draumrûna rites, where she holds particular power and provenance.

The Path of Lanus

Altered states play a prime part in any therianthropic and essentially shamanistic set of practises, and the methods of the devotees of Lanus are no different. As is the case with any Dark God, little is said of Lanus beyond Him taking the form of a great black wolf who presides over the Gloamingwood. It is up to the practitioner to come to apprehend Lanus' essence through direct communion with this deity.

The witch comes to know Lanus tentatively via a series of meditations, chanting the name of Lanus and so forth, before delving into exeatic shamanism via the ingestion of substances and performing austerities.

Sit in a comfortable position, focusing upon the breath.

Continue until you are fully relaxed.

Next, begin to visualise Lanus in his wolf form - black, with demonic red eyes. See His great hairy mass, his hunched shoulders, the steam rising from His dread canine jaws. See the silent, predatory wisdom and ferocity emanating from His fiery eyes. Chant *Lanus* throughout this meditation.

Feel yourself merge with Lanus, your body shifting and changing into wolf form. Your skin covers with fur, your arms extend, tendons stretching over lean muscle, hands elongating into razor claws. Feel every part of you truly transform into that of a great wolf beast.

Dwell in this form for as long as you wish to apprehend the energies of the Dark God.

End the meditation and return to normal consciousness.

Traditionally, this meditation was performed before every lycanthropic ritual, with certain substances ingested via a skin ointment, the ingredients of which can be discovered via historical research. This combination can often lead to hysteria and bouts of extreme rage. For this reason, followers of Lanus are often marked as solitary witches, who practise their rites in the depth of forests and other places well away from civilisation.

The Werewolf Rite

A wolf skin or other similar fur garment should be obtained to be worn during this rite (if this is impossible, your usual ritual attire will suffice). Nothing else should be worn, except oil and facial markings, drawn according to intuition and personal preference - the aim here being to tap into a racial atavism. The success of this rite occurs after consistent practise.

The rite is to be performed naturally on the full moon (experimentation with other phases such as the new moon is recommended).

It is important to forsake during the duration of the rite all semblances of civilized humanity, every faculty of speech and reason. Therefore, it must be performed alone.

The communion with Lanus, as detailed in the Lycanthropic meditation should be performed prior.

Find a place deep in a wooded area where you will not be disturbed. It is important to have fasted for three days beforehand, eating only uncooked meat products when food is necessary, and on each night to have performed the Lycanthropic meditation.

Clothed in black robes and adorned in musk oil, sit and meditate on the breath for a few minutes. Next, begin a counter clockwise dance or pattern, circling slowly inward, whilst vibrating the word SATANAS. When you are spent, sit and say the following:

Satan, Dark Master of the Forests, Lord of Awe and Derision - come forth from the shadow of the woods and bring your wild hunt!

Lanus, O Hound of Satan, O steward of the Eternal Forest - come forth from the shadow of the woods and anoint me as one of your kin!

May the Wolf possess me; may I be reborn as a Beast of Satan!

Begin your dance again, outward this time.

Focus on transforming your body into that of a wolf. As you continue your dance, feel your skin coated in black fur, your hand elongate into talons, your jaw snap forth and be filled with sharp teeth. Vibrate the name *Lanus* as you do so.

Commune now with the Dark Master, the ancient Keeper of the Forests. Attendant to him are werewolves who run with Him as hunting dogs of mundane flesh. Feel now the pleasure of the Werewolf, go out into the night and taste the pleasures of the Will.

If a correct state of mind is reached and bloodlust is not overpowering the practitioner, astral travel should be attempted taking the form of the wolf, after having worked the ritual to the point of physical exhaustion or delirium via ingestion of substances. Explore in this form and recount your experiences.

In time, Lanus will draw near, and may even grant the werewolf access to the wintry realm where He presides, where all things are possessed of claws and razor teeth.

Clear the area after the rite, leaving by sunrise at latest, and leave an offering to the inhabitants of the forest.

Exile in Lanus

Having practised the Lycanthropic meditation to

proficiency, and then the Werewolf Rite, the next step is to combine the two rituals with the following.

A week should be spent living in a secluded and heavily wooded region, somewhere humans will not discover you. No sleeping equipment may be brought - all that can be accommodated for are tools for making fire and perhaps boiling water. A blanket may be utilised for keeping warm during the night, as you will be expected to sleep on the forest floor.

All food eaten must be caught. A primitive weapon such as a composite bow may be utilised, or else one may employ traps and a survival knife. The aim here is to break the mind down into a primary racial atavism, thus opening the gates for communion with Lanus to enter. Those possessed by His spirit will choose to live in the wild for longer - medieval England was replete with tales of the 'wild men of the woods' who donned wolf skins and shunned human habitations. The Norse Berserkers were also believed to have lived largely hermetic existences.

Practise the Werewolf Rite each night. Fasting can be reduced to one to two small meals per day in this case, with the minimum sleep being adhered to. On the final night, take the leaves of *Atropa Belladonna* and consume one to two of the smaller variety. Enough water should be kept nearby, as Belladonna will dry the mouth and throat considerably.

It is acceptable to have drunk alcohol prior to ingestion of the Belladonna, and alcohol was traditionally used as a deliriant alongside other drugs for entering a frenzy during these lycanthropic rituals. Often, the juice of Belladonna berries was mixed with a light alcohol such as mead.

Another method involves brewing the roots to make a tea (usually around four grams of root per dose), with topical application of Belladonna oil being especially conducive to astral projection during this time.

A Visionary Rite

To induce lycanthropic visions and receive further guidance from the wolf god, the witch must take the fat of a slain animal and mix it with aniseed, camphor and wolfsbane and smear this ointment upon their chest.

Next, make a small fire from the wood of a black poplar tree. Over this fire in a thurifer or similar vessel should be burnt around an ounce each of Hemlock, Henbane, Poppy seeds, Opium, Asafoetida, Solanum and Parsley.

The smoke is allowed to billow out generously, with the witch inhaling its suffused essence, all the while chanting *Agios O Lanus*. Alongside this should be employed a scrying bowl filled with animal blood and into which the witch should peer and receive visions from the Gloamingwood.

Simpler and similar methods involve placing a small drop of Belladonna and cannabis oil under the tongue prior to scrying into the blood mirror.

Appendix IV - Coenobitic Vampyrism

Toward A New Community

One of the principal goals and intents of the Drakon Covenant is to encourage a move away from the urban centres and cities to a more agrarian way of living; a way of living which will allow its adherents to establish a monastic community where genuine novitiates of the tradition can abide and pursue the Sevenfold Way free from the external circumstances and demands of mundane living.

Such an agrarian/monastic environment would allow the novitiate to fully integrate themselves into the world of the Dark Tradition removing as it would the barriers and pressures which arise from the everyday world and which barriers and pressures can hinder optimum development.

A monastery would of course require an area of land, preferably located somewhere within the British Isles, as well as considerable funding to purchase said land and to build a structure which can house the monastic settlers. This could be as simple as a collection of dormitory rooms and a communal hall, as well as several areas such as a temple, a teaching area and an outdoor ground.

As well as this, the monastic community would strive

toward total self-sufficiency (such a communal religious living arrangement was historically known as a *coenobitic community*). For this, a well would need to be built, along with small crops or a small collection of livestock. Alternatively, monastery members could take employment in the mundane world, with a portion of their earnings going toward the maintenance and running of the monastery itself.

Religious monastic living has proven to be highly effective throughout the ages - whether exemplified in Christian or Buddhist contexts, for example, as well as fully fledged communities such as the Amish or various Mormon sects.

A monastery devoted to the Sevenfold Way would also be a great advancement of the tradition itself, becoming a sort of pilgrimage for serious seekers. It would also become a Falciferian focal point of power against the White Lodge, hidden away and known only to a very select few; thus, it would exist in total secrecy and safety.

Two methods could be given for this approach - as well as the aforementioned 'compound' approach with an area of land bought and built upon, individuals could work to subtly infiltrate and take over an already existing rural community.

For example, a small village consisting of circa 50 houses could be made a target for a future coenobitic community. Coven members could purchase or rent all available houses within the village, with other members buying or renting houses in a village as and when they become available. Over time, the coven would comprise a majority within the community, perhaps - over generations via seeding families there - making up the entire village's populace itself. With coven members being a sizable minority within the village, they could yield a proportional voice in community matters, thus subtly directing the community along the aims of the coven itself.

On Rural Living

There are many self-professed Satanists and practitioners of the Sinister tradition in this latter day of instant communication and self-expression who spend much time and energy (amongst other things) writing grand tracts or posturing their unique view on how the aims of an order such as the ONA or a satanic movement should be presenced and enacted in the modern age. The author is no exception from this observational critique, of course.

Many admittedly creative and bright individuals have for some years and decades all lent their efforts to how acausal forces can be presenced and give rise to a change within society, leading to the emergence of Vindex in its eventual and inevitable form, whatever that may be.

So few however, it seems, question their place in the very system they claim to be opposed to; so few are painfully aware of just how necessary these mundane governments and rules of law are to their continued survival and safety as individuals. How many can (or will) eke out a living off the land, expressing and living a truly Pagan way of life by learning the ways of the soil and the natural world of which they claim to channel energies from?

So many talk of revolution, thinking only in terms of the ephemeral urban sphere, thinking only of urbane political upheaval, urbane political street fights, urbane political propaganda (that is, those select few who manage to progress beyond the online ego-posturing and roleplaying and who have the gall to recognise such struggle may very well be a necessity in the future, should the aims of the Sinister be seriously considered).

This conditional approach, relying as it does upon the existence within and reliance upon the cosmopolitan edifices which the Magian has built for the very purpose of entrapment and subjugation, is inherently flawed; childish in its belief that one can fight against a foe whilst expecting this foe to feed, house and clothe it. A true revolution against a system such as the current Western one (and many such agrarian revolts exist as examples), infected as it is with the cosmopolitan Magian worldview, must essentially be that of willful emancipation from the urban sphere, a return to a more rural way of living and a move toward becoming more self-sufficient, no longer relying upon the apparent wretched system to feed and nurture us. Instead, we should begin to develop and move toward self-reliance, self-integrity and a slow, pernicious return to a more genuine existence - a removal from the rush and slavery of city life.

You cannot overthrow the current order by yourself. And you cannot claim to fight against it whilst paying taxes and perpetuating its consumer capital memes and produce. You can however remove the influence which it has upon you, thus achieving a very real and genuine liberation in life beyond the vague notions of such espoused by largely modern and largely inept 'satanic' ideologues.

This then, is how we create a new society. By establishing these self reliant and honorable homesteads and communities, who choose to co-operate together and who work free from impersonal concepts such as profit and debt based monetary gain, ultimately free from the chaos and conflict that such urban living inevitably breeds.

It is through such a Numinous way of living that a new species may arise, one imbued with a natural empathy which comes from an intimate living with the soil itself.

And it is from such a Numinous society and its consequent species (and only from such) that the energies and personages of Falcifer, Morgatha and Vindex may eventually emerge.

Vindex and A Numinous Rural Society

Who is Vindex then, ultimately? Many strive to compare Him/Her/It to historical figures such as Julius Caesar or Adolf Hitler, making the (innocent) mundane mistake that Vindex is a simple expression of warrior might or conquest, a rebellious figure to rightfully emulate and assume will eventually, in full messianic fervour, emerge from the rank and file of Sinister Initiates and Adepts.

However Vindex will emerge is currently unknown; however, it can be safely said He/She/It has not emerged yet. This alone should be lesson enough that the current system and approach of the aforementioned Initiates and Adepts is not conducive to such an emergence. A defiant and deliberate change in the manner in which we live must emerge among us.

Vindex can be most adequately expressed by the concept of Expansion: the spread of life through its environs, the overcoming of the challenges these environs may pose, and the evolution wrought via such a natural dialectic of this expansion and challenge. In short, Vindex will be the essential avatar of the West.

There is no need to envision a brutal overthrowing of the old order, nor a need to think in terms of old Aeon revolutions and civil wars; what Vindex is and can be is simply the evolutionary growth of the Numen embodied in an intelligent and aware species. We will become Vindex when we evolve and spread beyond the confines of this Earth planet (those of us who choose to do so, that is).

The evolution necessary for such a change is exemplified most perfectly in the Pathei-Mathos of a tradition such as ours, that of Sinister Hebdomadry; the combined experience and lessons of all those who have come before us exists for us to draw upon and guide ourselves through life with - be it the traditional followers of the Sevenfold Way, the reclusive wild witches known as the Rounwytha, or those Dreccian rebels who live according to no law beyond that of Personal Honour and Kindred.

Yet all these things have been written many times before, and undoubtedly will be written again. Such words will fall upon deaf ears until the individual reading them has gone forth and truly lived what is being argued for here; when the Initiate has merged with the Dark Gods and seen through the chaos into the Numinous essence; when he/she has come to learn of and appreciate a wordless flowing with the spirit of the land and listened to the quiet Grail within the blood (when he/she has grasped the inner meaning of Blood & Soil, that is).

Such a way is simple, and requires only an emancipation from the urban struggle and the beginnings of a new way of living. From such new ways will come new folk, and from such new folk, new societies. Thence will we witness the emergence of Vindex among us.

This move toward non-urban emancipation and the founding of a monastic centre will potentially one day be realised by adherents of the Drakon Covenant tradition. Where this centre will actually be located should be easily discerned by those familiar with the spiritual beliefs of the Covenant and the locations pertinent to it.

Appendix V - Draumrúna

Causal reality may be regarded as a great collective dream. If one is aware of the dream, one can in theory alter it and change its properties and outcomes. However, reality is a dream dreamt by many, a consensus reality upheld by many minds. Thus, to change the properties and outcomes of reality itself is a monumentally difficult task, and one which is beyond the scope and ability of most individuals.

To therefore alter reality at a macroscopic level (or to use common parlance, to 'cast magick') requires the individual will to be strengthened to the amplification of a thousand minds unified in purpose.

The Magians are succinctly aware of this dream-like nature of reality; however, being essentially magickally inept, they operate on a basis of being only able to control the dream by streamlining and restricting the apparent limitations of the dream according to those who exist within it. If one can control what people think about, and how people think about certain things, they can ensure the dream will go somewhat according to their vision, if not be able to outright control it. It is for this reason that the principle ethos of the Magian is abstraction and censorship. If one believes certain things cannot be dreamt, those certain things will simply never arise.

Abstraction is the placing of abstract ideas and forms above genuine, personal experience. So many people accept 'isms' and ideologies in lieu of a personal Weltanschauung sculpted by pathei-mathos and the application of this to life experience. More and more people are becoming detached from the inherent reality of living and instead placing their values into preconceived models and systems.

Censorship involves the enforcement of mental tyranny, aided greatly by the aforementioned concept of abstractions (the medieval era notions of heresy and heretical knowledge were a prime example of this desire to not only keep certain knowledge from the masses, but also to actively and subtly condition the masses into rejecting said hidden knowledge. We see the same today, not least in regards to modern heresies, such as so-called Holocaust denial, among other things).

To break free of the tyranny of Magian abstraction then, the magickal initiate must cast aside all abstractions and the patterns which lead to acceptance of abstraction over numinous reality, instead creating for themselves a philosophy based on life affirming principles and life experience. For that to occur, genuine life experience and an increased consciousness need to be cultivated. This is the reason for the Sevenfold Way in the initiate's quest.

Censorship must be combatted via insight roles and indulging in conventionally heretical pursuits and beliefs (see the *Mass of Heresy*). Only when one has surpassed these dogmas can real individuation begin - magickal adeptship. Adeptship cannot be achieved until one has expanded consciousness via the Dark Pathways, Spheres and magickal workings of the Sevenfold Way; until one has observed, understood and transcended the notion of causal abstractions; and finally, until one has cast aside the notion of censorship (an issue most detractors of the ONA's magickal system seem infected with at this present point in time).

Reading the various ONA corpus with these key concepts in mind will help the novitiate truly advance along the path toward Adeptship.

Altering the dream

Any lucid dreamer knows that to alter one's dream, it must be sufficiently guided toward a direction and desired conclusion; simply imagining a considerable change interrupts the process and forces the mind to wake up. To apply the analogy of a dream to the question of magickal ability, the will must be strengthened, and the 'dream' must be guided toward a goal via various ways. This is the essence of Aeonic magick.

Of course, the longer the witch dreams, the longer he/she can work to alter and guide the dream. This is one of the many reasons why we strive for Lichood - our quest for mastery cannot be halted by death; human life is very short in the grand scheme of things. Within the teachings of the Sevenfold Way, the final stage - that of Immortal - can only be attained after one's causal death. Within the Drakon Covenant, this is of course also true. However, the methods to achieving Lichood are more detailed than the attainment of acausal Immortality, and the vampyric Masters of the Covenant strive to remain close to this world to guide and shape future minds to help mould this dream into something more fitting, more liable to aid evolution. For unless the Magian is countered, and unless the sickness that is their ethos is purged from this planet, we will never leave this planet. We will never expand as free individuals into the starry cosmos. We will never truly grasp adeptship - and individuation, mastery, wisdom - these will be the reserve of the very few.

It is thus imperative that evolution be maintained by the genuine initiates of the Sinister Tradition. Whilst the Magian tyranny enthralls Mankind into ever more servile and urban ways of living, they will stifle and bring evolution to a grinding and irreversible halt. Removing challenge, conflict and natural selection, they will turn this species into a mass of weak, directionless units capable only of consumption, domesticated goyim who keep their sickly masters furnished and in unquestionable rulership. They will drive this planet into crisis, leading eventually to the extinction of Homo Sapiens, known more fittingly as Homo Hubris.

We alone stand as stewards of Cosmic Change, and with the opening of the gates to the Acausal, we usher in the very forces of evolution which will destroy the Magian plan once and for all - the Dark Gods.

128 year of Fayen

Lamia Dei, Commune cum me

Agia Ha Morgatha

Sources and Further Reading

A. A. Morain
Codex Aristarchus
Forsworcennes
Weald Hagtaesse

Order of Nine Angles
Naos, A Practical Guide to Magick
Hostia
The Deofel Quintet
The Sinister Tradition
The Sinister Way

Tempel Ov Blood
Liber 333
Tales of Sinister Influence
The Book of Dark Mothers

David Myatt
Vindex - The Destiny of the West
The Numinous Way of Pathei-Mathos
Seven Essays Regarding Vindex

Donald Mackenzie
Wonder Tales From Scottish Myth and Legend

J.G. Frazer
The Golden Bough

Arnold J. Toynbee
A Study of History

Oswald Spengler
The Decline of the West

Sylvan J. Muldoon & Hereward Carrington
The Projection of the Astral Body

Robert Bruce
Astral Dynamics

David Ellis
Medicinal Herbs and Plants

Ptolemy
Geographia

W.Y. Evans-Wentz
The Fairy-Faith in Celtic Countries

Julius Caesar
The Gallic Wars

Patrick W Joyce
The Origin and History of Irish Names of Places,

Alexander Carmicheal
Carmina Gadelica, Volumes 1&2